Parmenides, Plato, and
Mortal Philosophy

Continuum Studies in Ancient Philosophy
Series Editor: James Fieser, University of Tennessee at Martin, USA

Continuum Studies in Ancient Philosophy is a major monograph series from Continuum. The series features first-class scholarly research monographs across the field of Ancient Philosophy. Each work makes a major contribution to the field of philosophical research.

Parmenides, Plato, and Mortal Philosophy
Return from Transcendence

Vishwa Adluri

continuum

Continuum International Publishing Group

The Tower Building	80 Maiden Lane
11 York Road	Suite 704
London SE1 7NX	New York NY 10038

www.continuumbooks.com

© Vishwa Adluri, 2011

First published 2011
Paperback edition first published 2012

British Library Cataloguing-in-Publication Data
A catalogue record for this book is available from the British Library.

ISBN: HB: 978-0-8264-5753-0
    PB: 978-1-4411-6600-5

Library of Congress Cataloging-in-Publication Data
Adluri, Vishwa.
Parmenides, Plato, and mortal philosophy : return from transcendence /
Vishwa Adluri.
    p. cm.
Includes bibliographical references (p.).
ISBN 978-0-8264-5753-0
1. Parmenides. 2. Plato. Phaedrus. 3. Finite, The. I. Parmenides. Nature. English.
II. Title.

B235.P24A34 2010
182'.3–dc22
                                            2010018302

Typeset by Newgen Imaging Systems Pvt Ltd, Chennai, India
Printed and bound in Great Britain

In the cold waters of Lēthē you will remember that the warm earth meant a thousand heavens.

Reiner Schürmann, paraphrasing Osip Mandelstam,
Brothers, Let Us Glorify Freedom's Twilight

To my beloved mother, Suguna

Contents

Foreword

On reading this book, I was struck by Dr. Adluri's insight into the nature of Parmenides' poem as a whole, and his arguments for the relevance of ancient thought to contemporary philosophy, and I was touched by the relationship established between this research in the history of philosophy and contemporary philosophical problems.

Dr. Adluri argues for a "mortal philosophy," that is, a philosophy that is aware of and maintains the tension between the mortal desire for transcendence, whether understood as eternity or as the timeless truths of metaphysical propositions, and the irreducibly tragic "mortal condition" which implies a return from transcendence to our finitude. In my view, Dr. Adluri holds together these opposing elements admirably in his book and, in doing so, provides a thought-provoking and brilliantly original analysis of Parmenides' poem with extensive notes, written in a fresh and lucid style. His work, which is very interesting on the level of scholarly work, provides new insight into Parmenides' poem that goes well beyond the logical analyses to which one has attempted to reduce it over the most recent decades. Above all, he proposes a description of Parmenides' approach that does not reduce him to being the philosopher of Being and of Eternity. Parmenides speaks of the universe, and confronts not only immortality, but mortality as well. The importance of argumentation in the poem is considerable, and continues to be admitted by all, but the role played in it by myth is decisive in it.

By focusing on the poem's long-neglected proem, Dr. Adluri sets out to demonstrate that the theme of journey is the central motif unifying Parmenides' poem. Dr. Adluri conceives of philosophy itself as a kind of unique journey from life to death—a journey that each one of us *is*. Dr. Adluri suggests that the journey of the Parmenidean *kouros* to the realm of the goddess continues even beyond this metaphysical realm where change (and thus journeying) have been abolished; the *kouros* returns to the mortal cosmos in the goddess' second speech. This return gives the book its subtitle: *Return from Transcendence*. Through this interpretation, Dr. Adluri shows how hard it is to see Parmenides simply as a "monist" who rejected all change and movement, as he is still read all too often.

But Dr. Adluri's book will be of interest to scholars of Platonic philosophy as well, as he applies the same analysis to Plato, defending him against the charges of "Platonism" or of "metaphysics." Dr. Adluri shows how the striving for timeless truths in the dialogues always takes place against the background of Socrates' impending and tragic demise. Thus, he argues that "[b]y etching the immortal Forms onto Socrates' perishable body, Plato shows the Forms to be impotent and irrelevant" (Introduction). More generally, Dr. Adluri considers that there are two poles in Plato's philosophy. Eternity remains attached to the hypothesis of the immutable Forms, whereas the mortal character is associated with the quest for self-knowledge. How can one participate in eternity while remaining a particular human being: such is the dilemma Plato must face in his dialogues, which usually present a Socrates in whom this twofold reflection is concentrated.

Finally, Dr. Adluri's work provides interesting thematic links between ancient thought and modern and contemporary writers, including Nietzsche, Heidegger, Arendt, and his teacher and mentor Reiner Schürmann. It argues for the relevance of the pre-Socratics to a "post-metaphysical" age, especially as an important corrective to modern technology.

As one can observe, this book attempts to establish a correspondence between the beginnings of philosophy, represented by the figure of the *kouros* in the poem of Parmenides, and the most contemporary reflections on the question of death, or, more precisely, the relations between death and discourse. No one doubts that human life runs in only one direction, one leading to death. Yet philosophers try to anchor within the atemporality of discourse the deepest human desire, the desire for immortality, even if at the end of the day they must backtrack and admit that man is mortal. It is the same approach, moreover, that manifests itself in love: "In love, I recognize the singularity of my lover, while in death, his loss brings home his singularity with exceptional force to me" (Chapter 6). In sum, we encounter once again the dialectic between immortality and mortality.

At the limit, this book can be read as a work of consolation following the death in 1993 of Dr. Adluri's teacher Reiner Schürmann, who taught from 1976 until his death at the new School for Social Research (the home of Hannah Arendt as well). By invoking the mortal singularity of his teacher, Dr. Adluri is able to talk about something that is pervasive in ancient philosophy though neglected by most contemporary philosophers: the link between mortality and philosophy. Indeed, this book may be considered not only as a homage to this master, but also as a prolongation of his reflection on Heidegger, and the latter's definition of authenticity as linked to the experience of death. In the end, Dr. Adluri repeats for the man who was his teacher Plato's approach to Socrates.

All this results in a book that is clear and engaging, for philosophical reflection anchored within the history of Greek philosophy remains linked to a personal approach, consisting in a twofold reaction with regard to love and death. Dr. Adluri thus escapes two pitfalls: that of pure erudition, and that of intellectual biography. The erudite reading of ancient texts is constantly oriented by a contemporary philosophical questioning. This is what makes this book so engaging.

Luc Brisson
Translated by Michael Chase

Acknowledgments

My deepest gratitude naturally goes to Reiner Schürmann. I also wish to acknowledge my intellectual debt to my teachers Joan Stambaugh and Seth Benardete. I also gratefully acknowledge John Lenz for his challenging questions. I acknowledge Luc Brisson, Gianni Vattimo, Hal Thorsrud, Svetla Slaveva-Griffin, and Arbogast Schmitt. Finally, my thanks to Deborah Nails and Harold Tarrant for their support and to Fr. Nathan Vail, Felix Griesbach, Alberto Martinengo, and Matt Newman. For great love and faith, I thank Joachim Eichner, Thomas Komarek, Joydeep Bagchee, and Manfred and Milly Eichner. Last but not least, I acknowledge the support I received from Dr. Madhava Agusala.

Introduction

Parmenides and Renewing the Beginning

There is probably no greater beginner in the history of philosophy than Parmenides.
Reiner Schürmann, "Tragic Differing"[1]

Of Parmenides, Heidegger says "The dialogue with Parmenides never comes to an end, not only because so much in the preserved fragments of his 'Didactic Poem' still remains obscure, but also what is said there continually deserves more thought. It is a sign of a boundlessness which, in and for remembrance, nourishes the possibility of a transformation of destiny."[2] This study renews the dialogue with Parmenides as a series of reflections upon ourselves and our mortality. The dialogue with Parmenides never comes to an end because Parmenides is, above all, a thinker of mortal being. The traditional characterizations of Parmenides as monist and founder of logic, of rationality, overshadow his true genius: an appreciation of what it means to be human, that is, to stand at the crossroads of mortality and immortality.

Parmenides the Pre-Socratic

Scholars have traditionally held the following view of Parmenides' place within the pre-Socratic tradition. "Pre-Socratic philosophy is divided into two halves by the name of Parmenides. His exceptional powers of reasoning brought speculation about the origin and constitution of the universe to a halt, and caused it to make a fresh start on different lines . . . Whether or not he directly attacked Heraclitus, had Heraclitus known of Parmenides it is incredible that he would not have denounced him along with Xenophanes and others . . . philosophically Heraclitus must be regarded as pre-Parmenidean, whereas Empedocles, Anaxagoras, Leucippus and Democritus are quite certainly post-Parmenidean."[3]

In this work, I demonstrate the one-sidedness of this view. Contrary to this characterization, I argue that Parmenides, in fact, shares and perfects a pre-Socratic cosmology. Such a cosmology has as its central concern a description of natural phenomena, and a commitment to preserving *phusis* in *logos*. But this cosmology oscillates between two poles: one mortal, deriving from a Homeric view of man's mortal destiny, and the other immortal, deriving from the magical anti-chronic properties of *logos*. Thus the neat distinction of a pre- and a post-Parmenidean phase in pre-Socratic philosophy is a phantom of the history of philosophy. Parmenides' affinity with Homer also links him to the fifth-century tragedians, whose central theme is a clear demarcation of the boundaries and interactions between mortals and immortals. This engagement with what I call the monstrous *aporia* of temporality, where mortals and immortals appear and converse, grants mortals the possibility of metaphysical transcendence, while also making a return unavoidable. Parmenides thus belongs within a (pre-Socratic) tradition that not only extends back to Homer, but also forward to the tragic poets and Plato. Contrary to traditional scholarship, Parmenides, as we shall see, is not zealously attached to the monism he portrays as a feature of the goddess' realm. His use of the motif of journey deconstructs such a simplistic view. As Schürmann writes, "Could a thinking that is meant to utter ultimately one single word—*hen*—begin with a narrative? And furthermore a narrative of a journey, involving places and displacements, hence time?"[4] Parmenides was well aware of the world of becoming, and the finitude of mortals: both in the temporal realm and with regard to their epistemic faculties. Parmenides' "double speech," one of static being and another of cosmological becoming, brings him closer to Heraclitus' apparently paradoxical *legomena*.

Further, I argue that the true "pre-Socratic" element in Parmenides remains his commitment to preserving mortal temporality and thus dignifying mortal individuality and existence. *Logos*, as Parmenides understands it, is not a happy escape into a suspicious metaphysical eternity, but rather deadly in that it could strip mortals and their universe of the legitimacy of their existence. In this sense the immortality of *logos* is pernicious: it does not grant us immortality, it robs us of our mortality. Parmenides therefore presents a metaphysical realm, and then returns to the mortal universe. Plato, as I will show, inherits this pre-Socratic concern with mortality as can be seen in the way he articulates the dangerous fatality of *logos* as the *pharmakon* in the *Phaedrus*. The first and second speeches of the Parmenidean goddess recur as the realm of Forms (and its alleged copy, the world of becoming) on the one hand, and the *real, existing, mortal Socrates on the other*.[5]

Parmenides the Father/Beginner

But Parmenides is not merely a pioneer father, he is also a founding father, involved in the constitution of ultimate foundations. As Schürmann puts it, philosophy since Parmenides "provides evidential moorage for the sake of consoling the soul and consolidating the city: some single first law governing all regional laws, be they cognitive, practical or even positive."[6] The goddess' demand for an atemporal *logos*, which is by its very nature an overcoming of mortality, is an example of such a law. A henology, a monism, or even a monotheism is thus a "foundation" upon which human mortality can be sacrificed for a metaphysical structure. By questioning the legitimacy of any single first law, Schürmann questions the role of the goddess' first speech, that is, of her *transcendental logos*. He finds that the beginning is not a single unified beginning of philosophy in the One (as Parmenides has usually been interpreted), but a tragic knowledge, a knowledge of our mortality and its contrary (championed, in Parmenides' work, by the goddess herself). By questioning the *origin*, understood both as a beginning and as a *foundation*, his interpretation shatters the sedimentation of "Father Parmenides" understood as a prophet of a monism. By denying exclusivity to the transcendental interpretation of *being*, as the goddess' sole theme, this new parricide reincarnates Parmenides again as thought-worthy at the end of metaphysics and within our mortal cosmos. In pluralizing a hitherto monistic first principle, philosophy as ontology, theology, and logic withers away. This reincarnation has a twofold significance:

1. It is our mortal responsibility to claim our own beginning within the cosmos, wresting it away from fascistic, totalitarian, metaphysical tyranny, that is, by rejecting monistic ontology once and for all. The beginning that lies ahead of us and which we must claim lies not in a philological, scholarly, or historical past that we may or even could return to.[7]
2. This reading also makes the human life-span once more into a philosophical problem. No monistic god, no monistic state, no monistic law shall bind all humans in one static unity: the mortal journey is irreducible to any single paradigm.

This reintroduction of temporality and mortality breaks up the "ultimate immutable foundation" of metaphysics and makes a reintroduction of mortals in their "ultimate concern" into philosophy possible again.

Biography: Reclaiming Socrates and Other Beloveds

Socrates: "[T]hose who really apply themselves in the right way to philosophy are directly and of their own accord preparing themselves for dying and death."

Plato, Phaedo *64a*

The accepted convention demands that every written piece end with a bibliography, but let me begin with a biography.[8] This juxtaposition of biography and bibliography is one of the central themes of this study. The word juxtaposition is a woefully neutral one, politely covering over the awkward antagonism between mortals and deathless words.[9] The Platonic drama is the drama of a condemned man trying to wrest the secret of immortality from *logoi*. Living through this drama constituted my own philosophical education.

When I came to the New School for Social Research, I came to study under Prof. Reiner Schürmann. My undergraduate mentor, Prof. Joan Stambaugh, was unambiguous in her advice: Reiner was one of the best teachers available. So I began my graduate studies, bright-eyed and bookish, having studied books as mainstream as Plato's dialogues and as esoteric (for an undergraduate 15 years ago) as Heidegger's very late works. I was registered for Prof. Schürmann's lectures on medieval philosophy. I was armed with the books, *ta biblia*, but quite unaware that these would be inadequate to any future biography of mine.

Although publicly Prof. Schürmann was name-tagged the "Heidegger man" (a classic case of missing the forest for the trees), what he taught me had nothing to do with bibliographic *Wege*. When I first saw him in class, I was shocked. He was frail, emaciated even, but robust in his speech and brilliant in his eyes. He was awesome in a daemonic way, and although easy to respect, few could truly love him. Although I took copious notes, no philosophical questions occurred to me. I dutifully read all the recommended books, and submitted shamelessly clever papers. Yet I sat uneasily in class, fearing the time when the retrovirus would defeat so great a man. He incarnated all the *telē* of a graduate student: he was an accomplished teacher, an admired scholar, and a respected thinker. He seemed invincible, yet I knew this virus very well. It had already effaced many of the best men I knew.

It is hard to say which came first: my love for him or the fearful knowledge of his ever-present mortality. But both seemed somehow to feed on each other. When I saw him in his office and later outside campus, we never talked about "ideas." And when I went back to Plato's dialogues, the comfort food of philosophers, their epistemological pretenses deconstructed themselves. I began to see Socrates the man, condemned to die as Reiner was, and I could no longer believe in the seriousness of the "theory of Forms." The everlasting landscape of the *topos noētos*, with its immortal, perfect Forms, now mocked all men, especially the one I loved. Within the deadly isolation of the epidemic, my subculture learned the lesson of survival learned long ago by the children of Israel: believe in your community. My community was the community of mortals. The Platonic dialogues, I learnt through my association with Reiner, do not "immortalize" Socrates; they preserve the ephemeral: his mortal face. By etching the immortal Forms onto Socrates' perishable body, Plato shows the Forms to be impotent and irrelevant. Yet, tragically, he also proves their indispensability. Scholars now debate whether Socrates was a character in Plato's dialogue and whether he was just a mouthpiece for the younger man's philosophy. To them, I say: no more accurate, more moving, more personal, and more complete a biography was ever written. Is it historically accurate? Or is the dialogue mere fiction? I try to show in my work that history and true accounts only produce bibliographies—*biography requires preserving the individual, the lover, the mortal, and the singular.* The body of this study will not mention Reiner's name on every page, but it is his biography in this fundamental sense. Of course, he would have written it better, but I claim with a certain pride that no "historian" could have done a better job. The life and loss of each one of us is neither as basic as a fact nor as capricious as fiction.

Philosophy: From Particularity to Singularity

Philosophical writing can be a form of idolatry. Not all forms of writing are, of course, and I do not believe that writing itself is to be blamed. But hardly had Reiner passed away, when his "philosophy"—that is, his bibliography, not his biography—supplanted him as a cheap idol (Greek *eidōlon*) would. In one seminar, I was amazed to hear this ultimate condemnation of him: "a nice guy, but influenced by an errant philosophy." Though bibliographically defensible (its opposite can also be proven by more careful readers; facts can be used in any way), biographically this is wrong on three counts. Reiner was not a "nice" guy. He was mercilessly intolerant of pretension and just about as polite as Socrates. In terms of "influence," his philosophical *praxis* consisted solely of the discovery of cracks in all foundations. Reiner was less susceptible to fashionable philosophies than Socrates was to Alkibiades. The term anarchy, which had many levels of meanings for him except the most obvious one, also means the susceptibility of all "influences" to critical questioning. Finally, errant philosophy is a sword that cuts both ways: as soon as a philosophy becomes conspicuously errant, such as Heidegger's is alleged to be, it begins to teach even greater and subtler philosophical lessons.

Biographically, Reiner taught me the difference between particularity and singularity. In his writing, he clarifies the difference as follows: "death as mine temporalizes phenomena because it is absolutely *singular*. But the singular cannot be treated as the determinate negation of the universal; the contrary opposite of the universal is the particular. It takes a neglect of the persistent tie between time and the singular, a tie signified to me by my death, to append these conflicting strategies to the list, long since Antiquity, of terms that are mutually exclusive within a genus and jointly exhaustive of it."[10]

For Reiner, interested in the public sphere, the singular was a tool to demonstrate the illegitimacy of univocally binding "phantasms," such as totalitarianism. For me, interested in Reiner, the singular was happily the object of love, tragically the object of death, and ultimately, the face and fate of all *phusis*. Knowing Reiner in his last days was nothing more and nothing less than what walking with Socrates must have been for Phaedrus. In one way or another, all shadows of the immortals that covered up the mortal singular—be it the city, hyperurania, philosophical or erotic genera—fell away from my eyes like scales falling off the eyes of a blind man. No more generalizing philosophy for me in the style of Lysias! Like Parmenides (I argue), no matter how seductive the realm of eternal, simple being may be, we must return to our pluralistic mortal cosmos, where singulars are possible. In this work, which is a continuation of the journey I began with Reiner, I extend his notion of mortality to redefine (if definition is even possible in the realm of singulars) human beings and *phusis* in terms of mortal temporality.

Speaking with the Ancients: From End to Beginning

Once I displaced eternal Forms by mortal finitude and embraced mortal fate instead of the seductions of epistemology (which natural science pursues more fruitfully than philosophy), I found my concerns resonating with the voices of the pre-Socratics. Their suspicion of knowledge for its own sake and their awareness of mortal finitude endeared them to me. I have learned many things from Heidegger, but I differ from him significantly, especially in his approach to the pre-Socratics. I find that his Parmenides lectures chart an altogether different landscape than the one in which I am journeying. Whereas his paradigmatic description of temporality is historical (*Seinsgeschichte*), I champion the individual life-span. Man, in general, does not appear to me in *Geschichte*, or in its narrative; the opposite is more convincing to me. For me, there is no "history of being," there is no "history" at all; there is only the life-story of the singular. Nor does metaphysics satisfy me. Metaphysics has no history and is insufficiently heedful of time. The various forms of evasion of temporality and erasure of the singular all set themselves up beyond man in the same way: through a forgetting of mortal time. Thus the end of metaphysics for me is not an event in the history of being; it is the loss of relevance and dignity of these interpretations, inadequately respectful of time as they are, in the hour of death of a loved one. The end of metaphysics is a function of the end of a singular life-span. The beginning, which invokes the pre-Socratics, becomes in a certain sense no beginning at all, but an enduring in this end, an enduring that is, ultimately, not possible. We are as metaphysical as we are mortal. I will demonstrate that the very faculty that impels us to seek nutrition and guides our growth also gives birth to metaphysics (I call this faculty of the soul *thumos*). Thus the task of enduring at the end is practically a returning to the beginning again and again, an endless homecoming.

Thus Socrates returns from the vision of the forms to hemlock, and the youth in Parmenides' poem returns, I argue, to the mortal cosmos, and my philosophical journey leads away from metaphysics to live and die among mortals— without succumbing to philosophy's bibliographic temptation.

Plan of This Work

This work reflects my interest in making mortal individuality significant to philosophy. To do this, I engage in a dialogue with the founding fathers of Western metaphysics: Plato and Parmenides. Were they exclusively concerned with immortal forms and eternal being? Does mortality, as a painful but real condition, not play a crucial role in their philosophy? I think it does. Parmenides gives us not one, but two *logoi*. One is the goddess' famous argument for eternal being. But her second account, the mortal *doxa*, retains mortality as an irreducible reality. Plato also retains mortality, in an even more powerful form: the individual mortal, Socrates, remains incarnate and in dialogue with immortal Forms.

I frame the issue of mortality and immortality in *temporal* terms, arguing for a tragic return to a philosophy of mortality.

In Chapter 1, I show the centrality of *time* to philosophy. Rather than engage in a "philosophy of time," I shift the focus from general arguments to concrete individuality. To do this, I reinterpret individuality, extending from birth to death, as the primary mode for understanding temporality. Analysis proceeds not through abstract argumentation, but through paying attention to various expressions of individual being in the philosophical texts under consideration: *thumos* or the *mortal* soul, and journey. I contrast individuality and its mortal temporality to the accounts of time traditionally given in metaphysics. Indeed, I interpret traditional metaphysical denials of time as an attempt to deny painful mortal temporality.

Chapter 2 introduces Parmenides and his work. In his philosophical poem, we find the clearest articulation of mortality and immortality, and their irreducible opposition. Previous scholarship has ignored those portions of the poem that complicate the traditional obsession with his argument for eternal being: I briefly discuss these interpretations and their limitations and point out the complex multiplicity of Parmenides' poem taken as a whole.

The following three chapters deal with each of the three parts of Parmenides' poem: the proem (his journey to the realm of the goddess); the goddess' speech on eternal being, its unity and immutability; and finally her returning him (in speech) to the world of the mortals, a cosmological description we may not overlook.

Chapter 3 focuses on the proem in which Parmenides recounts his protagonist's journey to the goddess. His text introduces two crucial themes, those of *thumos* and journey. *Thumos* (or, as I call it, the "mortal soul") propels the youth on his journey from mortality to an immortal realm. *Thumos* embodies both mortality, since it is rooted in *phusis* (marked by individual birth and death), and the painful awareness of its own finitude, which it manifests as a desire to transcend its own mortality. The motif of journey best maps the trajectory of mortal individuality. *Journey is not a metaphor, but a mode of being in phusis and thus a primary mode for philosophy as well.* To paraphrase John Dewey's words (pertaining to education): journey is not a metaphor for life; instead "journey" is life itself.

I attempt to subvert the dominant hegemonic paradigm of eternal being in Chapter 4. Here I discuss the goddess' speech on *alētheia* or true being. I expose its dependence on multiplicity, contradiction, and duplication—features she suppresses through logical argumentation. Her monologue on true being only works at the level of abstract reasoning or *logos*, because *logos* by its nature is unable to express the temporality of *phusis*: coming-to-be and passing-away.[11]

Chapter 5 deals with the Eleatic's breathtaking cosmology, which returns the mortal youth's attention in the poem to his proper *topos*: the cosmos of becoming and change. Here it becomes clear that the journey Parmenides undertakes is a "round-trip" to the goddess' metaphysical realm. Scholars have previously read the contradiction of the goddess' two speeches as denying phenomenal reality (something unthinkable to a pre-Socratic),[12] but I argue that it is meant to draw limits to the *logos she unfolds in her* ontological demonstration.

From Parmenides, I turn to Plato in Chapter 6, and read his *Phaedrus* with these themes in view. The *Phaedrus* is Plato's most Parmenidean work. Many commentators readily grant that the two thinkers share the theme of *immortal being*. But I suggest another, deeper connection between the two thinkers, one that I call the *mortal journey*. Plato and Parmenides engage in dialogue with each other not only about issues of epistemology, but also about other crucial issues: mortality, living in the physical world of change, and the longings of the soul (whether *thumos* or *psukhē*). Such a reading of Plato relates him back to the pre-Socratics as well as to our contemporary existential concerns.

I focus on Plato's obsession with individuality, pluri-vocality, and his juxta-position of a living mortal individual, Socrates, with the generality of *logos* (writing). These themes, often ignored in favor of an epistemology of Forms, become crucial in his dialogue the *Phaedrus*.[13] Along the way, my discussion offers a critique of Derrida's influential theory of the *pharmakon*.

In the Conclusion, I return to Heidegger's influential thesis of the "end of metaphysics" and argue that the tragic reading of Parmenides presented here points a way beyond Heidegger's thought. I underscore the theological resonances of Heidegger's philosophy and argue that Heidegger fails to understand the tragic wisdom of the Greeks.[14] The retrieval of singularity in Reiner Schürmann's thought enables a return to the Greeks, in which the fate of the mortal singular once again becomes a powerful tool for deconstructing metaphysics. The need to return to Parmenides is thus implicitly bound up with the need to rethink our own present "post-metaphysical" anti-tragic age.

The Appendix presents a new, complete translation of the surviving fragments of Parmenides' poem, "On Nature," with some notes on reading it.[15] I comment on particular readings of the Greek text and offer my interpretations of them. I pay close attention to the nuances of Parmenides' brilliant poetic language. For practical reasons, not all of these remarks have been fully developed in the thematic accounts in the preceding chapters. Therefore these textual notes are an integral part of my reading of Parmenides and should not be overlooked as mere technical addenda.

I hope that this book with its title *Return from Transcendence* will be the first stage in a larger project where transcendence is rethought beyond metaphysics. I will address this in a separate work. Ever since Socrates defined human mortality as the single preoccupation of philosophers, philosophy has had a unique and original relationship to death. In the modern period, Nietzsche gives the question of mortality new urgency through proclaiming the death of god.[16] Heidegger defines human being in terms of its unique relationship to death: only humans are capable of death as death.[17] Despite his questionable political entanglement, Heidegger's philosophy decisively shaped twentieth-century philosophy. His student Hannah Arendt made the question of "singularity," that is, of the unique trajectory between birth and death each one of us is, central to philosophy. Reiner Schürmann applied the concept of singularity as an ethical and political force in his work *Broken Hegemonies*.[18] I would like this book to be read as a philosophical engagement with this tradition.

Part I

Beginnings: *Arkhai*

Chapter 1

Radical Individuality:
Time, Mortal Soul, and Journey

If we wish to retrieve the temporality that makes the existence of individuals possible and their death a real loss, we must move beyond the static temporality *epistēmē*[1] presumes (a temporality that is preserved in *logos*), to the temporal existence of mortals such as Parmenides and Socrates. Philosophical *logoi* in their generality can never give a complete account of why living creatures die. As ephemeral creatures inescapably subject to mortality, our philosophical self-knowledge must address the issues of time, change, *phusis* (natural growth), and the individual. Mythic discourse captures individual mortal existence without reducing it to a static entity.[2] It thus differs from *logos* in a crucial respect, namely, in being able to maintain the irreducible plurality and individuality of existence.

This work describes a philosophical trajectory that returns us, through metaphysics, to our mortality, and that leads all the way back, through Plato, to the pre-Socratics. The journeys of Parmenides' *kouros* and of Plato's Socrates trace a common theme. Each begins with a concern for metaphysical permanence, then deconstructs metaphysical atemporality, and finally accepts the mortal condition. Philosophy (as ontology) arguably begins with Parmenides' attempt to dissociate time from being. Henceforth, this enduring description of being is understood as delineating a fixed and static entity—either eternal or atemporal. When temporality is taken into account, philosophers speak of a flux of becoming. However, I wish to show that static being (or flux, for that matter) is problematic for both Parmenides and Plato.

The central problem, as I see it, is philosophy's exclusion of time from its subject matter. Before tracing their journeys, I would like in this chapter to describe my understanding of basic philosophical themes such as time, mortality, metaphysics, "radical individuality," and the double soul. I understand existence in time cosmologically in terms of *phusis*,[3] existentially as a journey between birth and death, theologically as the existence of a finite being in need of salvation, epistemologically as the one confronting the *aporia* of eternal being and fluxing becoming, anthropologically as the being that knows what it means for it to die and thus bears responsibility for its life, and psychologically in terms of *thumos,* a spatio-temporal and historical identity. These elements interweave themselves into a discourse that replaces epistemology and static *logos* with an unsubsumable (*unhintergehbar*) mortal individuality, an experience that lies at the heart of philosophy.

Time

What, then, is time? If no one asks me, I know; if I want to explain it to someone who does ask me, I do not know.

Augustine, Confessions *XI.14*[4]

Time and Its Importance for Philosophy

Philosophy and the natural sciences approach the problem of time in diverse ways. No consensus exists on the nature of time, but I will describe it provisionally as follows: time is implicit to all phenomenal experience. With this statement, I insist on time's inseparability from the life of the individual—the trajectory extending from inception at birth to termination in death. Time is not to be understood in the Kantian sense as a form of sensibility. No one can truly die on Kant's view of time, because death is robbed of its concrete temporality, being merely a subjective form of experience. We can, on Kant's view, at most *perish,* but are incapable of experiencing our death *as* death, that is, as an event which brings a unique mortal journey to an end.[5] Newton, by contrast, provides an entirely objective account of time, as an absolute container within which all phenomena occur.[6] Both Newton and Kant, in their own ways, abstract the existential experience of time away from phenomena.

The experience of time is divided into past, present, and future. The pre-Socratic philosophers (followed in different ways by both Plato and Aristotle) articulate this experience through the terms "coming-into-being" (*gignesthai*), "growing (or being nourished)" (*phuein*), and "perishing" (*ollusthai*) respectively. This view of time is biological or *kata phusin,* "according to *phusis*" (where we might define *phusis* as "nature" or more comprehensively as phenomenal nature unfolding in the threefold manner of becoming described above).[7] While retaining the Greek sense of "all that is," my definition of *phusis* especially emphasizes the elements of coming-to-be and passing-away, thus preserving both the natality and fatality of all beings on the one hand, and the "prior to human intention" of the unfolding of being as beings on the other. By incorporating the birth and death of beings into the word *phusis,* I also retain the sense of *nasci,* which in Latin signifies birth.[8]

By following this explicitly biological model of time,[9] we can say that time is unidirectional, irreversible, and unique to each existing individual. This does not mean that time has no universal component, but I wish to stress the uniqueness of each life-trajectory. As individual mortals, we manifest time in a concrete way. A lifetime, as the basic manifestation of time, does not reduce time to space or to motion within space. In a universe where science declares the relativity of time and space, an individual lifetime offers an irreducible standard against which to understand all other senses of time. Man is the measure of all things temporal: those that come to be and pass away, as well as those aspects of reality that are immune to generation and perishing.

This anthropocentric understanding of time contrasts with the atemporality of many scientific and metaphysical *logoi*. As a metaphysical *logos*, ontology typically asserts that being somehow transcends time; theology often asserts that being (as divine) is eternal; and logic insists that its propositions are a-historical in nature.

I wish to propose a mortal view of time, taking my cues from a variety of sources, including grief over the death of loved ones, quantum physics (which reiterates the pre-Socratic view of time as the fundamental nature of *phusis*), and Continental philosophers such as Nietzsche and Heidegger. I will not go so far as to argue that the various laws of science, logic, and epistemology are unfounded or incorrect, but I do claim that they are fundamentally incomplete: failing to capture the experiential aspect of time, they banish it. The retrieval of time as experienced by human beings will doubtless complicate rather than simplify our account of reality. Nevertheless, the experience of time is fundamental,[10] even for an understanding of the gods—the immortals. The atemporality of science, metaphysics, and theology clashes with human temporality, thus revealing time as ultimately unthinkable, paradoxical, monstrous, and aporetic. In one of its aspects (metaphysics), time is disclosed in the mode of stasis, erasure, or indifference. This makes knowledge of beings possible. In another aspect, time challenges and withdraws the stable foundation of knowledge. This is the aspect of time that defines *phusis* and our mortality. In the realm of the non-metaphysical experience of *phusis*, *epistēmē* can never be secured on stable foundations, so that only *doxa* is possible: hence, "mortal" *doxa*.

Even the foundational accounts of static being by Parmenides and Plato, I argue throughout this work, are not as unambiguous as they may seem. Take Plato's *Theaetetus*, for example, a dialogue devoted to securing an understanding of *epistēmē* (true knowledge as opposed to *doxa*). In the dialogue's introductory dramatic setting, Eucleides and Terpsion are conversing, the former having returned from a meeting with Theaetetus at the harbor. "Alive or dead?" asks Terpsion (142a) about Theaetetus, who is on his deathbed. "Alive, barely," is the response (142b). Eucleides then relates the earlier dialogue between Theaetetus and Socrates. Socrates interrupts the dialogue by leaving (210d) to hear the indictment against him: the first step toward his execution is already enacted.[11] The proximity of impending death overshadows the *Theaetetus; its dramatic setting thus stands in the starkest* to its subject matter, an account (*logos*) of the nature of stable knowledge as it relates to objects in a realm beyond the fluxing temporal *phusis* in which mortals come to be and pass away (Plato's *topos noētos* ("intelligible realm")).

But the origin of the question of stable knowledge and being is not itself immortal; it originates in mortality itself. Theodorus introduces Theaetetus in the following way:

> Truly, Socrates, it is well worthwhile for me to talk and for you to hear about a splendid young fellow, one of your fellow-citizens, whom I have met. Now if he were handsome, I should be very much afraid to speak, lest someone should think I was in love with him. But the fact is—now don't be angry with me—he is not handsome, but is like you in his snub nose and protruding eyes, only those features are less marked in him than in you. (*Theaetetus* 143e, trans. Benardete)

At this painful slap in the face for Socrates, the reader flinches. Yet Plato immortalizes this instant through conveying it to the reader. No, Plato does more: the very origin of the question of knowledge begins here. Socrates beckons Theaetetus, wishing to examine his face in order to *know* his own (144e). The conversation then moves to examining knowledge as perception. The ugly perceiver and the ugly perceived (Socrates and Theaetetus) lose their individuality and dignity in a dialogue about *epistēmē* (certain knowledge).

Later in the dialogue, the definition of knowledge requires a criticism of Eleaticism. Here, Socrates shows the problematic exteriority of the mortal knower to unchanging knowledge, by refusing to criticize Parmenides. Socrates draws attention to the individual who remains outside the sphere of *epistēmē*:

> *Theaetetus*: No, Theodorus, you must not be released until you, and Socrates, as you proposed just now, have discussed those others who assert that the whole of things is at rest.
>
> *Socrates*: Well, but, Theodorus, I think I shall not comply with Theaetetus' request . . . A feeling of respect keeps me from treating in an unworthy spirit Melissus and the others who say the universe is one and at rest; but there is one being whom I respect above all: Parmenides himself is in my eyes, as Homer says, a "reverend and awful figure". I met him when I was quite young and he quite elderly, and I thought there was a sort of depth in him that was altogether noble. I am afraid we might not understand his words and still less follow the thought they express. Above all, the original purpose of our discussion—the nature of knowledge—might be thrust out of sight, if we attend to these importunate topics that keep breaking in upon us. (*Theaetetus* 183c–184a, trans. F. M. Cornford)[12]

Socrates declines to criticize Parmenides, even in the epistemological context of his discussion with Theaetetus. Parmenides, the "reverend and awesome" individual, exceeds the constraints of an epistemological setting. The individual escapes being hunted down (to take an image from the *Sophist*) by epistemic *logoi*. Rather than being identified with his thesis of static eternal being, Parmenides is here understood in terms of his individual life-span. When Socrates was young, Parmenides was quite elderly. In the *Sophist*, a dialogue that is a dramatic continuation of the *Theaetetus*, Parmenides is dead, and a nameless disciple continues his philosophy. The individual Parmenides persists in the living memory of Socrates as "*one being* whom I respect above all others,"[13] whereas epistemology requires nothing more than the signification: Eleatic stranger (*Sophist*). In the third dialogue, *Statesman*, another generational turn is introduced: a certain young man also named Socrates becomes a stand-in for a completely silent Socrates. *Individuals exceed the* logoi *concerning knowledge— whether mathematical, ontological, or political.* As generations, generated and perishing—indeed, Socrates describes himself as a midwife to Theaetetus' conceiving of "embryo thoughts" (201b–c, trans. Cornford)—individuals retain a temporality that is problematic to the stable entities presupposed by *epistēmē*.

Being, abstracted from time and rendered as unchanging and stable, makes knowledge possible. But the *knowers* themselves are subject to a different temporality: that of being born, growing, and perishing. Parmenides, whatever his arguments for static ontology may imply, is clearly experienced by Socrates as a living mortal. Epistemology requires that this fluxing temporality be extinguished, and Parmenides be subjected to a metaphorical "parricide" (*Sophist*).[14]

Time's *Aporia*: The Crossing of Mortals and Immortals

We can approach the paradox of the coexistence of fluxing being and stable knowledge in a different way, by turning away from the ontological/epistemological interpretation of being to *phusis*, understood as a mortal cosmology.[15] This entails a new view of metaphysics, in which the artificial separation of being and time is rooted in *phusis* and its temporal properties. We err when we interpret *phusis* exclusively as either being (as understood in metaphysics) or as becoming (as understood by the Sophists);[16] we also err when we reduce one to the other. By ignoring one of the two principle aspects of time, both metaphysics and Sophism produce incomplete accounts of reality. We should appreciate the inherent contradiction of asserting the existence of both fluxing becoming *and* immutable principles, as a basic feature of *phusis* (nature) itself. This contradiction, I argue, is real: whereas every individual man must die, the *genus* "man" does not die. *Phusis* itself manifests itself in this contradictory manner. We may argue that such definitions exist "only" in language, but attributing atemporality (or eternity) to language is an incomplete solution, for language itself is rooted in *phusis*. *Phusis* includes both mortality and immortality. It is constantly becoming, yet knowable (when appropriate) by such universal definitions as grammar, logic, and universal categories.

The paradox of time's two aspects may be termed temporal *aporia*[17] or the crossing of mortals and immortals. By "immortal" I mean that which transcends an individual's lifetime (Greek *aiōn*).

This paradoxical double nature of *phusis*, rooted in its temporality, is not a new problem in philosophy. Since Nietzsche, we have been aware of our psychological inclination to repress the philosophy of becoming and to focus exclusively on being. Metaphysics, understood as an account of *phusis* as stable, knowable being, dissolves the paradox. Metaphysics, understood as an ontology, theology, and logic, enables us to evade the monstrous duality of permanence and change in *phusis*. A destruction of metaphysics, begun in a self-conscious way by Nietzsche, becomes crucial to philosophers of the twentieth century, most notably Heidegger. This destruction of metaphysics requires us to rethink the paradox of time.[18]

Thinking about time leads us to an unknowable, unavoidable, and frightening *aporia*. The ambiguity stemming from this *aporia* is, at least for human beings, irresolvable and primordial, and we can find it in the work of many clear thinkers, despite the fact that Western metaphysics in general tries to gloss over it. Though it shields our eyes from the abyss of time, this practice of glossing over devalues our temporal existence. The converse is also true. When we stress the historically contingent aspects of our existence, we become desensitized to the abyss of time, in that we identify with our historical and cultural identities while evading our inevitable death.

The *aporia* of time occurs in two loci: *phusis* and the soul. Both cosmology and psychology address the paradox of time. Cosmology is not enough. At the individual level, the bifurcation occurs not as body and soul (the traditional metaphysical dichotomy) but as the doubling of the soul as fragmented—as either tripartite or bipartite. I will retrieve the early Greek twofold account of soul, as *psukhē* (immortal) and *thumos* (mortal soul), and apply it throughout. I explain this distinction in the next section. The crossing of mortals and immortals, that is, the *aporia* of time, occurs in the individual soul as well as in *phusis*.

What is the nature of the distinction between mortals and immortals? As Greek tragedy thematizes this distinction,[19] it is an inviolable separation: crossing over to immortality is an act of *hubris* that implies violating, jettisoning, our mortal life. To trespass into the domain of immortals is impossible; any attempt to do so is punishable. Immortal "lifetime," *aiōn*, exceeds and is opposed to the mortal *aiōn*. Ultimately, the real distinction between mortals and immortals is a matter of exceeding the mortal life-span, not of eternity versus singularity. Thus mortal time is the fundamental sense of time, and immortality is explicable only in terms of it; the beauty of the Greek gods is that they are defined by reference to mortals (rather than being eternal, like Augustine's God). The Greek gods

(1) are defined as a negation of mortality (*a-thanatos*), and (2) validated by duplicating mortal life-spans: they are born, have bodies, they eat and are nourished in their own ways.[20]

Metaphysical *Logos* is Temporally Deficient: Myth as a Cure

The goddess' speech in Parmenides and Plato's theory of Forms are two of the clearest articulations of metaphysical reality in the history of philosophy. In the following chapters I interrogate these two ancestors and explain my conception of metaphysics.

The term "metaphysics" is of late origin, originating as a description of the books following the Aristotelian *Physics*. In the absence of a common, unifying theme that could suggest an appropriate title, these books simply became known as *ta meta phusika*, "the ones after the *Physics*." Kant reinterprets the term "metaphysics" within the framework of his philosophy of experience to mean that knowledge which is independent of sense-experience.[21] In the latest major formulation (or metanarrative), Heidegger describes metaphysics as the history of the withdrawal of being from the time of Plato onwards in favor of a merely scientific or utilitarian study of beings (of their essences and particulars).[22] Heidegger argues that Nietzsche put an end to metaphysics and he wishes to return philosophy to its proper subject matter (through what he calls fundamental thinking): being as the coming-forth of phenomena.[23] To accomplish this, he renews the philosophical dialogue with the pre-Socratics, who, he believes, predate the birth of metaphysics.[24] The pre-Socratics' poetic conception of being, in which phenomena are described in their coming-to-be and passing-away, attracts him especially. As a substitute for the study of being according to categories, he emphasizes the *phuo/phusis* (natural growth) of being and its disclosure in phenomena.[25]

In this study, I define metaphysics in a new way—neither as a history of being nor as a theory about beings. Metaphysics is not *only* transcendence of nature, although it includes and requires transcendence, *it is a way of thinking that lays aside temporality in an attempt to evade mortality*. Metaphysics is a *pharmakon* (potion) that purges our cosmological account of the temporality that reminds us of our mortality. Thus the natural sciences, along with the dreams of the ghost-seer, history, logic, laws, cults, and religions, are all metaphysical. By metaphysical I mean: *atemporal, non-mortal descriptions of reality, often referring to some atemporal or eternal foundation, whether in being, knowledge, method, or law*. Thus metaphysics is nothing special; rather it is our most ordinary mode of being-in-the-world.[26] Metaphysics includes any explanation that shares the atemporality of *logos*, especially the atemporality of laws (including grammar).[27] I contrast the atemporality of metaphysical *logos* with another kind of *logos*, one that preserves the singularity of the individual human experience—Platonic dialogues would be an example of this latter sort of *logos*.[28] Nietzsche is correct in labeling as metaphysical the elements of other-worldliness in both Socrates and organized Christianity;[29] furthermore, Heidegger is correct in labeling technology as metaphysical.[30] Metaphysics is, in its essence, the flesh become *logos*, existence defined according to principles and laws.

Both universals and particulars, in the traditional logical-ontological-theological senses, belong to the lexicon of metaphysics. Opposed to these is the phenomenon of the inescapable radical individuality of each concrete individual life-trajectory from natality (birth) to fatality (death). Metaphysics posits certainty, predictability, control, project, and method as ways of evading the epistemological impossibility of knowing our own death; hence the need for the anxiety induced by Socrates, to know that we do not know. We cannot eliminate or overcome metaphysics any more than we can cure our mortality. However, given the pervasiveness and banality of metaphysics (in this sense), the task of philosophy becomes primarily ethical. Philosophy must not allow the fictions of metaphysics to obscure our mortality.

The closest traditional metaphysics comes to accounting for individuals is by assigning them proper names, such as "Adam" or "Reiner." These names, however, like labels, function like common genera or species names such as "cat," "dog," or "tree," in that they deceptively attribute static being to individuals who are essentially temporal. In every case, we make an assumption that there is *some unique* being we name by this name—the nominalist prejudice. (Parmenides, we will see in a later chapter, draws attention to the role of names and naming in a universe of *phusis*.) Proper names, though they may sometimes be unique, do not address individuals, any more than do social security numbers (which are always unique). They conceal living-and-dying individuals with symbols.

How, then, do we restore the individual? In the next section, I will discuss radical individuality. First, I will follow up the foregoing criticisms of metaphysics as static *logoi* with some remarks about myth as a cure—an alternative means of presenting *phusis* in language. I do not use "myth" in the trivial sense of falsehood or "mere" story, but in the original Greek sense of *mūthos* as narrative. The poem of Parmenides and the dialogues of Plato are neither historically accurate nor completely capricious, and they are not intended to be mere rhetorical tools or literary devices. Both are narrative forays into *phusis*. In this fundamental sense, these philosophers are myth-makers. I thus advocate rejecting the standard, normative picture of the evolution of philosophical thought as progress from *mūthos* to *logos*.

Myth has the advantage of moving away from the metaphysical obsession with truth toward a depiction of *phusis* as individuals in the context of their life-worlds. Myth is not concerned only with facts and entities that we can deem "true" or "false"; instead, myth presents us with shapes of existence (*Gestalten*). Instead of certainty and its counter-concept, the equally metaphysical concept of chance, myth elegantly provides us with probability (*tuchē*, chance) and lucid accounts—as opposed to necessity (*anangkē*), certainty, and predictability.

Of fundamental importance is myth's power to preserve individuals (Akhilleus, Socrates) without factualizing them. Myth preserves individuality through anecdote and focuses on the mortal life entangled in *phusis*. It addresses this individuality by highlighting the individual's *thumos* rather than his *psukhē*. The following two sections present my views on individuality and the soul.

Individuality

Individuality and the Self

Understanding time according to its biological mortal life-trajectory amounts to a critique of traditional metaphysics. Atemporal metaphysics ignores the individual human being as a unique, finite, and irreversible singular. Individuality *per se* is, of course, far from being a new concept in philosophy. Every metaphysical system entails some understanding not only of the world but also of what it means to be an individual in the world. Such systems, however, fail to account for individual temporality.

My concept of individuality is not the same as the modern conception. Specifically, it is not the Cartesian concept of individuality, in which the individual is either an objective spectator or a *res cogitans*. Either way, individual mortality is suppressed. According to Descartes, the basic activity of the individual is not coming-to-be, enduring, and passing-away (the terms of Greek *phusis*), but secondary mental actions: thinking and perceiving. Nor is my concept of individuality Kantian—that is, identical with a transcendental "self," described again in terms of a mental activity: synthesis. Romanticism in general fails to give a positive account of the individual. It posits the individual as a hero against the world, and accordingly, sets nature in opposition to the world. Finally, I do not define the individual in terms of consciousness, freedom, or citizenship, which all play an important role in Hegel's philosophy and German Idealism. It is commonly assumed that Kierkegaardian existentialism focuses on concrete individuality. But this is not the case. In *Fear and Trembling*, for example, the concrete analysis of Abraham's dilemma immediately dissolves into general comments about faith. Kierkegaard indulges in ironies, masks, plays, and, in many cases, posturing—a far cry from a real concern with the singularity of actual persons and an urgent response to their tragic loss. Thus, while Kierkegaard valorizes the "existent individual," he actually has very little place for the death of the other. In positing the other as an unknowable "absolute," that is, as God, Kierkegaard makes "fear and trembling" the most basic attitude in which we relate to the other rather than the attitude of *erōs* threatened by loss that is characteristic of the tragic condition of mortals in love. Tolstoy, in contrast, in his *The Death of Ivan Ilych*, comes close to what I mean here by a philosophy of radical singularity.

Whatever categorical determinations we might make of a person, these do not adequately give us the individuality of a person. The notion of individuality that I am arguing for here, unlike the "thinking ego," has a temporal structure. In *phusis*, the individual life-trajectory can be called "mortal individuality," as a condition of being which manifests itself through specific, existing individual beings. In everyday life, we continue to live as if we were mortal and yet have somehow transcended mortality. Metaphysics is the prephilosophical condition whereby we employ *logos* to protect us against our own mortality. A properly philosophical discourse deconstructs the metaphysical linguistic structures that shield us from mortality and *returns* us to our mortal *phusis*, namely, our mortal existence in our mortal cosmos—knowingly and willingly. This philosophical trajectory that returns us to our mortality is inscribed in the journeys of Parmenides' *kouros* and Plato's Socrates. Both begin with a concern for metaphysical permanence and later willingly accept their mortal condition.

Radical Individuality

By "radical individuality" I mean a non-egoistic, non-transcendental, non-conceptual, non-resurrectable, non-reincarnatable, non-reversible, non-repeatable, non-reducible, and non-reifiable space-time trajectory that is the being of one who belongs to his own death in an inescapable way, is aware of it, and bears untransferable responsibility for himself and his actions.[31] The journey begins with an awareness of mortality and ends with the elimination of all metaphysical delusions and the heroic acceptance of death.[32] This philosophically purified mortal rectitude is what I call "radical individuality."

The Mortal Soul

Thus far, I have argued that temporality and individuality are necessary for an account of *phusis*. Now, from *phusis* in general, I turn to the human element in *phusis*, and interpret this being according to the dual themes. To that end, I take up early Greek psychological terms and interrogate them according to their relation to temporality and individuality. I develop a theory of the two souls, which I call *psukhē* and *thumos* and which I appropriate from early Greek thought and from its modern critics such as Gomperz and Onians. I call attention to *thumos* or "mortal soul" as the domain where temporality and individuality coincide. This concept will figure prominently in my reading of Parmenides and Plato.

I define as "soul" all human transcendence, insofar as we are never exclusively a body existing in space. The temporal dimension of human existence, in the sense that man does not merely exist in space-time but also constitutes it, is the soul. Soul is not merely knowledge of temporality or a condition for existing or experiencing—it is our primary mode of being. As transcendence, our soul is also self-awareness, and it corresponds to time in its twofold manifestation: *logos*-based immortality (*psukhē*) and unavoidable mortality (*thumos*).

Two-Soul Theory: *Thumos* versus *Psukhē*

Early Greek thinkers and writers, including epic poets (such as Homer and Hesiod), poets (such as Sappho), tragedians, and philosophers, employed a rich psychological vocabulary, including *psukhē, thumos, noos, kardia,* and *phrenes.* Besides the body and soul (the one mortal but hardly the entire individual; the other—the *psukhē*—individual but exceeding mortal temporality), there is a third: something that is distinct from the body and yet distinctly individual, and, more importantly, that does not exceed human temporality. This something (hardly a thing, more a faculty) is the *thumos.* The *thumos* has appetitive, nutritive, trophic, and affective functions.

More than one hundred years ago, Theodor Gomperz identified and described the dualistic character of Empedocles' psychological teaching.[33] Following the standard division of Empedocles' extant fragments into two books—*peri phuseōs* and *katharmoi*—Gomperz describes this duality as a physics of the soul on the one hand and a theology of the soul on the other. He marshals evidence from the Empedoclean fragments with eloquence and acuity. I quote Gomperz *in extenso:*

[Empedocles' psychological teaching] was dualistic in character. It comprises on the one side what is practically his physics of the soul. Turning to this first, we see that he reduced the psychical to the material without exception and without intervention. He did not even postulate an intermediate soul-substance, but he based all differences of psychical properties and functions on corresponding material differences, as well in the species of beings as in individual beings, and in the varying states of the individual—

E'en as the matter at hand, so man increaseth in wisdom.

Ever as men do change, there cometh in constant succession one thought after another.

The other side of the dualism we mention is found, if the expression be permissible, in the Empedoclean theology of the soul. Every soul is a "demon" that has been thrust out of its heavenly home to "the unamiable fields," "the joyless place," the valley of lamentation. There it assumes the most diverse shapes. Empedocles himself claimed to have passed through the metamorphoses of a boy, a girl, a bush, a bird, and a fish. The soul is bound to that habitation by its native guilt, especially of bloodshed or perjury, and the vagrant fugitive cannot return to its original home, if at all, till after the lapse of 30,000 ὧραι, or 10,000 years . . . It is a reproduction of the Orphic-Pythagorean psychology depicted in glowing colours and fervid eloquence; . . . He describes in moving verse the fatal mistakes to which orthodoxy itself may impel those who are uninitiated in metempsychosis. There was the blinded father, for example, who was fain to offer an acceptable sacrifice to the gods and slew unwittingly the son of his own loins, thus preparing a fatal meal for himself with the very words of prayer on his lips . . . The road to purification was a long road, and its steps were marked by centuries; nor could sinful men regain their lost divinity till they had climbed the topmost rungs of the ladder of earthly existence as seers or poets or physicians or princes . . .

Here, then, we have the two parts of Empedoclean psychology, and it may reasonably be asked how two such different doctrines, which practically exclude each other, could have found a common resting-place in one mind.[34]

Gomperz suggests a brilliant solution to this paradox. He reminds us that, for Empedocles, "the 'soul-demon', like the 'soul' or psyche of most of his predecessors, was not the vehicle of psychical qualities denoting an individual or a kind of beings."[35] As evidence, he mentions Empedocles' assertion that he was now a bush, then a bird or a fish. By stripping the soul of its egoistic, emotive functions, Gomperz is able to relate Empedoclean psyche to a background of Homeric psychology: "The psyche of Homer played precisely the same idle part in the existence of man on earth as the 'soul-demon' in Empedocles . . . Psyche's *sole* raison-d'être *would appear to be her separation from the body at death and her survival in the underworld.*"[36] This finding is not surprising, when we consider the survival of the individual soul after death. But it is rather shocking that what really defines individuality (which I, with Gomperz, will locate in the *thumos*) remains alien to the soul; it is not *psukhē*'s function to preserve the individual's individuality. Here, Gomperz faces a problem: how does Akhilleus recognize the soul of Patroklos? To be sure, Homer describes the dead and avenged Patroklos speaking to an ill-fated but living hero as an oneiric (dream) sequence. The soul is clearly not the individual, but its double. This is a common feature of the soul; its vagaries are independent of the body, and Bremmer[37] provides a great wealth of evidence (such as instances of bilocation) to prove this. The dream context in which Patroklos' soul appears underlines the nature of *psukhē* as a double: it is an *eidōlon*.

Thumos: Historical Overview

The word *thumos* undergoes an interesting transition in early Greek literature. Beginning as something like "life-soul" in Homer, *thumos* later attenuates to denote simple emotions or appetites. To understand Parmenides, we must understand his role in this evolutionary process. I will begin by briefly discussing the etymological history of *thumos* without specific reference to Parmenides. Subsequently, I will be in a position to discuss its meaning within his text and philosophy.

Thumos in Homer

Consider Caswell's lucid account of the meaning of *thumos* in Homer. She names five contextual categories in which we can locate the meaning of *thumos* in early Greek epic poetry:

1. *Loss of consciousness/death*

Two "inner entities" mark the loss of consciousness (syncope), revival, and death: *psukhē* and *thumos*. In general, *psukhē* departs at syncope, and the *thumos* returns.[38] It is the loss of *psukhē* that determines a man's death and the *thumos* that experiences woe at this possibility.[39] I cite one example, quoting the anguished Akhilleus:

> The same fate comes to him who holds back and to him who fights, in equal *timē* (honor) are the coward and the brave man. Likewise, the man who has done nothing and the one who has accomplished much both die. Nor is there any profit for me, from the time when I suffered grief in my *thumos*, always to fight, setting my *psukhē* at hazard.[40]

It is worth noting that, the *psukhē* is curiously understated in Homer, only later attaining philosophical prominence in the writings of post-Homeric thinkers beginning with the pre-Socratics and reaching an apex in Plato. Gomperz, after noting that the *psukhē* does not seem to have any function in the living body/ person, as quoted above, continues:

> Not a single instance can be quoted in which she appears as the agent of human thought, will or emotion . . . Those functions, far from being performed by the Homeric psyche, actually belonged to a being of quite a different formation—to a perishable being which dissolved in air at the death of animals and men. To that extent it is even legitimate to speak of a two-souled theory in Homer, and this second mortal soul went by the name of Thymos.[41]

I will argue for the value of this *thumos*, the "mortal soul," to philosophy at the end of metaphysics.

2. *Intellect/cognition*

To understand what the epic poets mean by "intellect," we must first relinquish the modern belief that cognition and emotion are diametrically opposed to each other.[42] Such a neat distinction does not exist in epic poetry. For example, Homer's depiction of thought, motivation, and action is complicated by and interwoven with emotion. His treatment of *thumos* illustrates this point nicely. As S. D. Sullivan writes: "The passages of θυμός with verbs in the active or middle show that it was frequently an active agent within man. Unlike φρένες, which very rarely functions as an active agent in Homer, and far more frequently than νόος, θυμός actively performs a wide range of activities in a person. It engages in intellectual activity, feels emotion; it wills, hopes, desires, orders, and urges on."[43]

The intermingling of cognition and emotion is perhaps easy to demonstrate in Homeric texts, but difficult to comprehend. *Thumos* is used synonymously with both cognitive and emotive words such as *noos, noēma, phrēn/phrenes, kardiē*, and it appears with the verbs *manthanō, oida, phroneō, phrazō, noeō*, and *gignōskō* to describe intelligence.[44] Evidently, what fascinates Homer about his own language is not its *instrumental* precision but its richness; he employs *descriptive* precision for the realities described through language. It is useless to try to identify exactly what the meaning of each term is. Rather than build a lexicon of well-defined words, Homer keeps at his disposal elastic terms like *thumos* with a wide range of meanings, in order to depict a complex reality. It is therefore a daunting task to identify the various original meanings of *thumos* in Homer, and to identify which of these meanings become sedimented or lost in later Greek thought.

In summary, we can say that the function of *thumos* in Homeric poetry is somewhat elusive. It is the most prominent psychic entity in these texts, but it lacks a clear and unambiguous structure.[45] It is a word that informs the individuality, behavior, motivation, and action of a person, but not one that entails a defensible thesis on thought and cognition. That emotions play a significant role in thinking and making decisions does not seem to bother Homer. Looking ahead, it is the development of an inquiry into "knowing" and its corresponding universality that subjugates the role of *thumos*, a word loaded with unsubsumable particularity, individuality, and that bane of philosophical thinking: emotion.

3. Emotion

Caswell's third category is emotion. As discussed above, it is difficult to separate emotion from cognition in Homer.

4. Inner debate/conflict

Well-considered decisions also involve the *thumos*, as in Hektor's speech to his wife concerning his decision to fight in the Trojan ranks.[46]

5. Motivation

Thumos motivates action, chiefly impulsive action. The *locus classicus* of this example is Akhilleus, "who, having yielded to his great force and mighty *thumos* . . ." (*Iliad* xxiv.42–3).

The primary functions of the *thumos* remain almost unchanged from the epic poetry of Homer to Hesiod and other lyric poets—although careful philological work has detected some particular differences, these need not concern us here.[47]

Development of *Thumos* in Greek Thought

However, with time, the emotional aspect of *thumos* eventually comes to dominate its other meanings. As other words, such as *nous*, take over the task of describing intellectual activities, and as *psukhē* takes over the functions of life-force and individuality, the meaning of *thumos* becomes narrow and sedimented; it comes to refer only to the emotions. This attenuation, moreover, continues into the *New Testament*, where *thumos* means only one specific and negative emotion, namely, anger.

We begin to see this in the work of Plato. In the Platonic dialogues, *psukhē* becomes more important than *thumos* as a designation of the inner life of the individual. *Thumos* becomes subsumed within the *psukhē* as parts two and three of the tripartite soul in the scheme of *Republic* IV: these parts are *logistikon* (rational), *thumoeides* (passionate), and *epithumētikon* (appetitive). Plato arranges these three parts of the soul in a clear hierarchy according to a rationalistic prejudice. For him, the second and third parts should be subordinated to the *logistikon*. The *thumos*, formerly the most important psychic entity, is stripped of its intellectual and cognitive functions. It retains its emotional sense, but with a somewhat negative connotation. A clear dichotomy between the rational and emotional, which was absent in Homer, now becomes operative.

But this traditional account of the Platonic soul, as presented, is simplistic. When we follow the path of *thumos*, it leads into a more complex reading of Plato. In Chapter 6, I provide an interpretation of the *Phaedrus*, arguing that Plato inherits the Homeric polysemy of the word *thumos* by way of Parmenides. I conclude that, in this dialogue at least, *thumos* resists subordination to *psukhē*.

Thumos or the Mortal Soul

The foregoing discussion of *thumos* yields two insights into the soul as *psukhē*. First, we see how the concept of *psukhē* evolved from its initial appearance as a dormant principle in Homer to its later employment as an animating principle in Plato, naming the vital functions that had once belonged to *thumos*. Second, we see that *psukhē* retains its postmortem functions, while acquiring the noetic and individualistic functions of *thumos*. The changing conception of the word *psukhē* is thus a history of appropriating functions that had once been solely the province of *thumos*. The individual, by increasingly identifying himself or herself with this *psukhē*, forgets *thumos*, and with it, mortality. In terms of this development, we may safely conclude that all functions of *thumos* are appropriated by *psukhē*, *except mortality*, which remains associated with the body in a sign of its perishability. In Plato, we see evidence of this transformation in which the *thumos* literally becomes a part of the tripartite soul (in the *Republic*). With the waning of *thumos* as the psychological description of a living being, human self-understanding of mortality and finitude is also lost, stripping the world not merely of death, but also of temporality.

I want to stress the ephemeral nature of *thumos*. Gomperz himself does not relate the *thumos* to a philosophy of mortality, but he provides useful etymological, anthropological and textual support for it. He writes: "The word [*thumos*] is identical with the Latin *fumus*, or smoke, with the Sanskrit *dhumas*, the Old Slavonic *dymyu* and so forth." Cultural anthropological research, he explains, especially into the beliefs of the "oriental people," reveals the widespread conception that "the steam ascending from freshly-shed blood" is indeed a kind of soul. This "blood-soul" reveals an original conception of soul, dating to a time long before both Homer[48] and the later domination of psychic agency by the *psukhē* or the "breath-soul." "When the breath-soul came in the field, the ground was already occupied by the smoke-soul or blood-soul—and the later comer had to be content with a more modest though nobler part."[49]

Why do we even call the *thumos* a soul at all? For an answer we can look to Nietzsche's friend, the philologist Erwin Rohde. The answer is twofold. *Psukhē* and *thumos* are both detachable from the body and distinct from it, while residing in it and animating it. Furthermore, both entities are unique to the individual.[50] S. D. Sullivan writes "in all cases, θυμός is distinct from the person."[51] In this, it resembles the *psukhē*. However, unlike *psukhē*, *thumos* does not possess an independent existence once separated from the body, although the *thumos* may be briefly scattered or even temporarily escape the body. It must, if the person is to live, return to the body immediately. Should it fail to so do, the body will perish and so will the *thumos*. The *psukhē*, on the other hand, purely a shade, flits underground to Hades. The *psukhē*, unlike the *thumos*, has nothing in common with the body, and it mournfully remembers this distance in its insubstantiality (see, notably, *Odyssey* xi).

It does not even help to posit the "soul" as a unified self in Homer, because there are two souls. Even if one of these (the *psukhē*, for example) were posited as a self, we would still confront the problem of the soul's nature as a "double," an *eidōlon*. As a double, the soul is not an image in the sense of a "mere image" (in Plato's sense of a copy of a Form or a copy of a copy). Duplication is not primarily about an "original" as opposed to its "image." *Duplication is a fundamental feature of being itself.*[52]

We return to the idea of *thumos* as the mortal soul. As such, its functions are mortal in two senses: it aids the body while it is alive and delimits its mortality. When Parmenides writes, "as far my *thumos* reaches," this has to be interpreted as the limits of his mortality.

The purpose of the two-soul theory is to provide a psychological framework within which to understand human temporality. Human temporality itself is twofold. In accordance with *logos*, on the one hand, there is a certain continuity after death, something that transcends our worldly existence. This is the metaphysics of the soul as a "principle" or a "form" that animates and surives material existence. This temporally imperishable substance, on the other hand, does not provide a full explanation of human being. Just as humans have unique access to *logos*, they also have a unique awareness of their mortality. The "*logos*" in Aristotle's famous definition of man, "man is an animal having *logos*," summarily evades and fails to capture this mortality. Refocusing our attention on mortality as the fundamental mode of human existence opens philosophy to a temporality entirely distinct from metaphysics. This is the awareness of time as finite, unidirectional, unique, and unrepeatable. If we are to understand our soul as a human soul, this mortal temporality (*thumos*) must be understood as equiprimordial with the immortal temporality given through metaphysics. The two-soul theory does justice to these two temporalities. We need both *psukhē* and *thumos*.

Thumos: Implications for Philosophy

Thumos is the cornerstone of my philosophy of radical individuality (understood as mortal temporality) as well as a key to my interpretation of Parmenides. I translate *thumos* as "the mortal soul." Its basic elements are: (1) it represents the temporal trajectory of a mortal life from birth to death, (2) it possesses unique individuality or singularity, and (3) it desires to overcome its own mortality. Thus, in my view, *thumos* is the unintentional source of metaphysics. In Homeric psychology, "It is the loss of *psukhē* which determines a man's death, the *thumos* which experiences woe at the possibility."[53] Although, we have a two-soul theory here, their unity does not present a problem, because there is an essential relationship between the two: without *psukhē*, *thumos* vanishes.

Thumos allows us to define "self" as a temporal trajectory between natality and fatality. The *thumos* is a way of addressing individuality; epic poets use the word *thumos* only in the singular, and the plural never occurs. Common epithets of *thumos* (such as *agēnōr, hilaos, megas, sidērios, huperbios*) suggest a close relationship between person and *thumos*.[54] The nutritive, emotional, volitional, and intellectual aspects of a person are closely related to *thumos*.

Thumos acts autonomously for the most part, embodying a kind of "independence." "In this varied activity within a person, *thumos* differs strongly from *phrēn/phrenes*, which only rarely act independently in Homer. The large number of instances of *thumos* as an independent agent also distinguish it from *noos*, which appears less frequently as an independent agent."[55]

Thumos is a non-reifiable temporal structure, not an entity. It is the precognitive source of our knowledge of mortality as well as the seat of our desire to transcend mortality. Thus we may speak of the "structure" of *thumos*, while remembering that it is not an organ, but rather a physiological, psychological, and intellectual function. These functions can be metaphorically described as a "tripartite *thumos* soul," the three parts being:

Appetitive function: *thumos* is related to hunger and nourishment.

Emotive and non-conceptual knowing: Besides the standard emotive functions of the *thumos*, such as anger, desire, and so on, a kind of precognitive awareness operates here: the implicit awareness of mortality.[56] With the awareness of mortality and the resultant fear thereof comes a desire to overcome it. *Thumos* also experiences a desire to transcend mortality. Desire is the first seed of the mortal mind and an important element in understanding. Transcendence belongs not only to *noos* and *psukhē*; the *thumos* also has a component of transcendence. Such transcendence leads the *thumos* to both grasp itself as a "self" as well as become aware of its finitude. The awareness manifests itself not as conceptual knowledge (such as the statement "all men are mortal"), but rather emotively— as anxiety, either experienced or postponed.

Intellectual (explicitly cognitive) function: In Plato, this function belongs to *noos/ psukhē*. Nevertheless, in the tradition that precedes him, intellectual function can be found in *thumos* as well. The intellectual function is implied in decision-making, in the Homeric understanding of the psychological self, and finally in an attempt to "cure" mortal anxiety. This cure consists of a palliative escape from the *phusis* that generates *logos*, into the timeless interpretation of *phusis* in *logos*. This cure, in other words, is metaphysics. Plato erases the proximity of mortality, and the metaphysical cure for it lodged in *thumos*, when he takes away the intellectual faculty from *thumos* and relates it to the immortal *psukhē*. Thus metaphysics loses its "mortal" context and the *psukhē* becomes immortal. Only in post-Platonic philosophy can Parmenides' *Peri Phuseōs* disintegrate into two disconnected parts whose unity becomes an interpretive problem: the unity of the speech on immortal being (metaphysics) and mortal *doxa* (mortal conviction) is lost. The unity of these two parts, previously made possible by *thumos* and by *phusis* itself, is destroyed by Plato's epistemological interpretation of the structure of the soul. However, Plato retains the mortal context, as I will argue, in a concrete mortal: Socrates.

Journey

If the notion of stasis in metaphysics is to be remedied, and the birth-to-death trajectory of mortal life-span is to be made central again, then philosophy itself must adopt an itinerant structure. Philosophy is a journey away from—not to— certainty. Being in time is understood cosmologically as *phusis*, existentially as a journey, theologically as finitude, epistemologically as *aporia*, anthropologically as mortality, and psychologically as *thumos*. Journey is understood ontologically as *phusis* (coming-to-be, growing, and passing-away), existentially as finite life-span, epistemologically as a move away from the certainty of metaphysics to mortal *doxa* (which is merely probable), theologically as search for ultimacy, and psychologically as flight from death.

Journey is the Basic Structure of Existence within Time

There are two traditional senses of 'journey' in philosophy, and to these I will add a third. The three senses I wish to draw attention to are:

1. A philosophical journey (actual or metaphorical) is a search for knowledge, undertaken to explore new lands and meet with different people and query them.[57] Journey, as dislocation from one place to another, may be voluntary (as in the case of Parmenides) or it may be forced, either by oneself (Odysseus' searching for his *nostos*) or by exile (Empedocles). These journeys share, in varying degrees, existential features such as isolation, hardship, nostalgia, and mental and emotional unrest. Geographical dislocation is the first, but not the primary, sense of a journey.
2. Knowledge itself can then be traversed, using the metaphor of journey as a pedagogic tool: for example, the philosopher can lead a student on a "path to knowledge."
3. Mortal life is the primordial journey—all other journeys are metaphors in comparison. The journey begins with desire or *thumos*. Mythical narratives, which are inescapably temporal and preserve the individual, are the best vehicles for conveying this sense of journey, as opposed to generalizing *logoi* (as discussed above). (In Chapter 3, the temporality embodied in the journey becomes a central theme of my reading of Parmenides' poem; it sheds light on the goddess' surprising thesis of being as immovable and atemporal.)

The journey, in other words, has an existential meaning, which can and should be central to philosophy. The journey is neither the external form of knowledge nor the context in which it is sought; rather, it informs the very content of knowledge. Mortal life is the journey. Individual mortals follow a unique life-trajectory from natality to fatality. The very capacity of movement existentially modifies the philosophical description we can give of beings, both mortals and immortals: the description can no longer rest on stable epistemological foundations yielding certain truths.[58] An account of being by one on a journey is different from an account of being by one at rest: the former is a *mūthos*, the latter a *logos*. When a philosopher casts his philosophy in terms of a journey, the journey is not merely a literary device or a poetic motif.

Traveling for the sake of knowledge conveys the idea of gathering knowledge from a wider world. Geographic, ethnological, cultural, political, and even commercial interests motivate the journeyer to acquire something that transcends his own location. Even the acquisition of knowledge can be explained in this way. However, acquiring knowledge is not like acquiring a piece of property: the journeyer is irreversibly transformed by it. Therefore, I prefer to downplay the philosophical journey as an acquisition, and suggest that it is primarily one of irreversible transformation. In this sense, the philosophical journey represents less a displacement of the mortal and more a changing of his life.

The "aptness" of the journey as a metaphor for philosophy is perhaps as old as philosophy itself. In common parlance, we speak of an "intellectual quest," a "philosophical journey," of "stages in the way." Modern philosophy retains the journey metaphor, but only as a pale shade of its original meaning (a *psukhē*, not a *thumos*), by placing "method" (*meta-hodos*), the road or the way (*hodos*), at the center of the philosophical enterprise.[59] The emphasis, however, shifts from the journey to the road itself: "method" loses the sense of "meta-," a journey "with" or "after," in the sense of wonder, discovery, *nostos* (homecoming), an intellectual adventure—all hallmarks of early Greek thought. In modern thought, "method" becomes the guarantor of "certainty," the hallmark of truth understood in the modern sense. An emphasis on certainty and "proper" methods obscures the existential experience of the journey. A journey takes us from place to place (Parmenides' *kouros* travels over "all cities," *pant' aste*, 1.3, as does Odysseus). A road, however, without the journey, is static—a mere essence.

Heidegger forewent a lengthy preface to his collected works in favor of a simple sentence: "ways, not works" (*Wege—nicht Werke*). Is the close affinity between philosophy and the motif of journey a mere accident? It would seem so at first glance, because what does visiting various places have to do with the unfolding of thought? Here we confront the hidden meaning of the journey. The "journey" motif is not primarily concerned with space at all; instead it is concerned with experiences extended in time. Traversing various points in space is not the central meaning of journey, but rather the paradoxical unity of different experiences in a unified extension of time. In this way, the notion of journey demands that we understand it beyond spatial conceptions, incorporating it into such fundamental temporal trajectories as life and narrative. Philosophy, forever swinging between "being" and "becoming," that is, between unity and change, cannot hope for a more fundamental motif than journey. To put it succinctly, journey is the chosen symbol (not a metaphor) for philosophy, because its primordial nature is to express the unified unfolding of existence in time. When it stresses the unity of time, it can indicate being; when it speaks of time's extension, it stresses becoming. The motif of journey in Parmenides' poem and in Plato's *Phaedrus*, I argue, is no mere literary device, no mere external, capricious adornment. It is the *praxis* of philosophy itself—it is more than searching for a method, it is a being-on-the-road (*hodos*).

Mortal life itself is journey, beginning with birth and concluding with death. Here, the sense of geographical dislocation is underplayed, or irrelevant. The distention of time, not space, makes this journey possible. The temporal journey of the mortal life-span is not an isolated example of *phusis* (coming-to-be, growing, and passing-away) brought to light in a journey. In fact, the entire phenomenal world of change can be understood in terms of a journey, as irreversible change in passing time.

The Tragic Return from Metaphysics

My sense of philosophical journey also includes the notion of *return*. According to my analysis of the *aporia* of time, time includes both fluxing and static dimensions (what I called a crossing of mortals and immortals). Consequently, we saw that *phusis* allows descriptions of itself as both being and becoming. Even at the level of human beings, the dichotomy of time entails a twofold description of the soul as *psukhē* and *thumos*. Inherent in this dichotomy is the unavoidable possibility of metaphysics, which, however, represents only one side of the dichotomy. We may tie these elements together in a notion of journey understood as a return.

The philosophical journey has the following components:

1. The unidirectional journey of mortal life.
2. The flight from mortality into the metaphysical realm of certain knowledge and its atemporality made evident in "method." This metaphysical segment of the journey, despite my criticism of it, is crucial, unavoidable and an inherent feature of the mortal soul (*thumos*); my criticism of metaphysics is that one cannot remain stuck in this static realm; the realm of eternal being, promised by metaphysics, is ultimately unavailable to mortals (and their longing for it hubristic).
3. A philosophical, ethical abandonment of static eternal metaphysical being and a return to the cosmos.

Return is the structure that permits us to understand these three senses of journey in relation to one another. Mortal life is always a unidirectional journey. The second journey is that of metaphysics, which is made possible by *logos* and has its origins in the *thumos'* psychological longing to overcome its mortal nature. A realization that our mortal nature and our mortal cosmos are incompatible with eternal being necessitates a *return* from metaphysics to our mortality. This return, translated into epistemological terminology, is a tragic return.[60]

My philosophy stresses the return as crucial to the philosophical journey: we begin by going forward in a metaphysical leap, but continue the journey as a return, a homecoming. Parmenides' *kouros*, for example, seeks a home in the realm of being; but, crucially, he is not satisfied with this and returns, I argue, to his true home (the cosmos), understood with a new philosophical depth. Likewise, what makes the *Odyssey* great is Homer's genius in seeing the unity of Odysseus' well developed *nous* and craftiness of *logos*, on the one hand, and his longing for a return, a homecoming, on the other.[61] The point is recapitulated in recent times by Heidegger, who quotes Novalis and identifies the philosophical enterprise as essentially homesickness, a desire to return home.[62]

Having established a vocabulary of temporality, *phusis*, metaphysics, *thumos*, journey, and return, I now turn to these themes in Parmenides and, later, in Plato.

Chapter 2

Parmenides and His Importance
as a Beginner

The Importance of Parmenides

Parmenides remains compelling to us for several reasons. Recent interest in the pre-Socratics reflects deep dissatisfaction with a certain style of thinking associated with the Enlightenment—a dissatisfaction that reaches its culmination in the twentieth century. It is not easy to say precisely what this "certain style of thinking is." Some candidates are the domination of reason, the rise of positivism, the explosion of science, the neglect of existential concerns, increasing materialism and technology, or even psychological/moral failure leading to nihilism. Nietzsche's scandalous phrase "god is dead" and Heidegger's controversial expression "the end of metaphysics" articulate a typical modern anxiety: that we are somehow at the end of a certain set of possibilities. Even Hegel's sober dialectical method envisions its completion when the progression of history reaches its end point.

Whether it be *hubris*, delusion, or a reality, philosophy is called upon to renew itself in our times, and, in slightly more ambitious terms, to make a new beginning. This new beginning cannot be separated from the history of philosophy, including our caricatures and criticisms of it (the rise and fall of metaphysics, the end of reason, the age of anxiety, etc.). This attempt to make a new beginning, to critique philosophy since Plato and somehow distance ourselves from it, leads us to look beyond Plato and focus anew on the pre-Socratics. Nietzsche and Heidegger, although different in their philosophical interests and tasks (and temperaments!), reach back to the pre-Socratics and articulate the importance of these early "pre-metaphysical" thinkers (in Heidegger's terms) to the philosophical challenge of modern times. Besides the philosophers, philologists since Nietzsche have contributed a great deal to our understanding of the debt Greek philosophy owes to the pre-Socratics. And finally, the charisma of the pre-Socratics themselves, who were creative profound poets and thinkers deeply concerned with nature and cosmology, resonates with our own interests. The rest is, as they say, history: we have seen an explosion in scholarship on the pre-Socratics as well as philosophies inspired by them.

Why another study on the pre-Socratics then—especially one focused on a thinker so closely bound up with the history of philosophy, the thinker that we most wish to distance ourselves from? In other words, why the "Father" of ontology, theology, logic, metaphysics—in short, the "Father" of Western philosophy? Why Parmenides, and more importantly, why another study? The most honest answer is that Parmenides' poem allows me to express my philosophy most fruitfully. This does not mean that the philosopher is merely a vehicle for my own project; that would be an oversimplification. Rather, as others have done, I look to Parmenides for a "way forward" in thinking about nature in the widest possible sense. In thinking and rethinking his poem, I have journeyed with Parmenides along his way for so long that it would be impossible to say which elements of this study are truly Parmenidean and which are properly mine.

In reading his poem as an integrated whole, thereby embracing both its eternal logic and its focus on the changing physical cosmos, I have attempted to remain faithful to Parmenides himself.[1] The apparent contradictions in his poem can be restored to their proper source, namely, nature, in a way that embraces both *phusis* and *logos*.[2] With this aim, I offer an interpretation of the much-neglected proem, a corrective to the exaggerated speech on truth in the second part of his work, and a rehabilitation of the problematic "doxa" of the cosmology in the third.

I begin by introducing Parmenides and his work and then describe my approach to interpreting his work, how it differs from others', and how Parmenides can be considered a beginner in a new sense.

Dates, Life, the Poem and Its Three Parts: Fragments and Testimonia

Much has been written about Parmenides' philosophy of eternal being, but relatively little is known about his mortal life. Plato tells us that he visited Athens when he was about 65, along with his nearly 40-year-old student, Zeno (*Parmenides* 127a–c). The occasion was the great Panathenaic festival.[3] Socrates, who was then a youth, met with the two Eleatic thinkers. Plato refers to this meeting in two other dialogues, the *Sophist* and the *Theaetetus*. Based on Plato's testimony, scholars calculate that Parmenides was born around 515 BCE.[4] This date contrasts with another, 540 BCE, given by ancient chronographers.[5]

But everything we read in Plato about Parmenides is not to be accepted on faith. A facetious remark made by Plato implying that Parmenides was a pupil of Xenophanes is, for example, probably not to be taken at face value. The influence of Pythagoras on Parmenides is more likely.[6] Recent scholarship also makes Parmenides' knowledge of Heraclitus plausible.[7]

We also learn from Plato that Parmenides was an "awesome, formidable figure" (*Theaetetus* 183c). Nietzsche, who does not hesitate to cast philosophers in the most unflattering light, says, "Parmenides . . . [by contrast with Heraclitus, is] a type of truth-teller but one formed of ice rather than fire, pouring cold piercing light all around."[8] It was Plato who first called him "Father Parmenides" (*Sophist* 241a), an appellation that he deserves even to this day. If there is anything original in Plato's epistemology, it is rooted in his dialogue with Parmenides and Heraclitus.

Since Plato, it has been the standard view in scholarship that Parmenides was a monist. While Parmenides certainly founds ontology proper, both in its non-empirical subject and in its logical structure, there are problems with interpreting him as a radical monist. Reexamining this topic makes him, once again, a beginner for us.

The Work

As far as we know, Parmenides wrote just one work, the poem *Peri Phuseōs*, "On Nature." This poem survives only in fragmentary form. Even so, some long stretches of the surviving work constitute what has been called the first extended philosophical argumentation in "Western" thought. Paraphrasing A. N. Whitehead, Gallop says, "Plato's own writings might be said to have consisted in footnotes to Parmenides of Elea."[9]

The extant fragments of Parmenides' work have been arranged into three parts,[10] traditionally called the proem, way of truth (*alētheia*), and the way of mortal opinion (*doxa*). The proem contains a detailed description of the youthful protagonist's ethereal chariot ride, escorted by daughters of the Sun. A goddess he meets at the other side of mighty gates delivers a speech concerning the way of truth, *alētheia*. Pushing language to new limits, the goddess argues for a unified, non-temporal, and unchanging being. Her argument is traditionally considered to be Parmenides' greatest philosophical accomplishment. The third portion, the way of opinion, is badly preserved, and since it purports to be a cosmology and a description of a dynamic universe, its relationship to the truth portion of the poem is problematic.

Problems with the Monistic Interpretation

Then there are problems with the relationship of Parmenides' "*meta*-physics" to any physics whatsoever, a point that Zeno is famed for demonstrating. Aristotle, who seems to have studied Parmenides' complete poem, accuses the Eleatic philosopher of dualism![11] Nehamas notes that the entire didactic poem is "dualistic with a vengeance."[12] But Aristotle and Nehemas are not alone in doubting Parmenides' radical monism. Curd notes that the highly contentious pre-Socratics, as a group, ignore this version of monism.[13] Logical argumentation appears to have been discovered, refined, and then set aside by Parmenides and the other pre-Socratics. It thus becomes plausible that Plato may have misrepresented Parmenides and his method of argumentation.

Parmenides as the Beginner

There is probably no greater beginner in the history of philosophy than Parmenides.
Reiner Schürmann, "Tragic Differing"[14]

Starting with Plato, Parmenides has been recognized as a thinker of immense importance. Plato even wrote a dialogue named after him, in which a young Socrates "meets" Parmenides, and Parmenides points out problems with Socrates' theory of Forms. In the *Sophist*, an Eleatic stranger represents Parmenides and meets Socrates again, this time toward the end of his life. By now, Parmenides is called "Father Parmenides," and Plato has his protagonist, the Eleatic stranger, suggest a "parricide." The proposed philosophical murder of Father Parmenides does not really work out, and the dialogue ends in philosophical *aporia*, with Socrates exiting to answer the charges brought up against him. Since then, a view of Parmenides as the father of philosophy has endured through most of its history. Epistemology, ontology, logic, and even theology: all can be seen as pioneered by Parmenides.

Heidegger suggests that at the end of our epoch and at the beginning of the next, the essential beginning, which is thought in Parmenides, becomes thought-worthy again. But what epoch has ended? And what epoch is beginning? Here we encounter Heidegger's controversial notion of the "end of metaphysics." He hails Parmenides as a beginning that is not behind us, but, as a radical beginning, always stays ahead of us.[15] Heidegger thus brings to the study of the pre-Socratics both a radically fresh viewpoint and a sense of wonder. As we saw above, Heidegger says of Parmenides that "the dialogue with Parmenides never comes to an end, not only because so much in the preserved fragments of the didactic poem still remains obscure, but also what is said there continually deserves more thought."[16] Expanding, Heidegger writes,

Chronologically, 2,500 years have elapsed since the outset of Western thought. But the passing of years and centuries has never affected what was thought in the thinking of these two thinkers . . . what is thought in this thinking is precisely the historical, the genuinely historical, preceding and thereby anticipating all successive history. We call what thus precedes and determines all history the beginning. Because it does not reside in a past and lies in advance of what is to come, the beginning again and again turns out to be precisely a gift to an epoch.[17]

Let us ask again: is Parmenides still the father of philosophy? What remains worthy of thinking in Parmenides, which is not yet thought? Reiner Schürmann points out that Parmenides is not merely a pioneer, but also a founding father, involved in the constitution of ultimate foundations. Philosophy, since Parmenides, "provides evidential moorage for the sake of consoling the soul and consolidating the city: some single first law governing all regional laws, be they cognitive, practical or even positive."[18] Schürmann calls into question the legitimacy of any single first law through his reexamination of Parmenides. What he finds is that the beginning is not a single unified beginning of being (as Parmenides has usually been interpreted), but a tragic knowledge—a knowledge of mortality and its contrary (championed, in Parmenides' work, by the goddess).[19] His interpretation shatters the conventional understanding of Parmenides; this new parricide reincarnates Parmenides as a thought-worthy figure at the end of metaphysics, when philosophy as ontology, theology and logic withers away. I use the word "reincarnates" in two senses:

1. The beginning is always ahead of us, a point Heidegger makes tirelessly,[20] and
2. This reading restores the human life-span as a philosophical issue. This reintroduction of temporality and mortality, as Schürmann points out, breaks up the "ultimate immutable foundation" of metaphysics. Parmenides' poem, I argue in this work, presents us not merely with a metaphysics of the One, but also a powerful problematization and deconstruction of it.

There are other readings of Parmenides, of course. Diels, Burkert, and Kingsley note the ritual influences of Orphism in Parmenides.[21] Plutarch notes that Parmenides was a lawgiver.[22] Inscriptions provide convincing evidence for Parmenides being worshipped as a healer after his death, and therefore, he may have practiced the profession of a healer. The wise man of Elea seems not only an expert on immortal being, *but also on mortal life.* On the eve of Socrates' trial and subsequent sentencing Plato invokes the ghost of Parmenides by having the Eleatic stranger appear in the dialogue, the *Sophist*, and poses the question "Is Socrates guilty?" to him.[23] Death lurks in the background of these great epistemological dialogues; Parmenides is dead and only his voice speaks, and Socrates, though living, remains silent. The interlocutor, Theaetetus, is a likeness of Socrates, representing him in an uncanny way, just as the Eleatic stranger is a stand-in for Parmenides. A group of dead men discusses the nature of being and the possibility of knowledge—Plato's own awesome accomplishment. The triad of dialogues: *Theaetetus*, *Sophist*, and *Statesman* are Plato's "late works" in the sense that Plato abandons the theory of Forms. Insofar as they are meditations on Socrates' death, they retain their continuity with the "earliest" dialogues like the *Phaedo*. Why does Parmenides appear at the end of Socrates' life as a departed soul? The posing of this question is a verification of Kingsley's thesis: Parmenides has something to say about death.

My Approach to Parmenides

In this study, I take account of not only the goddess' speech on truth (mostly in fr. 8) but also the proem that precedes it and the *doxa*/cosmology that follows. In so doing, I withhold judgment on what philosophy is *supposed* to be and take Parmenides at face value. The guiding intuition is that Parmenides' genius consists not in launching a method of logical argument, but in documenting a basic experience of life. Thus it becomes necessary to speak about the various ways in which a "beginning" can be understood, and in what sense Parmenides is a beginner.

I begin by paying heed to the very beginning: to Parmenides, the father of Western philosophy. He appears to us as a *kouros* (a young man), a traveler, a seeker, rather than as a dogmatist. Within the interpretive horizon of Parmenidean philosophy, we must remain open to something new and relevant, something that is more than a historical beginning of metaphysics inaugurated by the goddess' first speech. This "new" element is his mortal cosmology, understood as a deconstruction of this speech. In order to accomplish this, I eschew a narrow philosophical interpretation in favor of a broad one, embracing all clues. I wish to overcome a common negative prejudice revealed in the following critical dismissal:

> Ancients and moderns alike are agreed upon a low estimation of Parmenides' gift as a writer. He has little facility in diction, and the struggle to force novel, difficult and highly abstract philosophical ideas into metrical form frequently results in ineradicable obscurity, especially syntactic obscurity. On the other hand, in less argumentative passages of the poem he achieves a kind of clumsy grandeur.[24]

Let us read the text as we have it, as Parmenides wrote it.

The text describes Parmenides, in the first person, on a journey. This is important to note. It is a testimony, a confession, and closer to St. Augustine's *Confessions* in its entanglement with the world than to Descartes' *Meditations*. Augustine's "I" gives testimony to the world and its truth, while Descartes' "I" abstracts. What we have is not a detached work written by someone who has finished his thinking, arrived at a truth, and then composed a poem to express it. The philosophical truth of this poem was not first derived as a philosophical axiom and later reconstructed. The truth, rather, unfolds during the course of the journey. It is therefore problematic to search for a "philosophical core" embedded in this husk of poesy. In this work, the act of thinking and what is thought are inseparable.

How does Parmenides himself describe his work? Is it dogma or is it narrative? A clue is found in verses 2.1–2, where the goddess says, "Come now, I shall tell you, and you having heard carry away the story (*mūthos*), What the only roads of inquiry that are to conceive." This passage occurs at the seam between the initial proem, which recounts Parmenides' journey, and the philosophy lecture given by the goddess, which has earned Parmenides his reputation in the tradition of Western metaphysics. The word *mūthos* is no longer adequately translatable into modern languages. The least misleading translation is "account" or "narrative." Our modern understanding of myth has diverged from the original sense, and to retrieve the original meaning of *mūthos*, we must undo the conceptions and misconceptions we have about myth. Here is Heidegger on this issue:

> Μῦθος, ἔπος, and λόγος belong together essentially. "Myth" and "logos" appear in an erroneously much discussed opposition only because they are the same in Greek poetry and thought. In the ambiguous and misleading title "mythology," the words μῦθος and λόγος are connected in such a way that both forfeit their primordial essence. To try to understand μῦθος with the help of "mythology" is a procedure equivalent to drawing water with the aid of a sieve. When *we* use the expression "mythical," we shall think it in the sense just delimited: the "mythical"—the μῦθος-ical—is the disclosure and concealment contained in the disclosing-concealing word, which is the primordial appearance of the fundamental essence of Being itself.

We note the negative result that there is a twofold fall in the meaning of the term *myth*. On the one hand, the word *myth* is no longer understood in its primordial sense—as an expression of being. (Here I use "of" to indicate that the expressing belongs to being.) Secondly, the word *myth* has developed in a manner that is alien to the meaning of the term as we see it in Homer and Hesiod; it has come to denote what is false.

We must understand Parmenides' poem as a *mūthos*. It is an account, but an account that has value, meaning. It is not meant to be an objective description, but nor is it a subjective opinion or fancy. Although the term myth now means something untrue, or fantasy, particular myths show that this was not always the case. The myth of Oedipus is hardly "false." No one would claim it to be historically accurate, nor would we be willing to say, in this post-Freudian era, that it is a subjective fancy of the Greeks. Parmenides also begins with "The mares that carry me . . .," that is, with a narrative, a *mūthos*.[26]

Let us return to the words of the goddess, "you must carry my *mūthos* away with you." Here we see that the journey is not merely a preface added onto the second part. The goddess herself directs that he *carry away* her *mūthos* once he hears it. The correct way to understand the entire work is as *mūthos*. The first part is explicitly Parmenides' *mūthos*; the second part is the goddess' *mūthos*, which Parmenides must make his own by listening to it and carrying it away. After hearing the goddess' *mūthos*, he must resume his journey, the journey that began in the first line of the proem. The goddess' *mūthos* speaks of logic and immovable being; Parmenides' *mūthos* is forever in motion. *If* mūthos *is an expression of being, does this not mean that the being of Parmenides is something radically different from that of the goddess?* That being which is unchangeable and eternal belongs not to Parmenides, but to the goddess herself. Parmenides' *mūthos* strives to distinguish and hold together this contradiction in being, these two opposing *mūthoi*; he has the goddess say, "It is necessary that you learn all things, both the untrembling heart of persuasive truth and the *doxai* (opinions) of mortals (*brotōn doxas*) in which there is not true trust (*pistis alēthēs*)" (1.28–30).

Thus there are three separate *mūthoi* in this work by Parmenides:

1. The *mūthos* that is proper to the *kouros*, the person characterized by the journey, which keeps him forever in motion, except during his brief encounter with the goddess.
2. The *mūthos* proper to the goddess, characterized by unchanging being, from which all motion and becoming has been banished.
3. The *mūthos* of the poem itself which can articulate these two contradictory *mūthoi*.[27]

Previous scholarship, however, has neglected to take this last into account. To be sure, the goddess refers only to two *mūthoi*, the speech on truth and that on cosmology. However, if we recall that the entire poem *as composed* is itself a *mūthos*, then it becomes clear that we have here not two, but *three mūthoi*. The third, outermost *mūthos*, the didactic poem itself, constitutes *Parmenides' true view on the nature of being and becoming*. It is only by ignoring the first part, the proem, that we lose the *mūthos* of Parmenides the human being, and naively attribute the goddess' *mūthos* to him. Losing the human being, we lose the goddess too. We end up with only one *mūthos*, the one that speaks of immutable being. The rest of the proem seems like ornamentation—clumsy and obtrusive.[28]

Summary of My Reading

Parmenides' poem consists of three sections, *which form a coherent philosophical program*. The first part is the proem, where divine escorts lead an unnamed *kouros* to the abode of an unnamed goddess. Then follows the middle part of the poem, consisting of a preliminary logical speech about abstract being, and, finally, a lengthy, rich cosmology, presented as mortal *doxa*. The motif of journey holds the three sections together: initially it is a physical journey; later, the journey consists of "ways" of thinking and speaking.

The proem provides the key to understanding Parmenides. The first line tells us that he went as far as his *thumos* could reach. When a person dies, *thumos* "rises like vapor" and disappears, while the *psukhē* survives in the underworld as a disembodied shade. The realm of the goddess is beyond our mortal reach. Therefore, he enters the realm of the goddess *in logos*, poetically, through the persuasive words of the Muse-like daughters of the Sun. Dikē, who cannot allow a mortal across the threshold, allows the *kouros* to enter poetically, through *logos* only. Therefore for the rest of the journey, we speak of "ways" of speaking, not actual roads.

The goddess describes being as it is for the immortals, beings who know neither genesis nor perishing. She repeatedly stresses the logical inconsistency of time, and banishes the past and the future. Her abstraction allows for a single, changeless, timeless, motionless *logos* or an account of being.

Then she says, "from this point mortal opinions learn" (8.51–60), and upon these opinions (*doxai*) she pours much abuse. Here, we can compare the *Odyssey*. Kalypso detains Odysseus by deriding the ways of mortals, especially aging and death. She offers him immortality, but he rejects it and returns (in a homecoming or *nostos*) to his home, Ithaka. The third part of poem, the goddess' second speech, thus is a *return* to the mortal cosmos. Thus we are two-headed: while we can talk about immortal being, our *phusis* is one of becoming. This contradiction is the mortal condition. And Parmenides begins to describe our universe in stunning detail. Thus we return from our journey into the metaphysical realm of the goddess, where we experience a trip through *logos* back to the world.

Philosophers ever since have hubristically confused themselves with the goddess, believing that the goddess has granted them citizenship in her world of words. These wretched, treacherous and self-loathing mortals wrap themselves in the goddess' garb and denounce mortal *doxa*—*as if we can disprove the world!* This is the kind of metaphysics Kant calls "the dreams of a ghost-seer." Parmenides is too honest for this type of metaphysics; he preserves the mortal universe and returns the *kouros* to it. He is the first to thematize the seduction of immortality through the apple of logic, and also the first to reject this false paradise.

So *why* does Parmenides do what he does? Perhaps because we all want to escape mortality and the allure of fleeing into the immortal "other world" of metaphysics is seductive. We try to use logic for this, because logic is atemporal. But we must return, just as Odysseus does to Ithaka and the *kouros* does to our mortal cosmos. Our place is within the realm of phenomena, and philosophy's task is to provide an antidote to our illusions and be honest about our irredeemably mortal existence. This is the essence of "knowing oneself" as mortal.

Part II

Parmenides

Chapter 3

The Mortal Journey:
Thumos (The Mortal Soul) and Its Limits

Elements of Interpretation

Three Parts of Parmenides' Poem

The extant fragments of Parmenides' poem, about 150 lines in all, belong to a single work, a poem of immense significance to the Western philosophical tradition. Of this poem, dubbed *Peri Phuseōs* ("On Nature") by later doxographers, only about one third has been preserved;[1] some in fragments only a single word long (e.g., Gallop's fr. 15a: *hudatorizon*). Fortunately, Sextus Empiricus has preserved the first part of the poem, traditionally called the "Proem" and known to us as fragment 1. Simplicius also quotes fragment 8, which we consider "the earliest example of an extended philosophical argument." These are the two best-known parts of the poem. I wish to situate them in the context of the *entire* work.

The extant fragments fall into three parts: the first part is conventionally called the proem, where the protagonist, an unnamed youth or *kouros*, is conveyed by a chariot drawn by mares and escorted by divine maidens to the abode of an unnamed goddess. The second and third parts are the two speeches the goddess makes for the benefit of this *kouros*. The first speech, called the "*alētheia* speech" or the "Way of Truth," is a philosophical argument in which the goddess denies time and becoming, and "proves" the unity and motionlessness of being. The second speech, variously called the "mortal *doxa*," the "Way of Opinion," or the "Cosmology," is the third portion of *Peri Phuseōs*. Despite its extremely fragmented current state, it is thought to have been the longest portion of the work as composed by Parmenides.

While long passages of the goddess' speech on *alētheia* survive, and have attracted interest from Plato onward, only short fragments of the *doxa* survive. This elicits a false impression of the original work. Diels estimates that we have only one-tenth of the *doxa*, but nine-tenths of the so-called Way of Truth.[2] Besides the fragments, which Diels considers to be the genuine work of Parmenides (his B fragments), we have numerous testimonia (which Diels collected as the A fragments), many also about the *doxa*.[3]

The *alētheia* speech has always attracted the most attention, in ancient times and in modern academic scholarship, thanks to its strong metaphysical message, despite the problematic conclusions it bequeaths to the history of philosophy such as the denial of change and motion. The nearly complete preservation of this part of the work amplifies this problem of privileging the *alētheia* portion at the expense of other parts of the poem. I will show throughout this study the importance of reading the poem as a whole—all parts in relation to one another—resulting in a moderated message contained in their dialectical unity. In doing so, I hope to forestall some of the problems that arise from a one-sided metaphysics.

Journey as the Unifying Theme of Parmenides' Poem

Reading the work as an organic whole has the advantage of integrating the proem into the rest of the poem, as well as relating the *alētheia* and *doxa* sections. The unifying theme of the poem is journey, which begins with the first line and continues throughout. It would be a mistake to consider the first part (the transportation of the youth to the goddess) simply a "proem," external or extraneous to the poem's real content. It would be equally misleading to ignore the journey's end. Having listened to the goddess discourse on the nature of being, the *kouros* is finally returned to the mortal cosmos, bearing the words of the immortal goddess.

The journey appears even in the goddess' speeches. For example, she exhorts the youth to avoid the way of non-being and follow the "path" or "road" (*hodos*) of being (2.2–5). She frames her philosophical message in terms of two roads (*hodoi*) on which the *kouros* may (theoretically) travel (fr. 6). In the speech on truth, she again compares her speech (*mūthos*) to a single "road" (*hodos*). In describing mortals "wandering" on the "path" of *doxa* (fr. 6), she uses travel terminology to criticize them: their paths are "backward turning" (*palintropos*) (6.9). Parmenides keeps the theme of journey before his readers as a guide through the geographical, philosophical, and lexical landscapes through which the poem wends.

The work embodies a journey in another sense, however. Of course, it opens with the literal displacement of the *kouros* to the realm of the goddess—a place where many philosophical interpreters stop and focus their attention, feeling they have reached the culmination of her argument. But the journey of the *kouros* continues. As we have seen, Parmenides uses the vocabulary of journey in the goddess' speeches on being and *doxa*. More importantly, Parmenides does not linger in the metaphysical realm of truth (the goddess' first and most famous speech): he returns the *kouros* to the mortal cosmos. Indeed, the goddess entrusts him with her message, which he presumably brings back to mortals ("and do you listen to my tale and take it well to heart,"[4] 2.1). The goddess' mortal cosmology can be seen as a way of conveying the *kouros* back to the mortal realm. Finally, she teaches him "so that never any one among mortals might overtake (*parelassēi*, go beyond) you in knowing" (8.61), implying, of course, that he will be back among them.

I will apply the theme of "return" of the *kouros* to the mortal realm in four ways:

1. By integrating the three parts of the poem into a unified whole, showing that the contrasting speeches of the goddess are in fact related *topoi* on the intellectual journey advocated by Parmenides.
2. By "correcting" the problematic conclusions that follow from the philosophical demonstration in the *alētheia* speech, which denies the phenomenal world. Thus Parmenides avoids the pitfall of having to deny phenomenal appearances while explaining their underlying causes.
3. By legitimizing the longest portion of the poem, the mortal cosmology or the *doxa*. This elegantly criticizes the *exclusivity* of the logical demonstration as an account of the world.
4. By arguing that Parmenides emerges as a complex thinker whose work truly thought through both *logos* and *phusis*, finally reaching temporal *aporia*.

Contexts of the Journey

Scholars agree on the importance of journey in Parmenides' poem, but how is this motif to be understood? Some classicists, such as Mourelatos, focus on the importance of journey within the literary tradition in which Parmenides wrote, that is, the epic tradition represented by Homer and Hesiod.[5] Others compare the work of Parmenides to lyric poetry (such as Pindar's sixth *Olympian Ode*), or to Orphism, shamanism, or other early Greek philosophers. However valuable such textual studies may be for understanding Greek thought and words, they are attempts to place Parmenides in *his* time and tradition and do not exhaust the philosophical significance of the philosopher. An equally valid question is: what can we learn about *our* reality from the extant fragments of this pre-Socratic? To this end, we must read Parmenides, not only in light of his historical and literary context, but also in light of the phenomena about which he speaks. These phenomena are more concretely available to us and can serve as a background against which Parmenides' theoretical interests relate to our own. The task of describing such phenomena is, however, fraught with difficulty. We do not know reality apart from our interpretation of it, and any analysis must be understood within this framework.

I will begin from the poem itself, from its dramatic and grammatical elements. Where such evidence is scanty or inconclusive, I will incorporate, when possible, relevant support from the poetic tradition (rather than the philosophical tradition). My reading reflects my methodology: a literary reading versus a literal or strictly philosophical reading. I pay attention, however, not only to philological aspects such as grammar, meaning, syntax, and etymology, but also to dramatic poetic devices such as imagery, effects, contrast, ambiguity, suggestion, association, and *aporia*. Classical scholars have pointed out Homeric parallels in Parmenides' words and images.[6] The thematic resonances go even deeper, but remain unexplored. I will explore a few of these resonances in this section.

The theme of the poem, understood primarily as a journey, does not originate with Parmenides. Homer's *Odyssey* made the journey a respectable topic for epic, and stands in the background of Parmenides' poem, but Homer is not the only one. Parmenides' journey continues a tradition, and his beginning is a dialogue with other beginnings. This should not cause us to minimize his achievement: it makes his beginning even greater. His beginning is mindful of time persisting as tradition, a sense of time that persists as ways of thinking beyond historical data. Every true beginning is essentially a confrontation with time, to mark with specificity ever-renewing time without speaking "out of time." Let me explore some Homeric parallels.

Parmenides presents an "Odyssean" conception of the philosopher in two ways. The first is the choice of journey as a motif for philosophy; the second is the destination as a return, a "homecoming." Parmenides' poem traces many *topoi*; his protagonist is, like Odysseus, *polutropos*: a man of many ways. Odysseus is driven on far journeys, just as the mares carry Parmenides' youth. Odysseus was on a voyage of discovery: many were they whose cities he saw and whose minds he knew (*pollōn d'anthrōpōn iden astea kai noon egnon*, *Odyssey* i). The hero's self is described in terms of his *thumos* (*Odyssey* i), which suffers much, and he is contrasted with the many mortals, who (reckless fools, like Penelope's suitors) do not return home. These elements reappear in Parmenides' poem. The *kouros* here is also described as the knower of all cities (1.3), and here too his self is identified in terms of his *thumos* (1.1; I will return to this issue of the self in a later section). The goddess receives him by pointing out the way his self is distinct from that of the usual run of "mortals"—he is singled out by his arrival at the goddess' (1.27; cf. fr. 6).

Tantalizingly enough, it is the notion of *nostos*, homecoming, the *telos* of the *Odyssey* that Parmenides remains silent on. This "discrepancy" turns out to be even more significant than the correspondences, because it highlights the apparent absence of a *nostos* in Parmenides. But I will demonstrate that this absence is only apparent, and argue (as above) that the cosmology and the poem itself reflect the homecoming of Parmenides.

Even scholars who take the journey of the *kouros* seriously understand the trajectory of the journey as extending in a one-way route, from the cities of men (1.3) to the realm of the goddess. Scholars debate whether Parmenides travels into the heavens or underground (cf. Burkert's influential view of a *katabasis*); for our purposes, we do not need to enter into questions of topography. Kingsley develops at length the notion that Parmenides, in a *katabasis* to the realm of the goddess, reaches his true home.[7] For Kingsley, Parmenides comes to terms with death by taking refuge in a primordial reality that precedes all mortal life. Kingsley thus keeps Parmenides in a metaphysical realm, while simultaneously relocating that realm.

Havelock compares Parmenides' journey to Odysseus' and draws attention to Odysseus' stay on Circe's island. He writes, "So Parmenides remembered how on that island coming to be and perishing had been banished . . . For the philosopher, this is where the *nostos* ended."[8] This draws a sharp limit to the parallel with Odysseus, who, of course, by contrast, must *leave* the tempting islands of the goddesses, Circe and Kalypso (whose name suggests she is a "concealer"), in order to return to his home on Ithaka; throughout, he remains faithful to his mortal identity.[9] Even though Kalypso had offered him immortality, this would have denied his homecoming (*Odyssey* i.14) to mortality, and therefore Odysseus cannot stay with her. A central insight of my study is that we can extend this theme of a return to the mortal cosmos to Parmenides and his poem. The unnamed goddess similarly seduces Parmenides upon his arrival beyond the gates. In her speech she too (like Kalypso) offers the young man an alternative to his mortality in the form of a *logos* on unchanging being. Parmenides, I argue, makes clear that this realm is not accessible to mortals except in *logos*; that the voyager returns (as the goddess urges him to) is demonstrated by the fact that we have his poem written in his hand.

Journey: Temporality and Multiplicity

My interpretation rejects the search for a "place" to which the *kouros* ascends or descends. The journey, I argue, is not just geographical, but also logical in the sense of being a journey in and through language. There are three reasons to reject the purely geographical interpretation of this journey as a descent into Hades.

1. Parmenides' journey is not confined to the road between the House of Night and the Gates where Night and Day cross, but includes a return to the ways of mortals and their cosmos.
2. The speeches of the goddess have very little in common with what Odysseus learns in the world beyond.[10] Therefore an insistence on the Homeric precedent may not be doing full justice to Parmenides. Parmenides had the benefit of a much richer thought-world than did Homer or Hesiod.[11] I propose that we look to someone more contemporary with Parmenides for interpretive guidance, namely, Plato. Plato was not only familiar with the Parmenidean but also with the Orphic tradition.
3. Finally, the gates, which occupy most of the description, are placed high in the sky. Kingsley maintains that the underworld has both chthonic

and ethereal entrances,[12] but, nevertheless, what transpires between the *kouros* and the goddess is not characteristic of a mystical experience. The goddess does not "reveal" a "transcendent truth," but argues in a most sober, sophistic manner, using logic and reason alone. Her argumentative method seems to preclude a mystical experience.

Time, more than space, offers a clue to Parmenides. Scholars have usually looked for the literal, spatial dimension of the proem. However, Parmenides is not concerned with giving us an exact topography of the journey. More important is the essentially temporal nature of journey. In describing the journey of the *kouros*, Parmenides stresses action words, such as rapidity, direction, uniqueness, the ideas of being escorted and of following someone. These are all temporal categories. When it comes to spatial descriptions, Parmenides is vague and elusive. Attempts to chart the topography of the proem's journey are, therefore, bound to be inconclusive. Parmenides deliberately deflects attention away from naïve realistic interpretations, which map out a specific "mythic geography," a task altogether too crude to attribute to this thinker. As Mourelatos points out, Parmenides intentionally withholds topographic evidence.[13] Parmenides asks us to take the motif of the journey seriously without reading the proem as describing a real journey into the sun or into the underworld. I wish to argue even further that Parmenides plays with an exquisite understanding of journey, not so much as spatial extension, but as temporal distension.

In the proem, Parmenides achieves a sense of rapid temporal flux while using a paucity of geographical references. The mares are carrying the *kouros* forward, while the daughters of the Sun, having left the house of Night, guide him on. A sense of temporal flux is heightened both in style (the use of hypotaxis: lines with several subordinate clauses),[14] and content. Although the exact location of the journey is only hinted at, its speed (the turning wheels emitting a hissing sound), its direction (into the Light), and its driving impulse (*thumos*) are well documented.

In the Way of Truth, on the other hand (the goddess' main speech on being), spatial descriptions predominate. In its time-deficient and space-emphatic mode, the journey continues without motion in her focus on the uniformly extended and bounded "sphere" of timeless being at rest. In the "wanderings" of the mortals, which is the concern of the third part of the poem, the image of journey continues to include both space and time: the spatiality of the cosmos and the temporality of its genesis and extinction are brought together into a complex relationship.

Parmenides uses the journey as a vehicle to convey both a search for knowledge, and a means of writing about that search. This means the journey can shed its existential dimension and be conveyed in a narrative. All narrative in fact embodies an inevitable distension, and thus a temporal element. Every narrative has a beginning, a continuation, and an end in the same way that a journey—every journey—does. Every narrative is a journey and must obey a certain temporality. In *logos*, narrative then takes the place of literal temporal and spatial distensions and their implications.

We must therefore not ignore the temporal dimension of Parmenides' narrative poem. He journeys to a goddess who herself *narrates* to him a *mūthos* about unchanging being (among other things). We must preserve the paradox of how the goddess, although she herself *narrates*, denies temporality. The paradox is highlighted, when in welcoming the *kouros* she recounts his journey, only to go on to logically negate its reality. Her language of logical analysis not only denies phenomenal reality, but also the narrative possibility of the poem itself—something we ourselves cannot ignore.

The Proem

For the purposes of my translation and discussion, I read 1.1–21, up to the reception of the *kouros* by the goddess, as the proem (the journey). This differs somewhat from the standard usage (mentioned above) that refers to all of fragment 1 as the proem. I discuss 1.22–32, in which the dominant theme is no longer his journey, but the encounter with the goddess, in Chapter 4, "In the Realm of the Goddess." The current chapter focuses on the themes of journey and its philosophical importance in reading Parmenides, and the theme of individual *thumos* and the self.

The poem begins with Parmenides telling us that he is already on the way, being borne by the mares. The daughters of the Sun lead him. They, having left the house of Night, proceed into the light, guiding Parmenides on. The beginning of the journey is not as simple as it seems. It contains a hidden trace of origin and direction. It would be reading too much into the poem to say that Parmenides himself is coming out of the house of Night. But it would be reasonable to agree that behind him lies the house of Night, and that the maidens of the sun lead him on away from it. Parmenides is also not following the maidens blindly; the maidens escort him but it is his wish, his *thumos*, that first initiates the journey. Therefore, I call this segment of the journey "expectation." It begins with the house of Night and extends beyond the gates where the goddess receives him by taking him by the hand.

The Philosophical Significance of the Proem

The entire fragment 1 is commonly called the "proem" in order to distinguish it from the body of the poem, which scholars often misleadingly describe as the poem proper, comprising the dual speeches of the goddess. The poem (in that sense) is further called the "didactic poem," to note its special character: the philosophical reasoning of the goddess. Some commentators, including

Heidegger, object to these appellations on the grounds that philosophical prejudices color these distinctions.[15] Closer observation will reveal that the "proem" is not only richer in imagery and suggestion than the body of the poem, but also contains a distinct, implicit philosophy. Even though the poem reads more like a logical explanation, its "philosophical" form is deceptive. The arguments of the goddess' speeches must be seen in the philosophical, phenomenological context that the proem provides. Understanding the philosophy elaborated by Parmenides throughout his poem requires a full appreciation of the poetic context and imagistic clues supplied in the proem. Therefore, I consider the poem as a whole, including fragment 1 (and especially lines 1–32). As Kingsley says, in studying authors like Parmenides, we should begin at the beginning, "at the point where they start," and not in the middle simply because this coincides better with the presumed interests of modern philosophy.

The notion that the proem contains clues to the thought of Parmenides is not a new one, as Kingsley, most recently, has demonstrated.[16] However, the philosophical "beginning" which Parmenides inaugurates in Western philosophy with his metaphysical theory of being and truth (Heidegger) overshadows the literal beginning of his extant work. The proem contains a different kind of beginning of thinking, expressed through the motif of journey. This existential, less technically philosophical beginning is important. Parmenides, it is alleged, broke away from both the mythic traditions of Homer and Hesiod as well as the obsession with cosmology displayed by his Ionian predecessors. He begins a new form of argument, introduces a new ontology, and bequeaths a new set of philosophical problems to posterity. By comparison, the beginning he makes in the proem with the words "Mares which carry me, as far as *thumos* might reach, were sending me . . ." is trivialized or ignored.

Even when the proem is included in their interpretations, many scholars subsume or assimilate it to Parmenides' logical ontology, for example, by allegorizing its imagery. This puts the chariot in front of the mares, so to speak; the proem is read as a poetic prologue to Parmenides' philosophical poem, as is clear from the following example. Kahn writes, "[Parmenides] certainly does not begin with any discussion of the structure of the heavens, or with the problems of the nature and number of elements." He sees this as a problem. He is correct in distinguishing the beginning made by Parmenides from that of his predecessors, the Ionian cosmologists. Despite his intuition that "a close reading of the proem alone is sufficient to give us a definite answer to the question 'What is Parmenides' problem?'," Kahn succumbs to the standard philosophical bias and immediately skips over the proem to the speeches of the goddess, when he says, "The philosophical exposition opens quite abruptly with the statement 'Come mark my words: I shall tell you what are the only ways of search there are for knowledge or understanding' [2.1]."[17] In other words, he actually begins with fragment 2 rather than fragment 1.

This common prejudice ignores some important contextual points. It sustains an artificial, textually unwarranted separation of "philosophical" subject matter from its "non-philosophical" context, which is regarded as poetic (i.e., philosophically extraneous) ornamentation. It replaces the literal order of Parmenides' presentation (the text as he conceived it) with a hypothetical conceptual order. This reversal seriously distorts Parmenides' philosophical message. Above all it presumes to identify Parmenides with the goddess. Read in this manner, the proem no longer modulates the problems raised by the goddess' twofold speech. Interpretations of the proem, too often, merely anticipate and confirm the dogmatic claims that emerge from the body of the poem.

Similar criticisms apply to the relation between the two parts of the goddess' speech, the first on true being and the second on cosmology or mortal *doxa* (opinion). We cannot forget that the title of Parmenides' work is *Peri Phuseōs*, "On Nature." Although it may not have been chosen by Parmenides, it does serve as an accurate title. Therefore, in discussing the speeches of the goddess, we must remember she discusses both *alētheia* and *doxa* and we must be careful not to privilege the former unduly. The description "nature," however, only applies to the *doxa* portion about the mortal cosmos of becoming—*the only realm in which the journey described in the proem is possible.*

The philosophical bias, which valorizes the logical argument on being, fragments the unity of Parmenides' work by denigrating both the proem and the so-called *doxa*. Just as the proem is ignored as an irrelevant bit of poetry, so the cosmology is written off as antiquated prescience. For example, when a scholar like Kahn concedes that his reading will address only the truly philosophical doctrine expounded by the goddess/Parmenides, he is forced to remain silent on the *doxa*: "I shall not attempt to resolve the vexing problem of the *doxa*, the cosmology offered in the second part of the poem," he writes.[18] If we begin instead with the proem, and relate it thematically to the *doxa* (through themes of journey and return), the journey described in the proem forms an antidote to the sterility and immobility of being that the goddess argues for in her aletheiological speech. The third phase of the *kouros'* journey, the cosmology of the *doxa*, then frames the goddess' speech on being.

But first, a few more words on the "philosophical" reading of the proem. This reading usually takes one of two extreme and contrary forms. At one extreme is Sextus Empiricus, a philosopher, who allegorizes the proem into a journey of the soul beyond the senses. In so doing, his philosophical prejudice requires him to interpret the proem rather creatively and perhaps violently.[19] At the other extreme is the "non-philosophical" prejudice of Taran, a classicist, who feels that his analysis "definitely settles the question that the proem is only a literary device."[20] Taran offers a detailed criticism, with rigorous philological method, of preceding attempts to make sense of the proem. He concludes, "[t]he journey to the house of the goddess is only part of the literary device, an antecedent of which we find in Hesiod's meeting with the Muses."[21] This interpretation unfortunately begs the question, why does Parmenides continue with this curious tradition? Why does he choose a (supposed) metaphor of a journey as opposed to a straightforward meeting with the goddess? Why does he need the goddess at all? Parmenides' proem invites us to ask more questions, rather than ignore them as manifestations of "poetic style."

I wish to steer a middle course between these two extremes of philosophical predetermination and the depletion of meaning implied in reading the proem as a literary device. The proem is a first-person account of a journey. Parmenides portrays himself as a journeyer, a *kouros*, who is being carried forth by mares. The motivation for the journey is doubly determined (both mortal and divine): he is propelled by his *thumos* (1.1) or desire, and led by the daughters of the Sun. Let me therefore turn to a discussion of *thumos* and its role in the proem.

Thumos and the Self

We begin with the first line of the poem. It is important to remember that the entire poem is written in the first person. Here, Parmenides says, "the mares were carrying me." By using the pronoun "me" (1.1), Parmenides refers to himself as a unified being in both space and time. At first glance, this observation seems trite. However, Parmenides' interest in his individuality becomes obvious once we are alerted to it. In fact, he overstates it. For example, the mares, which might seem to be an accidental detail, turn out to be well chosen for Parmenides' purpose. Greek athletes preferred mares for horse racing events;[22] besides indicating speed, this suggests the rider is like a potential hero in a contest (an *agōn*). The *kouros* distinguishes himself from the run of mortals; he far outstrips other mortals, as the goddess marvels: "far indeed have you come from the way of mortals" (1.28). If the first aspect merely distinguished him from men in general—he is a victor—the second shows that he has distinguished himself even within this class: he arrives on a path as yet untrodden by other mortals.

The *kouros* is said, in the very first line, to be on a journey "as far as *thumos* might reach." Interpreters have taken *thumos* in various ways.[23] Surely, it refers to the *kouros*. In Chapter 1, I described *thumos* as the "mortal soul" in early Greek thought. Let us apply it to this passage. *Thumos* becomes important as a key to reading Parmenides. Since it motivated his philosophical journey, this word is of more than casual significance. A simple translation of *thumos* as desire would be not only anachronistic, but also impoverishing. The word expresses longing, desire, individuality, and mortality. The protagonist of the poem is on a journey "as far as *thumos* might reach." But since mortal *thumos* finds its limit in death, this should be understood as "to the full extent of mortality," that is, as far as his life as a mortal extends. *Thumos* links the journeyer and the journey, by being the "cause" of the journey, the *hou heneka* or that for the sake of which the journey is undertaken. It marks the extent of the journey, as well as the extent of the *kouros'* individuality in that it marks his inescapable mortal radical individuality. The *thumos'* aspirations, however, surge even beyond the powers of the *kouros* himself when he is aided by divine escorts.

The first line presents two motivations for the journey. Divine escorts lead the *kouros*, but his *thumos* also propels him. Greek scholars call this common poetic device, of attributing motivation to both human and divine forces simultaneously, "double determination."[24] As E. R. Dodds demonstrates in his analysis of *ate*, this device cuts away any notion of autonomy from the Homeric and in our case Parmenidean notions of self.[25] (I discuss this device later in terms of the crossing of mortals and immortals, a feature I locate in *phusis* itself.) The *kouros'* individuality is defined by its limits; if he thought he was an autonomous self, he would never reach the goddess. Dikē (Justice), who guards the gates between mortal ways and the immortal realm, makes clear that she only admits him through the gates because his divine escorts persuade her (1.11–21). The goddess herself, whom he then reaches, reiterates this (1.24: "O youth (*kouros*), companion of immortal charioteers"). An attempt by a mortal to get past the gates guarded by Dikē, unaided or autonomously—that is, an attempt to exceed mortal limits—would be a classic case of *hubris*.

Let us discuss the individual motivation for this journey. The journey begins with a decision. This decision is not the goddess' will or that of the mares or the escorts, but a decision made by the protagonist himself. We would be wrong to think that early Greek thought did not have a notion of self, capable of making decisions.[26] The self we speak of here is indeed a complex but unified reality: the *thumos* or "mortal soul." I argue that the *thumos* corresponds to the self in an important way. In looking for a notion of the immortal soul (*psukhē*) or of the body, we have ignored the *thumos*. The search for *psukhē* has been colored, I suspect, by a secret desire to discover a *res cogitans* in Homer, and likewise the search for the body has been a search for a unified *res extensa*. We moderns see these categories as the only way to unify the self.[27] We have overlooked the *thumos* because it is mortal (just as we have denigrated the body, because it is perishable), which disqualifies it as either soul or mind in the modern sense of these terms. The self as a unit, living, willing, making decisions, suffering, and dying is indeed present in early Greek thought (and in Homer); it is not understood as "body" in the sense of a counterpart to the Cartesian model of the mind. Snell wrongly claims that the Homeric man cannot make decisions because Snell's notion of autonomy is, as Williams demonstrates, very Kantian.[28]

The basic structure of the *thumos*, I would argue, is neither transcendental nor reifiable. The objectifying description of the *thumos* (e.g., that it is located in the *phrenes*, that it can be scattered or gathered) notwithstanding, it is, in essence, the mortality of an individual life. We must not just equate mortality with death. Mortality is the basic phenomenon of life, a way of individual-being-in-time; it is a unique temporal trajectory extending from birth to an eventual death (as discussed in Chapter 1). It is not a "life-force," it is the phenomenon which the metaphysical term "life-force" attempts to explain away. On this understanding, Parmenides' portrayal of a journey corresponds with his reading of the self.

In conclusion, *thumos* is a non-reifiable temporal structure, not an entity. It is the non-conceptual source of our knowledge of mortality as well as the seat of our desire to transcend mortality. The focus of my reading of the poem thus swings away from the logic of the goddess' speech (as emphasized in previous scholarship), to a concern with mortality. Self, life, temporality, and death are the chief themes of Parmenides' poem. We must interpret the goddess' speech on truth with the basic nature of *thumos* in view, and evaluate it not only for the validity of the argument, but also for its relevance to us as mortals. The other basic feature of mortal life in *phusis* is the journey, with its temporal distention and multiplicity.

Journey and Multiplicity in the Proem

The beginning is preceded by a decision. When we plan, we weigh methods and consequences, we think ratiocinatively, but we do not yet make a beginning. A beginning implies action, and demands a decision to act. The decision to begin cannot be computed abstractly or arrived at passively. The decision that drives Parmenides' protagonist is not impersonal, mundane, or calculated. The mares drive him onto incalculable territories, access to which is not possible through human agency alone, and on this journey he transcends the cities and knowledge of men. Therefore the decision is not a product of knowing, nor is knowledge its goal. Parmenides' decision is impassioned: to go as far as his *thumos* leads him. Desire cuts the Gordian knot of deliberation.

Neither is the beginning of the poem the inception of the journey. The journey has already begun; we meet the *kouros* already on the divine road, being pulled by the mares. The daughters of the Sun have left the house of Night toward the light and are now escorting the eager *kouros*. His *thumos* (1.1) impels him to his destination.[29] He is already prepared for his journey: he is the knower of all cities, since the road is described as one "which carries the man who knows over all cities"[30] (1.3). This is not a journey from darkness to enlightenment, a common view held by Kahn, Kingsley, and others. We cannot simply say that the *kouros* is on a "quest for knowledge," because he already *possesses* knowledge: he is spoken of in the poem as a "man of knowledge" (*eidota phōta*, 1.3). Parmenides uses the term at 6.4, 10.1, and 10.5 to refer to mortal *doxa*. So in a sense, the *kouros* already has knowledge related to the cosmos.

The youth's journey is not from dark to light, but from *night* to light. Night has connotations other than darkness, as I will argue later in Chapter 5. He has reached the limits of human knowledge and wishes to go further, beyond the paths of mortals (as the goddess puts it). At the end of the acquisition of knowledge, we see a new beginning.

Curiously, there is no mention of a specific destination, or of an arrival. Parmenides does not say that the chariot pulled into a cave or a palace, or how he arrived at the abode of the goddess. He does not mention that he descended from the chariot to greet the goddess. In one line (1.21), the maidens are driving Parmenides on the "broad way"; in the next (1.22) the goddess takes his right hand in hers and receives him warmly. The transition is abrupt (*kai me* joins grammatically, but covers a disjunction). There are no interruptions in the journey, and the goddess continues speaking about the road (as I showed in Chapter 2). This road, she informs the *kouros*, is far from the tracks of mortals (1.27). Parmenides assures us that the road is still "present," except it is no longer a part of his first-person narrative of the journey described in the proem, but henceforth carried over by the goddess' speech. Parmenides never speaks in his own voice again in the poem, which means that for the remainder of this work the journey continues in the goddess' speeches. Parmenides has achieved here, under our very eyes, so masterfully and subtly that we never notice, a change in the description of the journey from the road to the way. Without realizing this move explicitly, we naturally talk about the "route" when we talk about the proem and the "ways" when we talk about the speech of the goddess. The language of journey pervades the entire poem.

The poem *Peri Phuseōs* contains many paths, many journeys. These modulate Parmenides' famous monism, which I argue, is only one way among many ways.

The proem is rife with the language of multiplicity (*polu-* means "much," "many"): *poluphēmon* (1.2), *poluphrastoi* (1.4), *polupoinos* (1.14), and *poluchalchous* (1.18). The language of plurality and multiplicity continue into the goddess' speeches. Strikingly, the goddess says that "very many signs" point to the proof of her monism (8.1–3: *sēmat' easi polla mal'*). Her argument is "much-contested" (*poludērin elenkhon*, 7.5).

These clues of multiple journeys, several routes of enquiry, many speeches, pluralistic vocabulary, undercut our assumption of the unity of knowledge, and the univocality of the cognitive interpretation of reality. Assuming that the journey has one destination (such as to Persephone) or that it has one message (such as the monistic ontology) does not do justice to either the poem as Parmenides composed it or to reality as we experience it. The thinking, which brings together both the static unity of the goddess' *logos* and the plurality of phenomenal existence, requires a more complex interpretive strategy than that provided by a one-way journey in space or an argument in *logos*. I therefore propose temporal *aporia* (as described in Chapter 1) as a more adequate tool for explaining the coexistence of contradictory explanations of reality.

Technology

But as generation followed generation, metamorphosis became more and more difficult, and the fatal nature of reality, its irreversibility, all the more evident. Only a generation after Europa, Pasiphae would have to crouch inside a wooden cow, a big toy on wheels, and have herself pushed as far as the meadows of Gortyn, where the bull she desired was grazing. And from their union was born a creature that would never be able to go back to being either a beast or man. He would be a hybrid, forever. And just as the craftsman Daedalus had to invent an inanimate object to allow the mother to love the bull, so now he had to invent another object, the labyrinth, to conceal the son. The Minotaur would be slain, Pasiphae would die in captivity and shame. Humans could no longer gain access to other forms and return from them. The veil of epiphany was rent and tattered now. If the power of metamorphosis was to be maintained, there was no alternative but to invent objects and generate monsters.

> *Roberto Calasso,* The Marriage of Cadmus and Harmony[31]

Since nearly 15 lines (1.5–20) of the extant poem are devoted to technical details (of a chariot, bolts, gates, and locks and keys), a number of lines slightly less than the goddess' speech on "true being," we must try to understand the significance of these technological details in the poem. Here again, we lack sufficient external evidence, such as other early Greek evidence about technology. Nevertheless, with these fragments, Parmenides challenges us to think again for ourselves, and we must consciously bring our own world and its issues to the poem in order to begin a fruitful dialogue.

For sheer diligence, we must praise Hermann Diels, who, besides being the authoritative compiler of the fragments of the pre-Socratics, had an abiding interest in ancient technology. Diels offers many elaborate comparanda in his study of ancient locks and keys in the second half of his book on Parmenides.[32] In this work, he brings to these technical artifacts the same comprehensive and detailed scholarship that gave us "Diels-Kranz." In a recent book, Kingsley gives us a fascinating interpretation of some of the technical language of the poem. He sees the technical terminology as metaphorical, esoterically evoking the language of mystery rituals. "On his journey, everything that moves has to do with the sound or appearance of pipes."[33] He relates the hissing sound of the chariot, "the sound of a *syrinx* (shepherd's pipe)" (1.6–7), to a text concerning initiation into mysteries, in which the initiate is told to produce a piping, hissing sound—precisely that of a *syrinx*. "The noise of a *syrinx* is the ultimate password."[34] Kingsley thus provides a cult ritual basis for the proem's technical terminology, but does not address the question of why technical artifacts occupy so prominent a position in a poem titled *Peri Phuseōs* ("On Nature").

Let me begin here: with a comparison of *phusis* and *tekhnē*. *Phusis* has a double meaning, which the English word "nature" retains: nature is both what a thing is (its essence) and the way we encounter the universe primordially. Nature is contrasted with what is man-made.

In Homer, the noun occurs only once (*Odyssey* x.303, although Homer uses related words, including verbs), in a passage that illustrates my conception of *phusis* as a relation between mortals and immortals. Here, Odysseus is seeking a *pharmakon* (drug) because his men have undergone a metamorphosis: Circe has turned them to pigs. Hermes, in the form of a youth, takes Odysseus' hand and gives him the *moly* herb. This *pharmakon*, which inures Odysseus to Circe's witchcraft and her power to change the form of men, precisely emblematizes the point of distinction between mortals and immortals. Gods know about it, and name it (*Odyssey* x.304: "and gods call it *molu*"), while men do not know its name or its nature; for mortals, it is difficult to dig up (305–6), but it is possible for the gods (306). The word *phusis* occurs here: Odysseus says that Hermes, "drawing it out of the ground, showed me its *phusin*" (*Odyssey* x.303). The plant embodies metaphysical contrast in its very appearance: its roots are black but its blossoms white like milk.[35] *Phusis* here means more than outward appearance. This entire passage develops a contrast between the powers of mortals and immortals; a contrast that, I argue, is inherent in *phusis*. In Chapter 1, I argued for the primordiality of temporal *aporia*, or the crossing of mortals and immortals, in any explanation of *phusis*. The *molu* root in particular, and *pharmaka* in general, evoke the temporal distinction between mortals and immortals, a distinction ultimately tragic for mortals. I will argue in a later chapter on Plato that *logoi* also can function as *pharmaka*.[36] The fatal dimension of a *pharmakon* arises because, like *phusis*, it holds mortal temporality *for mortals* thus delineating them from the immortals. *Phusis* contains an inescapable temporality and therefore also shares in the duality of time.

Phusis contains two aspects, the immortal and the mortal. We must especially resist the temptation to understand *phusis* as only the "*phusis* of the thing," as a thing's defining essence, where *phusis* becomes unproblematically and univocally available as the object of our metaphysical enterprise. I call this the immortal aspect of *phusis*; metaphysics and epistemology are always immortalizing projects. They become phantasms in *logos* for mortals (although, I argue, *logos* is grounded in *phusis*) if they ignore the other, mortal, aspect of *phusis*. Keeping in mind that *phusis* is related to *phuō* or "to grow" is an excellent way to maintain its germinative, changing dimension intact alongside essences (its immortal dimension).

Parmenides is well aware of the mortal sense of the term *phusis*. The term appears neither in the proem nor in the goddess' first speech on unchanging being, both of which belong (in very different ways) to the realm of *tekhnē*. He reserves usage of the term *phusis*, which has so well served as the title of the entire work (*Peri Phuseōs*), for the speech on the mortal cosmos, where I argue he returns explicitly to the theme of the work. The title already hints at the problematic duality of time which separates yet articulates the goddess' two speeches.

The term *tekhnē* gives us fewer difficulties. It can be roughly translated as know-how involved in human production, *poiēsis*. By extension, artifacts produced by human agency belong to this realm. Just as *phuō*, grow, helped us understand the word *phusis*, it also helps us understand *tekhnē*, by contrast.[37] *Tekhnē* appropriates a certain knowledge of beings in which temporality becomes irrelevant. It is an activity that produces temporally deficient objects, even objects *allegedly*[38] immune to and resisting temporal change. Unlike *phusis*, which heeds the contradictory pull of temporal *aporia*, technical objects do not grow, and exist in only one dimension of time, one that exceeds a mortal *aiōn* (life-span). Thus the technical object not only surpasses mortal temporality, but *tekhnē* itself also promises to become an aid in surpassing it. The often-neglected link between our desire (e.g., to overcome mortality) and our drive to technology is articulated and exposed by Parmenides.

Parenthetically, I would like to add that in the realm of poetry, a similar desire to overcome mortality makes metamorphosis a satisfying genre. Metamorphosis, in providing the illusion of escape from this mortal human form, presumes to achieve immortality through a succession of mortal life-spans (precisely the opposite of metempsychosis, in which an immortal—the soul—experiences serial mortality). Metamorphosis, metempsychosis, and technology all attempt to conceal what tragedy and the motif of journey expose: finite temporality and its inescapability. This is precisely the temptation Circe represents to Odysseus.

It is thus appropriate that the *thumos*, our mortal, emotive, cognitive soul, fearing its mortality and desiring immortality, should use *technical* means in its flight to the abode of the goddess. These technical methods and *logoi* are the only means available to mortals to transcend their mortality. Ritual allusions, as Kingsley describes,[39] are not metaphorically hidden in the technical language of the proem: ritual *is* technical.[40] A complete explication of ritual as a vehicle of technology standing at the disposal of a mortal *thumos* ready and eager to depart to the abode of the immortals is beyond the scope of this book. In sacrifice also, the victim is consciously, ceremoniously and publicly uprooted from *phusis* and appropriated into the realm of *tekhnē/poiēsis*.[41] Whereas *phusis* displays the distance between mortals and immortals, technologies such as ritual, metaphysics, certain types of *logoi*,[42] metamorphosis, metempsychosis, and magic bring them closer, enabling their contact. In comparing the technical, poetic means of the *kouros* with a sacrifice, we see that the latter is more self-consciously "mediated"—the "guilty" victim is sent across the boundary between mortals and immortals and his guilt ceremoniously enacted. Outside of this specific (sacrificial) context, however, it would be *hubristic* for a human to seek to approach the gods. Both sacrifice and *logoi* are thus technical means of approaching the immortals without *hubris*.

In relating technology to metaphysics through the agency of the *thumos*, the *singular* individual *rather than* "being" becomes both the motivation and the "that-for-the-sake-of-which" (*hou heneka*) of technology. Technology is seductive to man because it controls *phusis* (as far as *thumos* leads). But the control also challenges man, and transforms him. Man as he occurs in *phusis* reveals himself metaphysically, in the sense in which I use the term in this study. Although *thumos* impels man to reside in a technological realm, as technological, man comes to understand himself as *psukhē*. As the "immortal" faculty in man, *psukhē* is not encumbered with mortal finite temporality. In the immortal, metaphysical, atemporal realm, man no longer defines himself in terms of *thumos*, *aiōn*, *phusis*, or mortality. *Psukhē* appropriates the technology developed by the desiring *thumos*, and presents itself in the mode of a technological, eschatological, eternal, and immortal entity.[43]

The immortality conferred by technology never addresses man in his *thumos*, as a radical individual existing in *phusis* and its temporality. In this sense, man loses his basic mode of existence as *thumos* and is transformed into information: immortal in the sense of being storable, retrievable, and controllable. With the loss of *thumos*, technology severs man's connection to *phusis* on the one hand, and its obligation to man's "desire" on the other. With the loss of *thumos*, technology ceases to be instrumental and becomes constitutive. By substituting *psukhē* for *thumos*, man becomes information. As information, man surrenders his radical individuality and singularity; and technology makes a claim (*Anspruch*) on him as *psukhē*. Information is not merely "generated facts" about "objects" that serve our purpose. *Information, at its core, imitates metamorphosis and metempsychosis in transforming phusis into tekhnē, thumos into psukhē, and man into a knowable object.* As data, all of nature is translated into a retrievable medium. While encouraging the illusion that it is a construct of man and man only encounters himself everywhere (through the use of instrumental reason), technology exiles man from his home in *phusis* and prevents his return to the mortal cosmos. In the technological world-view, especially as dominant in the world we currently live in, man no longer has a journey, or a *nostos*.[44]

Although in Parmenides' poem technology retains its basic nature of transgressing mortality, it nevertheless remains guided by *thumos*. It is precisely *thumos*, the mortal *singular*, who realizes the instrumental rather than constitutive nature of technology that has the "saving power" to which Hölderlin refers.[45] In Parmenides' poem, *thumos* is able to harness technology both as a vehicle to approach the immortals as well as a medium of metaphysics (*poiēsis*, especially the first speech of the goddess).

Justice and Limits

Where does technology take the *kouros* in Parmenides' poem? To his mortal limits.

The gates, which Parmenides crosses, are the gates dividing mortals and immortals. To cross them would be *hubris*, a trespassing of the boundaries of man, an act punishable by avenging justice. The first words of the goddess when she receives the mortal traveler are: it is not "ill fate (*moira kakē*)" that brings him to her side of the threshold. What exactly is this fate (*moira*)? Fate is the connection between the domains of mortals and the immortals. These two domains are radically separated, guarded by justice, crossed by a mortal only with the permission of fate.

The distinction between mortals and immortals is the proper subject matter of tragedy, as I stated in Chapter 1. Parmenides' poem is reminiscent of Homer and Hesiod, but also the Greek tragedians in precisely this deeper sense. What does tragedy teach us? The distinction between mortals and immortals is inviolable, and attempting to cross over to immortality, an act of *hubris*, requires jettisoning our mortal life. To transgress the domain of the immortals is impossible; the gods quickly and mercilessly punish such acts. Yet the separate domains of mortals and immortals are interlinked through fate.

The distinction between the Parmenidean *kouros* and the goddess can be summarized as follows: he partakes of mortal fate, finitude, motion, multiplicity, and *doxa*. Each of these features depends on the unfolding and distension of time; each is essentially temporal. Death itself, as a critical limit of time for mortals, guides all other distinctions. The fundamental temporality underlying this poem is not an abstract concept of time, but one that grasps human experience of time at its extreme limit, its ultimate mortality.

Despite the pervading motifs of flowing time implicit in the themes of journey, mortality, and return, there is a place in the poem where time stands still. Specifically, it is the place where the paths of day and night cross, beyond which there is no movement in time. This is the abode of the goddess, who transcends mortal time and its flux and is therefore immortal.

Parmenides crosses the threshold to timelessness Muse-ically. This means that this transgression is poetic, not actual. This interpretation, although it may sound trivial, is important. The daughters of the Sun persuade Justice "with soft words" (*malakoisi logoisi*, 1.15)—a phrase appropriate to the charming nature of poetry.[46] Parmenides' adventure into eternity and the audience with the goddess is therefore not a real transgression—which would imply that Parmenides is not seeking to subvert his fate by confusing his mortal fate with that of the goddess. Therefore, it is indeed not a bad fate (*moira kakē*) that sends him—not *hubris*, but divine inspiration. Divine escorts accompany Parmenides' wish to think beyond time because he does not confuse what he can think with what he can have. When the goddess says thinking and being are the same, then we have to keep these disturbing reflections in mind and interpret that line accordingly.

The journey, as we have seen, is initiated by two factors: Parmenides' mortal wish (*thumos*) and the mares and divine escorts. The narrative of time is split from the very beginning, and pierces these two notions of time—one lethal, the other eternal. This split in the narrative runs through the entire poem.

Distinction between Mortals and Immortals

The journey of the *kouros* takes him through the gates to the unnamed goddess. I see a new part of the poem beginning at 1.22. Here the mortal *kouros* confronts an immortal goddess who presents a new discourse on being. In the next chapter, I offer a new interpretation of her speech. I use the radical distinction between the mortal Parmenides and the immortal goddess as the main interpretive tool in reading Parmenides. Mortals and immortals are temporal categories, as discussed in Chapter 1. Much in the poem supports this distinction, a distinction Parmenides himself marks off with several signs:

1. The movement of the journey on which Parmenides travels is contrasted with the stationary goddess.
2. A locomotive contrast conveys this locative contrast: the road on which Parmenides' *kouros* travels extend beyond "all cities," whereas the being described by the goddess is completely at rest.
3. An analogous contrast is retained on a cognitive level, where the knowledge of many cities and the "two-headed" *doxa* of mortals are distinct from the henology and ontology of the goddess.
4. The cosmology the goddess later expounds dissolves this unified knowledge, and opens up the path, once more, upon which the *kouros* must travel back after his divine encounter.
5. We can read the encounter of the *kouros* and the goddess dialogically.

Chapter 4

In the Realm of the Goddess:
Logos and Its Limits

The Poem as Dialogue

Of all the pre-Socratic thinkers, Parmenides presents the clearest antecedent to the dialogue form central to Plato's own philosophical enterprise.[1] He casts the youth and the goddess as two persons engaged in a philosophically illuminating encounter. Like Plato's dialogues, Parmenides' poem develops the individuality of the participants through dialogue with the other. Although the *kouros* himself does not speak, and stands apart from "mortals" and their *doxa*, the goddess nevertheless invokes their views and engages them in her speech.

The goddess' speech, commonly considered the core of the poem, addresses the protagonist's "self." She greets him cordially, and her arguments are meant to persuade him. Indeed, her notion of Truth is intimately linked to Persuasion (1.29–30, 2.4, 8.28), and thus requires an interlocutor. Her doctrine, once expounded, is left for his final consideration: "judge (yourself) by reason (*logos*) the very contentious *elengkhos* spoken by me" (7.5–6; and cf. 6.2, "these I urge you to consider"). The *elengkhos* and its relation to *logos* (in various contexts: Socratic dialogue, argument, *aporia*, myth) blossom in Plato's dialogues and are central to Socrates' mission, as he confesses in the *Apology*. Critics have most often fastened on the logical rigor of the goddess' argument, including her critique of opposing, non-logical accounts of reality, and claimed this as Parmenides' greatest achievement.[2] Stripped of its dialectical, *elengkhic* context, dogmatism becomes the legacy of the goddess' speech, the "pure" philosophy usually extracted from Parmenides' poem. But, as we saw, the goddess herself sees her enterprise as one of persuasion. In the end, in true rhetorical fashion, she asks the young man to think for himself about the arguments she has made.

Reading the poem dialogically, rather than dogmatically, allows us to read the speeches within the context supplied by Parmenides. The *kouros* and the goddess encounter each other from within their own realms and temporalities, which modulate their points of view as well as their fates. Let us begin by trying to contextualize the goddess in the poem before we interpret her ontological perspective.

The Realm of the Goddess is Not Hades

"Night" is first mentioned in Parmenides' poem at 1.9, which reads "[the daughters of the Sun, were hastening] to escort me, after leaving the House of Night for the Light." The daughters of the Sun are Parmenides' escorts, and they are with him from the very beginning of the journey, leading the way to the goddess. Night herself is not mentioned either as a personification or as a principle. The House of Night marks the "previous" event of the journey's inception, from which the maidens spring forward, into the light, to lead Parmenides. The road on which they lead Parmenides extends to the gates, where the paths of Night and Day cross, and beyond. Here again Night is not referred to directly, but only *via* a reference to the path she traverses, a path she shares with Day.

These facts lead some commentators to interpret the journey as Parmenides descending into the underworld to obtain knowledge. Kingsley's description of the journey as an underworld expedition is a strong articulation of this idea. I do not agree with Kingsley for the following reasons: like Burkert,[3] he would have Parmenides just pick up Orphism and add nothing. Kingsley does not take into account the logical, deductive method of demonstration the goddess uses. Mystical procedure is experiential and does not use argumentation. Although Kingsley purports to talk about death and overcoming death, he does not really do justice to the notion of mortality because he does not make use of any notion of time. With other scholars, he persists in positing this underworld or "other world" as an answer to mortality. But the other world will not answer questions of this world. An interpretation of Parmenides that addresses issues of this world (the only world)—including death, mortality, immortality, ambiguity, and contradiction—is philosophically richer.

The final proof of the journey as *katabasis* would be the goddess' identity. Kingsley identifies her with Persephone, who rules over the underworld. But note that Persephone is precisely the opposite of what the goddess in the poem represents as her truth: unchanging being. Persephone is closely tied up with an existence that is closer to the mortals, spending her time now with her mother Demeter and now with Hades—representing the rejuvenation of mortal life on earth with the seasons. She represents cyclical repetition of time, whereas our experience of mortal time is as a unique, unidirectional trajectory from birth to death.

The two chief arguments by analogy—one relating Parmenides to Orphism and another to Odysseus—are both insufficient to prove that the *kouros* journeys underground. The former argument is unsatisfactory because the goddess' pure logical analysis, her method of division and commandment to the *kouros* to think for himself stand in contrast to a mystical experience. She enjoins him, "Judge by reason my strife-encompassed refutation" (294.5–6). If we take this mystical reading seriously, we must ignore the contents of the goddess' speech on being. The Odyssean parallel is also to be taken with caution, because, as I have demonstrated above, the journey of the *kouros* is an inversion of the underground journey, both in form (the gates high above) and in content (logic leading to eternity instead of intimation of death through prophecy).

The *kouros* reaches the goddess through the persuasive and magical properties of *logos*. I use the word "magical" to underline the suspension of Dikē's routine function, and the charm-like effect the entreaties of his divine escorts have. The goddess welcomes him warmly, assuring him that no ill fate has befallen him. Kingsley reads this comment in the context of a "dying while living," a magical ritual *katabasis* to a place where the living are usually not allowed. Maintaining that the entire journey of the *kouros* is a descent into Hades, Kingsley explains the goddess' comment as a reassurance to the youth that he is experiencing a ritual descent, and that he is not really dead. True, *moira kakē*, or ill fate, has strong associations with death, but that does not prove that a *katabasis* into Hades is the true meaning of the journey of the *kouros*, or that the youth is in the presence of Persephone. Although Kingsley is correct in pointing to the cult practice of this goddess of Hades, where she is alluded to simply as the "goddess" or "*korē*," I find this an unsatisfactory explanation for Parmenides withholding the name of the goddess. My main reason for disagreeing with Kingsley on the identity of the goddess is the concrete character she represents in the poem. Her arguments are anything but what an initiate expects to hear in the throes of a mystical encounter. Logical exposition is an unlikely candidate among the "healing" *logoi*. The central rite of mystery religions is *epiphania* (e.g., Eleusis), and not *elengkhos*.

The invocation of *moira* is to be understood on many levels. We already saw how "no ill fate" is a formula against *hubris*. In Parmenides there are several other implications. "Ill fate," in a straightforward sense of the term, can mean death because that would be a way for mortals to traverse their own mortality. "Fate" in itself is a powerfully operative term here, because it represents the necessary limit of all human endeavors. "Fate" also posits time in a distinct manner: as death for mortals and as eternity for the goddess.

From the moment the *kouros* reaches the gates and Dikē bars entry, *logos* dominates his journey. It is not only the means of entry into the goddess' realm; his two journeys only become one in and through her speech, that is, they become one in *logos*.

The Realm of the Goddess is *Logos*

Parmenides' poem portrays the goddess' realm as one of *logos*. The awesome figure of "much-avenging" Dikē (1.14) guards the gates to the realm, bringing the chariot ride of the *kouros* to a halt. She holds the keys to the bolted gates, and prevents the *kouros* from entering. The gates are not wide open, and the road he has traveled on thus far is blocked. The next step in the *kouros*' journey continues in a new mode: that of self-consciously explicit *logos*. The daughters of the Sun use soft words to persuade Dikē to grant access to the youth. Here, the poetic formulation "soft words" (cf. Kalypso's *malakoisi logoisi* to Odysseus) underlines the *poetic-* or *logos-* based access of the *kouros* into the realm of the goddess. Dikē, persuaded by the Muse-like entreaties of the sun maidens, throws open the gates, and the *kouros* continues on his journey.

Precisely this, her skill in *logos*, gives us a clue to understand the goddess and her actions. She was accessed through *logos*, albeit a very special form of it, achieved through divine intervention. Her words likewise steer the *kouros* through *logoi*. After receiving the youth with warm salutations, she proceeds to convert the entire journey the *kouros* has undertaken so far into *logos*. She repeats, in a curious doubling, what the poet has already told us, and what the *kouros* has already experienced. She doubles in *logos* the existential journey of the proem.

O youth (*kouros*), companion of immortal charioteers,
With mares who carry you reaching as far as (*hikanōn*) our house,
Welcome, since no evil fate (*moira kakē*) sent you forth (*pro-*) to travel
This road (*hodon*), for indeed outside of men's stepping-path (*patou*) it is (*estin*),
But [rather] Themis (Right) and Dikē (Justice) [sent you forth]

Interestingly, she reverses the order of the proem. She begins with her house, then describes the road, and finally states what sent him forth. Her *logos* achieves two purposes. First, she reverses the youth's journey; in her *logos*, the way to her and the way back are equivalent. Second, she substitutes the *kouros' thumos*, the original impulse for journey with *themis* and *dikē*. Her *logos* undoes the wandering of the *kouros*, his personal odyssey, and replaces his concrete individuality (*thumos*) with the most abstract and most time-deficient entity: law. Despite his warm reception, the *kouros* remains outside the gates in his own mortal realm: the goddess in retelling his journey *from* Dikē ignores his journey *to* Dikē. Her *logos* negates the youth's journey and his individuality. No ill fate has befallen the *kouros*; to be sure, he is still safely at home. No ill fate will *ever* befall the youth, because *in her realm*, space and time are banished. This is not the realm of the goddess as *Hades*; it is the curiously doubled realm of mortals in immortal *logos*.

The goddess negates, reverses, and translates the chariot journey into *logos*, but the journey is not terminated or cancelled out. Only certain elements of the journey, such as its temporal dimension, are lost in the translation, but the wandering continues in her realm of *logos* in a noetic, rather than an existential-poetic way. The road of the proem becomes a "way" of inquiry, of thinking. Wandering is a legitimate manner of *noein*. The link between journey as wandering and journey as *nous*, that is, as related to intellectual inquiry, is well developed in early Greek thought. In Homer, Odysseus the protagonist is *polutropos* with respect to his limbs and also his *nous*. "He saw the cities of many men and knew (*gignōskō*) their minds (*noon*)." Parmenides exploits this relationship, and in the realm of the goddess, the faculty of *nous* replaces the *thumos* which sent the youth impulsively to Dikē's gates. The journey continues *noetically* in the realm of the goddess, as ways of inquiry in her world of *logoi*. She pulls apart the *Odyssey*'s relationship between journey and *nous*. For her the *nous* can operate in static *logos*; in fact, her *logos* houses only *nous*, and permits no wandering once one arrives there.

The goddess wishes to deny temporal and spatial extension whereas the *kouros* wishes to attain immortality, which in the case of a mortal means a journey without end. Dikē permits the youth's journey in *logos* only, and the goddess exploits the atemporality of *logos* to deny the possibility of any journey. Thus the *kouros* does not attain immortality in the sense that his *thumos* is preserved indefinitely, he only achieves a *logos* on immortality, one that teaches the impossibility of his mortal existence. Mortal being can never satisfy the criteria of true being (*einai*).

Who is the Goddess?

Scholars have attempted to identify the goddess with a number of different mythical figures, situating the proem within the epic tradition and other forms of literature. Taran admits there is insufficient evidence to identify the goddess with any from the known pantheon. He explains her away as a literary device. Santillana tells us that she is "un-Olympian in her personality, ignoring purely and simply the constitutional gods of the Greek cult."[4] Although the goddess appears unannounced, like an "awesome spectral, the Sphinx of Metaphysics,"[5] commentators persist in trying to give her a proper name. Santillana continues: "Proclus informs us that her name is Hypsipyle 'High Gates' which is strictly a title . . . By careful comparison with Hesiod, we can work out her homologues in the *Theogony* as Themis, Hekate, the Oracle of Night." Santillana goes further in identifying the goddess with the daemon in the cosmology (12.3). "[H]ere, concentrated in one figure which is also given total cosmic power in the Second Part of the Poem—'The Daemon who steers all things' is . . . Aphrodite Urania. It is she who Lucretius invokes as *orbis totius alma Venus*."[6] Although there is some reason to identify the goddess as a form of Aphrodite, especially with the Empedoclean paean to this goddess as a cosmological force, it does not seem to me that Aphrodite could be the goddess who speaks to the *kouros* in Parmenides' poem. Even if we rely heavily on Empedocles, his description of Aphrodite is clearly as a synthetic, blending force, in stark contrast to the goddess in Parmenides who is eristic. This is in sharp contrast to the goddess in Empedocles, who is one half of a pair: Philotes and Neikos. The eristic goddess in Parmenides' poem bears greater similarities to Neikos, than to Philotes or Aphrodite. Besides, we must take Parmenides' descriptions seriously; the divinity in the cosmology portion of the poem is a "daemon," whereas the unnamed goddess of the speeches is "*thea.*" I agree with Santillana's project of trying to see both speeches of the goddess as a unity, although I disagree with his claim that, "That the two aspects, the intellectual and the physical, belong to one and the same figure, can hardly be doubted."[7] Instead, I argue for the safer conclusion, that the "intellectual and physical" come from the same *phusis*, and as such articulate themselves together in *Peri Phuseōs*. I wish to allow Parmenides' decision to stand, and allow this "Sphinx of Metaphysics" to remain anonymous, and as distinct from the Aphrodite-like daemon of the cosmology. An inner coherence between the goddess' denunciation of the error of mortals in naming things and her anonymity should be preserved. Further, by stressing nothing but her *logos*, Parmenides stresses her impersonal character. If, as mortals, we cannot help but giver her a name, we would nonetheless be on safer grounds if we were to derive her name from her *logoi* rather than from supplementary literature: I find "*Thea Metaphysica*" or "Sphinx of Metaphysics," or "the goddess of *logos* and *eristic*" suitable suggestions.

The goddess is not *alētheia* as Heidegger argues.[8] This is because she herself warns the *kouros* of her ability to deceive (c.f. "listen to the deceptive ordering of my words" [8.53]; cf. also *ouk . . . apatēlon* in Empedocles and the Muses in Hesiod's *Theogony*, who are said to be as well versed in falsehood as in truth). The realm of the goddess is *logos*, she is a goddess of *logos*, and the journey of *kouros* now continues in the spatially, and more importantly, the temporally deficient realm of *logos*. This goddess is the matron of all philosophers who follow in that tradition, the gifts she bears are rhetoric, eristic, logic, and dialectic. Her *logoi* freeze and nullify the itinerant and individual nature of *phusis* in *logos*, so that "stable *epistēmē*" is possible. This realm of *logos*, where the temporal properties of *phusis* are negated, I call the metaphysical realm, and the goddess of *logos* is the goddess of *metaphysics* understood in this sense. It is therefore inadvisable to seek parallels in the religious or poetical traditions, which are more immediately committed to material *phusis*.

The Goddess' Double Speech

The goddess' speech is double: a logical derivation of eternal unchanging being and a detailed description of the mortal cosmos. Much strife (*poludēris*) plagues her proof of eternal being, and many a sign is required to identify it (*sēmat' easi poll'*). Her method of derivation is eristic, distinguishing the way of being from the way of non-being, but the fluxing mortal universe is not explained as a true plurality. Rather, it is cast in a language of dualism. The mortals are double headed (*dikranoi*), they establish double knowing (*duo gnōmais*), and they distinguish opposites (*antia*). The *logoi* in Parmenides' poem thus double and separate or hold together, again and again. In this polyphony of voices, some are monistic, some dualistic, and some are pluralistic. These conceptual categories, (which are meant to address being as one or two or many) are insufficient (yet unavoidable) in Parmenides' journey through the *topoi* of being. When Empedocles utters the words *dipl' ereō* (17.1) he speaks in unison with his predecessor.

Whenever being is addressed in *logos*, such duplication is necessary. *Logos* has a unique ability to transcend temporality—as the Parmenidean goddess demonstrates. But the One being in her poem is duplicated in a way so subtle that readers often miss it: her speech is already a duplication of being in *logos*. Further, the temporality of *logos* overcomes the temporality of being. Schürmann writes, "when Parmenides precedes the present participle with an article (*t'eon*: a construct that marks the transition from epic to philosophical language) and follows it with the infinitive (*emmenai*), he sets apart the noun and the verb. He thereby 'accuses', makes explicit, the duality contained in the present participle."[9] I quote this in full because of the double duplication contained in this thought. The present participle "indicates a difference"; it precariously moves from verbal to nominal forms. But this double life of the present participle only brings to light a curious doubling effect of *logos* itself, a doubling which allows Socrates to make a speech against speech, and a speech against writing in the curiously double discourse of *Phaedrus*. *Phusis*, "accused"[10] by language, seems all too willing to give up its temporality and yield static essences. Thus the doubling of *logos*, laid bare in the double life of the present participle, is itself rooted in *phusis*. *Logos* imports *phusis* preferably in a time-deficient, nominal manner, and arranges it according to its own static categories. But the self-conscious attempt to capture the temporality of *phusis* sets apart the epic poets and the pre-Socratic thinkers from the philosophers who love categories.

The issue of doubling is thus a temporal one; the nominal and verbal doubling in *logos* is according to the dimension of time. *Phusis* itself grounds this distinction, and its temporal unfolding paradoxically contains atemporal elements, which makes *logos* possible. A poetic way of saying this would be to use the epic distinction between mortals and immortals. If there were only immortals, *speaking* would be impossible. If there were no immortals, there would *be nothing to speak about*. Parmenides, it is easy to see, fully exploits these relations, placing both the speech about immortal being and mortal beings in the goddess' mouth. Thus her double speech articulates what is unutterable and unthinkable: the mingling of mortals and immortals in *phusis*. I refer to this joining-separating of time in its twofold character of fluxing *and* static, temporal *and* eternal, as the *temporal aporia* of time. Within the doubling of temporal *aporia*, *phusis* articulates itself and reflects itself in *logos* as mortals and immortals. All true accounts of *phusis* are thus articulations of a doubling, and all true philosophers say, with supreme ambiguity: *dipl'ereō*.[11]

The Goddess' Incoherence

As a case in point, I wish to take up G. E. L. Owen's thesis. He writes:

> In sum: Parmenides' goddess does not claim that her cosmogony has any
> measure of truth or reliability in its own right; her subject matter and her
> assumptions are not inherited from earlier cosmology; and she does not
> argue for a world that is spherical and everlasting. Parmenides did not write
> as a cosmologist. He wrote as a philosophical pioneer of the first water, and
> any attempt to put him back into the tradition that he aimed to demolish is a
> surrender to diadoche-writers, a failure to take him at his word and "judge by
> reasoning that much-contested proof."[12]

Here, Owen brackets out the cosmology of the goddess' second speech, but
also the first, where the goddess says being is spherical and eternal. Owen goes
so far as to deny any cosmology lurking in the background, inherited from
Parmenides' predecessors. Thus all descriptive, speculative, and ambiguous
cosmology is neatly carved away from the philosophical meat of the poem.[13]
Owen's interpretation is an attempt to disambiguate the goddess' double
speech, inviting us to leave behind *phusis* in all forms and flee into the clarity of
her logical argument.

But all interpretations that turn away from *phusis* must posit a subject for
esti in B2 and B8. Despite taking extreme pains to avoid a subject for *esti*,
Parmenides is readily supplied with one by Owen. The subject, according to
him is "simply what can be talked or thought about." He thus interprets *esti* as
what *exists.* Curd, in criticizing Owen, says, "According to Owen, the result of
Parmenides' argument is that there exists only a single, unchanging thing;
thus the Ionian search for an explanation of plurality of changing entities
is pointless."[14] Curd relies on Kahn's view that *esti* is "not existential,"[15] and
interprets the *alētheia* speech as not speaking about existence as such, but
as setting forth "criteria that a successful theory of what there is must meet,
and showing that such a theory must be grounded in principles that are
metaphysically and epistemologically justified."[16]

A logical prejudice is already at work here. These scholars read the poem
as containing logical inconsistencies such as the truth of the *alētheia* speech
and the error of mortal *doxa* that must be resolved. Understanding the poem,
according to the paradigm of these interpretations, requires us to resolve any
ambiguity and contradiction contained in it.

I too recognize the incongruence of the temporal and logical orders of the
goddess' two *logoi.* However, it is not clear that a methodological, philosophical,
or literary analysis is enough to address the radical duality of the two speeches.
We must supply a third witness: the *phenomena* themselves. With the introduction
of *phusis* and its dichotomous temporality into Parmenides' poem, as that which
the poem in general and the verb *esti* in particular are about, the incongruence

of the two speeches is illuminated. I do not imply that the textual problem will go away: it will be restored to its original context in *phusis*. There, the temporal asymmetry of the being in *logos* and the being in *kosmos* will become a perplexing feature for continued thought, under the name "temporal *aporia*."

Contradiction and the Goddess

Although she does not state it explicitly, the goddess exploits the persuasiveness of the principle of contradiction. She uses it to guide the *kouros* on his continuing journey—this time with respect to his *nous*, not *thumos*. How many routes[17] of inquiry are available to the youth? The standard view holds that there are three, the route of what-is, the route of what-is-not, and a third route that combines what-is and what-is-not. The goddess says emphatically that there are only two routes of inquiry:

> Come on, I shall tell you, and you having heard carry away the story (*mūthon*),
> What the only roads of inquiry there are to conceive (*noēsai*)
> The [first] one, that it is and that it is not possible for it not to be,
> Is the path of persuasion, for truth attends upon (it);
> The other [second road] that it is not and that it ought (*khreōn*) not be. (B2)

I agree that there are only two routes: what-is and what-is-not (one positive and one negative). However, there are similarly two routes in the cosmology, and these are now combined in the double-headedness of mortal *doxai*. The goddess' speech, as I have shown, is double. There is a doubling of the two routes of *alētheia*, but these are fused into one in the mortal cosmology. *Phusis*, it seems, is better able to contain contrary, even contradictory characteristics within itself than *logos*.

The principle of contradiction is the bedrock upon which logic is built. It appears to be an atemporal principle, one that no being could *conceivably* violate. Thus, it seems to transcend not only the human life-span, but to even eliminate all time and contingency. Yet, matters are not so simple, since the principle of contradiction itself conceals a mortal component, as I will show; the principle of non-contradiction requires three identities: identity of time, identity of subject, and identity of attribute. The principle of identity requires a unity of a subject and a certain predicate to occur within the unity of time, radicalized as a present moment. A cannot also be not A at one and the same time. "At the same time" is the tacit and forgotten basis of the principle of non-contradiction, a basis that is taken for granted, as if the principle existed outside of time. The principle, which balances precariously on the sharp point of a temporal moment, is interpreted erroneously as if it were eternal. The goddess adopts the principle of non-contradiction from mortals precisely because mortals understand it, and it therefore lends "*pistis*" to her point of view. From the point of view of the goddess, however, who is beyond time, temporal phenomena such as generation and motion cannot occur. There is no possibility for diachrony, and the rigorous henology operative here prohibits variance, even in the subject.

The goddess must therefore resort not to "necessity," "evidence," or other forms of abstraction, but to *pistis*, or persuasion. This *pistis* is distinct from the necessity of the trajectory of time toward death. In a reversal of attributes, the goddess invokes *pistis*, and the mortal depends upon apodictic *moira*. The former allows the goddess to speak to a mortal, and the latter allows the mortal to approach the goddess.

And yet I argue a much stronger point: that each of the roads is an iteration of the contradiction between what-is and what-is-not. In order to understand the relationship between routes of inquiry and contradiction, we must return to the road the *kouros* travels in the proem, the road that brought the mortal and immortal face to face by poetically overcoming the limits of Dikē. What the *kouros* brings with him is his *thumos*. The *thumos*, which marks a life-span, is essentially a temporal faculty. The youth brings to the goddess' door a finite, extended, mortal temporality. In the goddess' *noetic* realm of *logoi*, there is no temporality at all, whether this atemporality manifests itself in the laws of grammar or in ungenerated spherical being. The essential nature of contradiction is always this temporal element, which is preserved in the modern formulation of the law of contradiction. This law is valid only when applied to one or two entities, with respect to similar attributes, and *at the same time*. Since mortal life has temporality, only mortals can truly articulate the principle of contradiction. The goddess must recast the principle in her own atemporal realm with an artificial and misleading separation of being and non-being. The goddess applies the principle of contradiction while explicitly denying temporality; in fact she uses this principle to deny temporality. *Phusis*, which contains both mortal and immortal dimensions, by virtue of temporal *aporia*, thus manages to *noetically* support the goddess' logical argument, while permitting the "unacceptable contradiction" her conclusions create in her cosmology. Thus, although the principle of contradiction produces logical problems in the immortal realm of *logos*, it is only deceptively problematic when applied to *phusis* which is capable of containing a plurality of viewpoints and oppositions within itself.

Atemporality of *Logos*

The goddess' grammar illustrates the dangers of following language by replacing actions with structures. This is what language does: phenomenal reality, which consists of actions like appearing and disappearing, is converted into stable structures. These structures are at once syntactical relations and relations between stable nouns. The poem illustrates not only the way in which action is replaced by structure, but also verbs by nouns.[18] Similarly, phenomena are replaced by logic, speaking with thinking, and dialectical thinking with mediation.

Some mechanisms that aid in nominalization (atemporal, metaphysical essence) of verbs (temporal) are:

1. de-tensing
2. third-person singular (least of the subjects)
3. no subject.

The final effect is the elimination of time, and thus abstraction from temporal phenomena.

Of course, everyone knows that Parmenides' poem is about "Being" with a capital B. What is his word for being? Greek had no such word at the time. Aristotle later coined *to on,* "being," "what-is." Parmenides uses the same participle, *on,* although often without the definite article *(to).* Must it be a noun, as most scholars take it to be? And, if so, is it *only* a noun? Can we, in the first place, understand Parmenides' *on* as Aristotle's *to on* without the definite article *to?* This would be an evolutionary, generative view which sees Parmenides as an incomplete stage on the road to Aristotle's being. Parmenides saw the *on,* but not the *to!*

Let us approach the question of *on* afresh. Significantly, the goddess does not introduce her subject with being as a noun. Most commentators take *eon* (8.3) as a gerund, that is, as "being." Let us read this line with the question open: what is *eon?* What are the relative qualities of verb, adjective, or noun of the word in this crucial line (8.3)? Also at issue: what is the subject of *estin* in this line (8.3)? Is it, in fact, *eon* as a noun? That is the common opinion. The goddess is resolutely anti-nominal. Throughout, she leaves the subject of *estin* unexpressed. This has engaged commentators to no end. A typical approach is that of G. E. L. Owen: what is the "x" we need to supply as the subject of *estin* to give us the assumed "x *estin*"? In his influential article "The Greek Verb 'To Be' and the Concept of Being," Kahn distinguished three different uses of the verb "to be": veridical, durative, and locative.

Veridical usage. This is the most basic meaning of the verb *einai.* It means "to be the case." Thus it is related to predication and to facts.

Durative aspect of *einai.* This is an "aspect" of the verb *einai.* Kahn writes:

I think it may help us understand (1) the Greek notion of Eternity as a stable present, an untroubled state of duration, (2) the classical antithesis of Being and Becoming, and (3) the incommensurability already noted between the Greek concept of being and the modern-medieval notion of existence. Let me illustrate these points briefly:

The gods in Homer and Hesiod are *theoi aien eontes,* "the gods who are forever." In this and in a whole set of related uses, *einai* has practically the sense "to be alive, to survive." The gods *are forever* because they are deathless beings, their vital duration continues without end. Now, strictly speaking, the gods are not eternal. As the *Theogony* informs us in some detail, they have been born; their vital duration (*aiōn*) had a temporal beginning. It is the philosophers who introduce an absolute *archē* or Beginning which is itself unbegun, a permanent and ungenerated source of generation. The initiator here is probably Anaximander, but we see the result more clearly in the poem of Parmenides. His being is *forever* in the strong sense: it is ungenerated (*agenēton*) as well as unperishing (*anōlethron*). Limited neither by birth nor by death, the duration of *What is* replaces and transcends the unending survival, which characterized the Olympian gods.[19]

Parmenides was also the first to exploit the durative connotations of *einai* by a systematic contrast with *gignesthai*, the verb which normally provides an aorist for *einai*, and which expresses the developmental idea of birth, of achieving a new state, of emerging as novelty or as event. In Parmenides as in Plato, the durative-present aspect of *einai* thus provides the linguistic underpinning for the antithesis in which being is opposed to Becoming as stability to flux. Kahn writes, "The connotations of enduring stability which are inseparable from the meaning of *einai* thus serve to distinguish the Greek concept of Being from certain features of modern existence."[20] The verb "to be" always has a locative value. The verb "*einai*," writes Kahn, "is quite normally used for 'to be somewhere' (with the place specified by an adverbial word or phrase), to be in the presence of, or remote from some definite point of reference . . . I am inclined to believe the locative as a distinct and fundamental use of 'to be', from which the truly copulative use (with predicate nouns and adjectives) might itself be derived."[21]

I stress the durative aspect and the locative value of the verb "to be," both of which relate to man as a mortal thinker, whose being is temporally finite and whose location happens to be in a cosmos of change. The goddess contrasts her eternal being with the being of mortals within their cosmos of becoming, as Kahn states, through contrasting *einai* with *gignesthai*. In her two speeches where she marks off two *topoi* of being, she relies on the "connotations of enduring stability which are inseparable from the meaning of *einai*" to describe her domain, while reserving the temporally extended sense of *gignesthai* for the being of mortal cosmos. Only in the "now," *nun*, are eternity and flowing time indistinguishable. In fact, the term is used only twice, in highly specific situations in the poem: once in the first speech on unchanging being, and then again in the speech on generated mortal being.

> Nor ever was, nor will be, since is now (*nun*), all together (*homou pan*)
> One, continuous; for what birth of it will you inquire? (8.5–6)

> In this way for you, according to *doxa*, these emerged (*ephu*) and now (*nun*) are,
> And henceforth, from this, after having been nourished, they will perish. (19)

The goddess' realm depends on the durative aspects of the verb "to be," and the locative value of the verb in terms of spatial references. The gates mark off the two contrasting "locations," one on either side. Her realm is merely grammatical, which is why stressing her use of deduction within the mortal universe can lead to problems. For instance, if we stress the veridical use of the verb *einai*, describing *what is*, it is impossible to find a sphere that exists forever. Zeno's paradoxes are possible only through a "category" mistake: describing events in the mortal cosmos using *logos*, native to the other side of the gates. Scholars have seen this throughout history: the incompatibility of her two *logoi*. My point is more humble: let us keep the second speech, and with it, our mortal universe.

Interpreting the First Speech

Thus far, I have argued that the *kouros* does not go to Hades, but to the realm of *logos* and that the journey is obstructed by Dikē, who ensures that the journey henceforth occur in *logos*. The goddess' speeches continue the journey in *logos*. The encounter is to be understood as a dialogue. Although it is not obvious that the *kouros* contributes to the dialogue, the principle of contradiction would be impossible without such a dialogue, for the law, although invoked by the goddess, actually only applies in the *kouros'* realm, the realm of change and temporal modification. Further, the dialogic nature of the poem keeps the points of view of mortals (*doxa*) and immortals (*alētheia*) apart and their temporalities distinct. The immortality of the realm of the goddess is a function of her exclusive appeal to *logos* and its time-eliminating properties. Let us now apply these insights to an interpretation of her first speech.

First the goddess *translates* the journey thus far into words, and repeats in speech the travels of the *kouros* to her domain. Her statement "This road, for indeed away from men, outside of [their] stepping-path it is," should be interpreted as leaving the realm of *phusis* and entering the realm of *logos*. While the goddess mentions all the elements of the youth's journey (the road, the mares, the immortal charioteers), she ignores the *thumos* that sent him forth, and instead says "But [rather] Themis (Right) and Dikē (Justice) [sent you forth]." By leaving out the *thumos* as well as the journey that carried him over, and by positing standards such as right and justice, she displays the metaphysical nature of her reiteration of his itinerary. Metaphysics has its source in the *singular's* desire, but always presents itself as both distant from the singular as well as from the general. Instead, it appeals to criteria such as "right," "truth," or "necessity," criteria that are altogether outside the temporality of *phusis*.

The goddess accepts the twofold nature of speech, according to the categories of mortals and immortals, as *doxa* and *alētheia*. Even as she valorizes her immortal point of view and criticizes the mortal viewpoint using *logos* as evidence, she reminds him that he cannot remain with her. "Come on, I shall tell you, and you having heard carry away the story." The double nature of *logos* yields two viewpoints (mortal *doxa* and immortal *alētheia*) which she then characterizes as ways of inquiry. Both viewpoints are analyzed according a single set of criteria, that of *logic*. Nowhere does she address the realm of the mortals according to its own criteria: *phusis* and temporality.

Curd is correct in noting that "In examining fragments B2–B7, it is difficult to determine just where the repudiation of the route of what-is-not takes place, it is even more difficult, perhaps, to determine the form the repudiation takes."[22] She is also correct in arguing that we must discount looking at the statements that embody the repudiation of the second way and, instead, look forward to what will be proved in arguments of B8, that is, this repudiation is proleptic. Curd rightly points out that the "rejection of birth, coming-to-be, and perishing is crucial for the arguments that follow, for the claim that what-is is changeless or immobile (*akinēton*) in B 8.26–31 is based on the unavailability of coming-to-be and perishing, and the changelessness of what-is is a reason for its completeness."

The proof of the superiority of the way of what-is over what-is-not is to be found in the exclusion of *phusis* from *logos*. By stressing the atemporality of the *nun*, now, the goddess is able to eliminate the antecedent generation and consequent perishing, thus effectively eliminating *phusis*. Within the *nun*, the temporal *aporia* is especially susceptible to collapse into the metaphysical univocality of eternity. Once temporality as experienced by mortals is eliminated, thinking and being coincide tautologically in metaphysics. Only in metaphysical *logoi* can thinking and being be the same. In the case of mortals, who live in *phusis* and also have access to *logos*, thinking and being correspond in *logos*, but they are asymmetrical in mortal existence. Change, mortality, probability, and the *aporia* of time resulting from thinking about being are lost in her *logic*. In the absence of change, mortality, to be sure, can no longer be experienced as a problem, for where there is no change there can also not be an underlying subject that experiences his loss as a problem. Yet, precisely this erases mortality in the stronger sense that it makes it impossible for us to be as existents. This is the loss that concerns me here.

Chapter 5

At Home in the *Kosmos*: The Return

Importance of This Section of the Poem, the Cosmology

In the previous chapter, I considered the goddess' speech on true being, or *alētheia*, the best-known part of Parmenides' poem (also called the "Way of Truth"). Philosophers focus on this segment as the principle message of the Eleatic philosopher. However, the journey continues in its multiplicity; the poem continues, the goddess' speech continues, and the *kouros*' pedagogical journey continues. The goddess continues addressing the *kouros*, but she now turns to a different subject: mortal opinions about the cosmos of change and becoming. Conventionally, scholars call this part of the poem the "*doxa*" (meaning "opinion"). This word suggests a Platonic distinction between true knowledge or *epistēmē* and false knowledge or opinion.

Privileging truth as the unequivocal conclusion of a rigorous philosophical method, as readers of Parmenides do, prevents us from seeing the complexities of both his method and of the opposing points in the goddess' arguments about competing views of reality. Parmenides' method embraces a journey, one that encompasses both the goddess' truth (the ontological exposition) and a cosmology that is no less true. With other words, the poem presents *two* truths: divine and mortal truth. The goddess' truth is based on *logos*; it lives in words and arguments. The cosmology is experientially more immediately available: it describes the world of appearances, and cannot be excluded from philosophy. Her rigorous method of logical argument is, in fact, anti-philosophical, insofar as it trades the concrete self-evidence of phenomena for non-phenomenal, merely linguistic constructs.

I use the term *phusis* in a special sense. *Phusis* signifies temporal phenomena unfolding as nature. We can say three things at the outset:

1. *Phusis* is marked by an essentially mortal temporality, for it unfolds as the processes of coming-to-be, growth, and perishing.

2. However, it also bears within itself an urge toward knowledge, expressed in the human desire to arrive at systematic, propositional knowledge of nature. However, when *phusis* is subsumed under knowledge, its intrinsic temporality (mortal temporality) recedes in the face of *logos*, to be replaced by a curious atemporality. *Phusis* thus includes *both* mortal and immortal temporalities within itself.
3. *Logos*, which tries to capture and imitate *phusis*, has its origins within the latter itself.

I contrast my understanding of *phusis* with the metaphysical view that interprets phenomenal nature merely as things with static essences (so that "nature" comes to mean, in *logos*, "essence"). The goddess gives two accounts of *phusis*: a metaphysical one which posits that which is knowable, stable and eternal; and another description of *phusis* which preserves genesis and destruction. At 10.1–3, she says:

And you shall know both the nature (*phusin*) of the aether and all the signs
In the aether and the obscuring works of the pure brilliant sun's
torch, and whence they came to be . . .

The word *phusin* is also used at 10.5–6 in relation to celestial phenomena.

Already in the so-called *alētheia* speech, she insists on the necessity of double speech and double knowing (the term *duo gnōmas* occurs later in the cosmology, at 8.53). She declares the comprehensiveness of her *logoi*, and her teaching, in these lines (1.28–32):

It is necessary that you learn all things,
both the untrembling heart of persuasive truth (*alētheiēs*)
and the *doxai* (opinions) of mortals (*brotōn doxas*) in which there is not
    true trust (*pistis alēthēs*).
But all the same even these you will learn, how it was necessary for things
    seeming to be (*ta dokounta*)
to be (*einai*) assuredly (*dokimōs*), ranging throughout all things completely.[1]

I argue that it is incorrect to choose between the double speeches of the goddess. I interpret "seeming" in a twofold sense: (1) In the value-neutral sense of "phenomena opening up to vision," and (2) In the epistemologically problematic sense of mere appearance. The latter is founded upon the former, for only where phenomena have at all become visible, can they then offer us a mere aspect, merely seeming to be something they, in fact, are not. Precisely on the basis of this violation, interpreters have written off the entire cosmos as having, according to this poem, no reality at all.

Rather than being necessary, such philosophical "science" is rhetoric of a problematic kind: it is rhetoric that denies its own rhetorical nature. This critique does not apply to the goddess, however, because she, being aware of the difference, subjects "necessity" to "persuasion." She does not place a "moral" value on the choices she offers him; indeed, he is invited to think for himself (7.5) and is free to choose his own "way" on the basis of her persuasion. At the height of abstraction, both she and her student remain two, not reduced to one "truth" as her theory of truth would demand. *Her monistic view of truth—in fact any rigorous monism—cannot permit a dialogue.* Yet she addresses the *kouros* in the language of dialogue.[2]

I call the speech on mortal *doxa* the third and next stage of this journey, after the proem and the "Way of Truth." With this speech, the *kouros* begins his return journey to the mortal cosmos of temporality and becoming. He cannot, in the end, reside in the goddess' ethereal realm of unchanging being. We cannot experience metaphysical eternity existentially, but only through *logos* (thought and speech).

Rethinking Mortal *Doxa*

The goddess presents her cosmological speech on the pretext of demonstrating the false opinions of mortals. To her, the false opinions of mortals serve to confirm her picture of true, unchanging, unitary being. In fact, her emphatic criticism of the opinions of mortals has led several scholars to doubt whether Parmenides really believed in the phenomenal cosmos![3] A milder form of the same interpretation is to look for some logical fallacy in the opinions of mortals, thus retaining the phenomena provisionally until a suitable *logos* can be given. There are several problems with the standard interpretation that something is "wrong" with mortal *doxa* either in the logic contained in these *doxai* or in the assumption of the *doxai* that the world of change exists. I argue that we can see these two parts of her speech in a different relation than that of deductive proof, of general truth followed by supporting arguments. I argue that according to the contrasting temporalities that inform her *logical being* and the *mortal being* of our *phusis*, juxtaposition of these two realms *necessarily* generates an *aporia*, one that reflects the *aporia* of time discussed in Chapter 1.

The goddess attempts to apply the truth derived from immortal *logos* to a mortal cosmos. Her previous *logos* denied *phusis* and time. In applying atemporal, *a priori* principles to the mortal world, she denies the most general truth of the mortal realm: becoming. However, she is rather schizophrenic. She describes features of what look like typical pre-Socratic cosmology, urging the *kouros*, her listener, to beware of these. She presents a cosmology, without simultaneously acknowledging its supposed non-existence according to the strictly logical dictates of the "*alētheia* speech." We have, in short, two worlds. *The goddess herself is "two-headed,"* just as she accuses humans of being (at 6.5): mortals and immortals each have two *logoi*, one of being and one of becoming, an irreducible feature of *phusis* I have called "temporal *aporia*."

No argument refutes, or can ever refute, the *doxa*. The only reason in Parmenides to doubt the truth of the *doxa* is the goddess' repeated warning. She warns against the errors of mortal opinions but she demonstrates nothing false about the opinions themselves. She herself says the *kouros* must learn them ("So that never any knowing [*gnōmē*] of mortals might outstrip you," 8.61). What she says is "plausible" (*eoikota*, 8.60).

The goddess even more explicitly refers the *kouros'* attention to the *doxa* with verbs meaning "to know" (forms of *oida*: 10.1, 10.5). The sun, by contrast, is *aïdēla* (10.3), "obscuring," an adjective etymologically[4] meaning "not (*a-*) knowing" (the verbal stem *-wid*, as in (*w*)*oida* "know," *idea*, or the Sanskrit word *Veda*). This is significant because the poem describes the youth's journey from Night into Light.[5]

The two parts of the goddess' speech, the *alētheia* and the *doxa*, are usually distinguished by the dichotomy of true and false. We have seen that this is problematic and nor is it even what the goddess herself claims. The goddess objects to the realm of *doxa*, that is, to cosmology, for another reason: what is offensive is its mortality, a key element in ever-changing *phusis*. The cosmology by definition refers to the phenomena of generation and corruption (or coming-into-being and passing-away; verbs of birth and destruction abound; cf. 10.3, 11.4, "hateful birth" at 12.4, fr. 18, 19.1–2).

The goddess begins her second speech, elaborating on mortal *doxai*, with the following words (fr. 9):

But since all (*panta*) things have been named light and night,
And the (names) [have been given] in accordance with their powers
   (*dunameis*)
to these things and to those,
All (*pān*) is full of light (*phaeos*) and obscure (*aphantou*) night together,
Of both equally, since in neither does nothing have a share.

Many commentators read this as a contradiction: light and night cannot exist together. They take this as an answer to the problem posed in 8.53–54: mortals have wrongly established two ways of naming. Curd characteristically ignores the goddess' error in applying a *logical* structure of atemporality to *phusis*, which cannot be thought aside from mortal temporality. She writes: "Despite thinking that they are on the positive route to inquiry, all theorists who depend on opposites and who insist that coming-to-be and passing-away are real (and this includes most of Parmenides' predecessors) are actually on the negative route, a route that leads nowhere, from which no tidings ever come."[6] She suggests that night and light, as opposites, are typical of mortal *doxa*. This enantiomorphism does not, according to Curd, satisfy the *logical criteria* set up in the Way of Truth (*alētheia*), especially in fragment 8. The very problem underlined by Parmenides, the incommensurability of *phusis* and atemporal *logoi*, is laid aside.

Night and Light

Although scholars commonly understand the goddess to present Night and Light as opposites, the poem itself does not support this view.[7] Consider another line (fragment 14), about the moon—one of the most beautiful lines in ancient Greek . . .[8]

Nuktiphaes peri gaian alōmenon allotrion phōs

. . . a line O' Brien translates:

. . . *claire dans l'obscurité de la nuit, errante autour de la terre, lumière venue d'ailleurs.*[9]

The above line (describing the moon) shows Parmenides' keen grasp of the interplay of night and light, and his skill in using this knowledge to make subtle distinctions of philosophical relevance. The light of the moon is borrowed, not its own, and it wanders, homeless in the darkness over the earth. The true, original source of light, the sun, is not visible in the night sky. As I noted in the preceding section, Parmenides surprises us by not equating Light with enlightenment. I wish to analyze this motif of Light, and its relationship to Night in Parmenides' extant work. Such an analysis will illuminate the journey he describes in the poem, and its philosophical relevance.

A brief historical note is useful. Night and Light do not have equal value in early Greek thought. Night has priority in two senses: it has power over the gods, and it comes first—a principle of generation. An example of the first is Homer's epithet for night, "subduer" (*dmēteira, Iliad* xiv.259). Sleep (Hupnos) says, "and he [Zeus] would have cast me from *aithēr* into the sea, out of sight, had not Night, subduer of gods and men, saved me; to her did I come in flight, and Zeus ceased, angry though he was; for he was in awe of doing what would be displeasing to swift Night" (*Iliad* xiv.258–61).[10]

Aristotle notes the archaic cosmogonical aspect of Night (*Metaphysics* N4, 1091b4), explaining that the gods are themselves generated from Night in ancient cosmogonies. In Hesiod, Night comes into being at an early stage, although not first, and accompanied by Gaia, Okeanos, and Ouranos (*Theogony* 21 and 105–9). But Orphic thought elevates Night to a first principle: Night, Aer, and Tartaros emerge at the origin of the world in these poems.[11] Light does not share such a privileged position in the cosmologies of this period. Night belongs with misty Tartaros, at the beginning of the world, and the often-supposed equiprimordiality of a Night-Light couplet, however reasonable sounding to us moderns, is without basis here.

Night, as Hesiod describes it (*Theogony* 763–4), holds in her hand special gifts for mortals: sleep and death. Night represents a different kind of knowing, which receives dignity elsewhere in Greek literature as tragic wisdom: knowledge of the mortal nature of human existence. We can also call this "physics." Night is thick in body and heavy (8.59); obscure and unknowable (*adaē*, 8.59), it conceals the nature of our existence beyond our mortal life-span. It weighs us down: down to Hades. In fact, as I noted previously, the sun itself shares the obscurity of night: it is *aïdēla* (10.3), "obscuring." Night and Light, then are not complete opposites, and Light does not unproblematically refer to enlightenment as a metaphor for true knowledge.

Light relates to the goddess' speech on being. Here we see phenomena in a unified vision of being. However, mortals do not know this yet. They have not yet heard her speech. Here is the problem our interpretation must resolve: how then can mortals be said to have "established" a "knowing" of this kind (our translation of 8.53)? This is metaphysics. It is non-mortal. It embodies the longing to go beyond mortality: precisely as Parmenides' *thumos* urges him in the first line of his work (1.1). The physical world provides a glimpse of this to mortals; the goddess here provides the example of fire, which is less physical ("gentle . . . light [in body]") and "everywhere the same in itself" (8.57). The moon may provide another example. However, the moon shines with a "borrowed light" (fr. 14). This is the heavenly light of metaphysics shining on earthly or quasi-earthly bodies.[12] The moon is no longer a goddess but a body doomed to encircle the earth, "always searching out the rays of the sun" (fr. 15). Mortals do the same, for their knowledge is, as a knowledge of mortality, a light that belongs to the night, an illumination that is unique (and proper) to man, as this *mortal* being, alone. Man (*phōs*) is also Light (*phōs*).

Two Knowings

These two knowings are usually interpreted as being and non-being and the latter is said to be impossible (8.54, "of which it is not necessary (*khreōn*) to name one; in this they have wandered astray"). But how can mortals establish being, when the goddess repudiates the knowing of mortals who are not aware of her teaching about being? In my reading, the "two knowings" weave together the strictly immortal knowing of the goddess and the strictly mortal wisdom of mortals in the passages on cosmology. But she places *both* of these in the mortal realm.

The goddess, however, quickly points out that one of these knowings is not necessary (*ou khreōn*, 8.54). Critics usually interpret this as implying the falsity of one of the two terms in a dichotomy.[13] This third part of the poem thus describes two paths of mortals, in accordance with the earlier imagery of mortals as *dikranoi* or "two-headed" (6.5). We need not join these critics in flatly dismissing one of the two terms, however.

Not Monism

What does the goddess criticize as wrong in this third part of the poem, the so-called *doxa*? The goddess does not in fact fault mortals' opinions for being dualistic (enantiomorphic) or pluralistic. The minimal positing of difference is not the mistake, as Taran holds: "What lines 53–54 imply is that consciously or unconsciously those who explain and believe in the sensible world posit difference as real and the minimum of difference is two."[14] Based on this misinterpretation, scholars attribute monism to the material world. Thus Taran continues: "Since the existence of this minimal difference is impossible, any explanation of the phenomenal world is *apatēlon*" (i.e., "deceptive," 8.52). But the goddess' teaching in this third part of the poem is neither ontological nor logical. It is in fact a clarification of the one kind of knowledge that is proper to mortals: the knowledge of the physical world (cosmology), with its essential, unforgettable, unavoidable principle of mortality (19.1–2). Recall that at the outset, the goddess offered to teach the *kouros* two ways of knowing: "both the untrembling heart of persuasive truth (*alētheiēs*) / and the opinions of mortals (*brotōn doxas*) in which there is not true trust (*pistis alēthēs*)" (1.29–30).

The goddess now becomes the arch-critic of metaphysics. In the third part, she claims that mortals have deceived themselves into positing a false metaphysics. And in reading Parmenides, they have allowed the goddess to deceive them with the first part of her speech. But mortals are incapable of achieving such atemporal monistic being. Mortals can achieve metaphysical immortality only through language.

Homer's Description of Man: Transcendence and Return

Parmenides elaborates a mortal cosmology. For an understanding of mortality he draws on Homer, the preeminent philosopher of mortality. This early Greek background presents us with an abiding interest in mortal existence that was later lost due to the domination of metaphysics, leading to devaluation of mortal aspects of philosophy.

Homer begins the *Odyssey* by evoking a mortal *andra*, "man," and the narrative unfolds toward the end foretold by Tiresias:

> And I will tell you a very clear proof, and you cannot miss it,
> When, as you walk, some other wayfarer happens to meet you,
> and says you carry a winnow-fan on your bright shoulder,

then you must plant your well-shaped oar in the ground, and render
ceremonious sacrifice to the lord Poseidon,
one ram and one bull, and a mounter of sows, a boar pig,
and make your way home again and render holy hecatombs
to the immortal gods who hold the wide heaven, all
of them in order. Death will come to you from the sea, in
some altogether unwarlike way, and it will end you
in the ebbing time of a sleek old age. Your people
about you will be prosperous. All this is true that I tell you.

(*Odyssey* xi.126–37, trans. R. Lattimore)

This prophecy is striking, all the more in relation to a similar prophecy in
the *Iliad*. There, Patroklos, Akhilleus' dead friend, appears in a dream to the
mourning hero of the *Iliad* and foretells his death. That prophecy (one of
many allusions in the *Iliad* to the death of Akhilleus) is already fulfilled in the
context of the *Odyssey*: Troy has fallen and Akhilleus is dead. In both cases,
Homer assigns the climax, the fall of Troy or the death of the chief protagonist
(Akhilleus or Odysseus), to prophecy. It is not an immortal god that predicts
the hero's death, but a mortal who knows death through first-hand experience.
In Homer, heroes are keenly conscious of their own mortality. Note, by contrast, that in Parmenides it is the goddess, rather than mortals, who presents
a "true" speech.

What is remarkable in the *Odyssey* is Homer's philosophical endeavor to
explicate the mortal life-span in terms of journey. All mortal life-spans are
journeys. However, Homer paradigmatically chooses the journey of a mortal
hero to explicate his philosophy of mortality. The hero's life-span, understood
as a journey, always includes two stages: the hero desires to transcend mortality
and acts on this desire, and the hero ultimately returns, through death or
homecoming or both. The Homeric hero, thus, on my reading, represents
a philosophical rather than a historical paradigm.

My own philosophical task attempts to define man in terms of Homeric philosophy. The first words of the two epics, *mēnin* and *andra*, demarcate the full
range of possibilities of mortal individuals. The former word, *mēnis* ("wrath"),
discloses a man, in this case Akhilleus, as an individual who traverses the ocean
and fights a war to win glory.[15] His wrath individuates him; it underlines his
commitment to achieve fame, while paradoxically seeming to undercut it
through threatening to withdraw Achilleus from the war. Through deeds,
Akhilleus ventures to transcend the anonymity and annihilation that threatens
mortals. This *desire* for individuation, of living beyond one's death, which
motivates all human transcendence, is one of the two basic components that
define man. This desire impels us on a journey.

Mortal life itself is a journey, inasmuch as an individual mortal life proceeds
from natality to fatality. A hero, who transcends as I just discussed, ultimately
forsakes the quixotic quest for quasi-immortality by heroically accepting his

mortal nature. This constitutes the subsequent stage of his journey. In the *Odyssey*, the first word of the epic, *andra*, "man," discloses man as returning to his mortal nature.[16]

Death is the proper end of man's—every man's—life-journey. What then is the beginning of the journey of life, its *arkhē*? Homer does indeed speculate about the existence of shades after death. But he never addresses birth or what lies beyond and before birth, the great mystery of *phusis*. Essentially he presents human life without answering the question of man's *arkhē*. In philosophical terms, Homeric man is *an-arkhic*.[17]

Homer goes further. He portrays Akhilleus and Odysseus as representing two distinct types of heroes, which I see as two stages in the life of a mortal. The *Iliad* portrays heroic man as *desiring* to transcend mortality, as an individual. A common Homeric term for the soul or inner life—I call it the mortal soul—of an individual human being is "*thumos*." We might see this as the "self." Thus although Homer does not explicitly say it, the Akhillean stage of man is dominated by *thumos*.[18] Akhilleus represents the intense desire of *thumos* to escape mortality, as well as his keen awareness of his individuality. *Thumos* distinguishes man as a solitary mortal, and urges him to embark on the journey of transcendence. This philosophical point is clearly seen in Parmenides' *Peri Phuseōs*: the protagonist speaks of a journey to the realm where coming-to-be and perishing are denied by an immortal.[19] The impulse for the journey as well as its reach or extent are described in terms of his *thumos*: "The mares were carrying me, as far as my *thumos* could reach," writes the Eleatic poet (1.1).

A very different psychological faculty dominates the Odyssean type of hero and the paradigm it provides for the second stage in the life of a man. Homer praises Odysseus' intellectual abilities. (He is shrewd, cunning, of many devices, *polutropos*, "the man of many ways.") The paradigmatic Homeric psychological faculty here is *nous*, "mind," more than *thumos* (since, to be sure, Odysseus also has "spirit" or "courage").

These fundamental descriptions of what it means to be a mortal are lost if we focus on other romantic interpretations of heroes as quasi-divine, closer to the gods.

To summarize, Akhilleus and Odysseus are not two different types of heroes, they are two phases of man defined as mortal. The mortal life-trajectory necessarily includes both mortal transcendence and return to mortality. Therefore, it is not wrong, but incomplete, to say that Homer is "completely subject to the fatalistic view that Death is unavoidable and not even the gods are able to protect man against it."[20] Given this, it is insufficient to say that Homer grants no postmortem transcendence to mortals.[21]

To say Homer is fatalistic betrays a metaphysical prejudice, as if a robust survival of death is the only transcendence possible to mortals. Heroes strive for *kleos*, and are sometimes privy to *kleos aphthiton* (undying fame).[22] We should recognize this drive—usually characterized as a quest for indirect immortality—as an important means of mortal transcendence. Homer is a *phenomenologist of mortality*, in that even death and the shades in Hades are recounted from a living and acting mortal's point of view.

Dynamics of Human Transcendence

The interpretation of the goddess' second speech presented here returns the *kouros* to the mortal *doxa* that discloses our mortal cosmos of becoming as such: changeable, and knowable with some probability but not with certainty, and never unequivocally. Before I state my reasons for suggesting this interpretation and describe it in detail, I would like to make some general remarks about "transcendence" as such.

In order to understand transcendence, I will return to the *kouros*' point of departure. In the proem, the protagonist is portrayed as a hero, being carried away by extraordinary mares and divine escorts. In Chapter 3, I described how he *already* excelled in a certain kind of mortal knowledge: he is described as a man who knows all cities (1.3). The singularity of this past accomplishment and his unique quest (upon which, he had told us, his *thumos* impels him; 1.1) are emphasized by the goddess, but with significant differences of emphasis:

> This road (*hodon*), for indeed far outside the stepping-path (*patou*) of men it
>   is (*estin*),
> But [rather] Themis (Right) and Dikē (Justice) [sent you forth]. It is necessary
>   that you learn all things. (1.27–8)

Her words make several points. The youth is some kind of a hero, who has left fellow mortals behind, and, through the longing of his *thumos*, has transcended his fellow mortals. The theme of *agōn* (competition) is repeated in her introduction to the speech on mortal cosmology: "So that never any one among mortals might outstrip you in knowing (*gnōmē*)" (8.61). The themes of mortal *agōn* and transcendence of humanity necessarily belong to an ethical *topos*. The goddess, exquisitely skilled in *logos*, and capable of the most rigorous and precise usage of words and arguments, surprisingly introduces a new dimension into her description of the youth's journey to her house. She substitutes Themis for *thumos*, and she underlines her choice of terms by further linking Themis to Dikē. Further, her account of the journey differs significantly from his: she claims that Dikē and Themis (1.28) sent him forth, whereas he said it was his *thumos* (1.1). Their accounts indeed can never be the same. His is mortal, hers is immortal, and her speech cannot capture the mortal experience of a journey. Dikē (Justice) did not in fact send the *kouros* on the journey; she merely permitted him to pass the gates, yielding only to the charming words of his immortal escorts. The goddess, in stressing the roles of Dikē and Themis, who reside in her realm of immortals, casts the entire journey in an ethical light. Ethics operates both within a community of mortals and as that which marks the boundaries of this community. The ethical principle expressed in the Greek notion of *hubris* marks the boundary between mortals and immortals. Does ethics among mortals depend upon their relation to the immortals? Clearly, the historical evidence is legion.

The goddess approves of and facilitates the transcendence of mortality. Yet, she is unable or unwilling to keep the youth in her realm. The youth returns to the mortal cosmos. In this return, the transcendence of humanity is reversed, the youth returns to his own kind. Here, too, in describing his return, agonistic language is used: if he listens to her and *returns having heard* (2.1), no mortal will outstrip him in thought (8.61). Hesiod gives us an interesting parallel to this *agōn* both within and between human communities. Whereas good *eris* is something necessary and not to be ignored, bad *eris* causes nations to war with each other. Likewise, Parmenides' poem contains agonistic elements, both positive and negative. By positive *agōn*, I mean the drive to transcend exemplified by the individual *thumos*, which carries him over the cities of men (1.3), far from the ways of mortals (1.28), to learn things in such a way that no mortal can surpass him (8.61). A negative *agōn*,[23] in my reading of Parmenides, would occur if he remained in the realm of the goddess, contrary to *dikē*; the goddess herself seems to refer to this as a "bad fate" (1.26). To transcend humanity either by coveting the *aiōn* (eternal life) of gods, or by betraying one's mortality, is abhorrent, and punishable by gods and *phusis* respectively. In both cases, the punishment is death, as Greek tragedy shows.[24]

Conclusion: The Fall of Parmenides

Parmenides "pours" into the journey the sum of his wisdom, his poetry, and his acute mind, and rises, incarnate, into the sky to shine with the goddess and partake of immortal being. Justice, if we are not to be childish and moralistic, is precisely this: the separation of mortals and immortals. Justice, in its primary sense, works with the arbitrariness, ambiguity and contingency of mortals, in concordance with an order established by the immortals. But the disembodied wisdom of the goddess (what else is her speech but this?) is not to be his. The goddess mocks Parmenides for being mortal, and her ultimate deception is this: she pushes him back into the mortal cosmos, and Parmenides tumbles, head first, through the entire universe, back to his only reality—conception in a womb (natality) and separation from eternal being (fatality).

But Parmenides has his revenge. As an aspiration, as a first principle, as an *arkhē*, the goddess and her *logos* turn out to be deceptive, and her dominion withers away, no longer the borrowed light of the night of our unknowing. Her *logos* is parasitic on (a denial of) human temporality. She derives her argument as a negation of mortal becoming. Parmenides, however, restores us to the only light there is, daybreak, and the only night there is, twilight of the idols. This fall is more heroic and tragic than any other, because all other falls presuppose a metaphysically prior paradise. Only Parmenides rises beyond the ethereal gates, on the power of his own *thumos*. Not a goddess of *logos*, but Persephone the queen of death,[25] or the unnamed generative daimoness of line 12.3 who presides over regenerative *phusis*, remains as a hope, an earth that receives Parmenides' mortality without deception.

Part III

Plato the Pre-Socratic

Chapter 6

Reading Plato's *Phaedrus*:
Socrates the Mortal

[T]he content of the dialogue [Phaedrus] *is by no means a jumbled potpourri. Its rich content is shaped so remarkably well that this dialogue must be accounted the most accomplished one in all essential respects. It therefore may not be taken to be the earliest work of Plato, as Schleiermacher believed; just as little does it belong to the final period; it rather belongs to those years which comprise the* akmē *of Plato's creative life.*

Martin Heidegger, Nietzsche[1]

Introduction: On Plato and Parmenides

The importance of Parmenides to Plato's philosophy is well appreciated.[2] As one scholar writes, "Plato's own writings might be said to have consisted in footnotes to Parmenides of Elea."[3] However, analyses of Parmenides' legacy usually focus on obvious dialogues, such as Plato's *Parmenides* and associated works (*Theaetetus, Sophist, Statesman*), or on the theory of ideas.[4] The Eleatic stranger in the *Sophist* is thought to advocate a theory that is a precursor to the theory of Forms developed in Plato's "later" dialogues.[5] But recent scholarship[6] shows that the picture is not so clear. The influence of "Father Parmenides" on Plato extends far beyond the obvious.

I consider that the dialogue *Phaedrus* most clearly displays Parmenides' influence on Plato. Although the *Phaedrus* is not usually considered in this context, Parmenidean elements pervade the dialogue. The *Phaedrus* offers several useful points of comparison with Parmenides' poem: the philosopher's journey, the trajectory of mortal life, *erōs* and the desire to overcome mortality, and the location of knowledge of eternal Forms as a brief *logos* within a mortal trajectory.

Modern scholars interpret Parmenides' poem primarily as a logical treatise on being (Taran, Barnes, Owen)[7] or as a foundation of epistemic conditions (Curd).[8] Plato's *Phaedrus* has recently gained notoriety as "a critical theory of writing" in the wake of Derrida's influential essay "Plato's Pharmacy."[9] Although the logical argument in Parmenides' poem and the discussion of writing in the

Phaedrus are important parts of their work, they are merely parts. In the case of Parmenides, scholars who analyze the goddess' speech on true being neglect the proem and the cosmology, or treat them as incompatible. In "Plato's Pharmacy," Derrida does not give us a convincing account of the hyperuranian sojourn of the soul, or of the philosophy of erotic love, to which no less than three "speeches" are devoted. By reading *Peri Phuseōs* and *Phaedrus* side by side, however, we can identify themes that we would otherwise miss. It is not my intention to show that the *Phaedrus* is a literal commentary on Parmenides' poem. I wish to point out certain thematic connections between the two works, and my argument, if successful, shows that Plato responded to Parmenides' "commentary on the mortals" as well his epistemological challenge.

With a "commentary on the mortals," I try to demonstrate a certain understanding of mortality common to these thinkers. The *kouros* in the pre-Socratic poem and Socrates in the Platonic dialogue appear in these dialogues as heroes. I interpret the works as being *about* them, and about their fate. That Socrates is a mortal is not just a logical proposition with the structure "S is P." Socrates, besides being a brilliant philosopher, is the victim of a politically motivated execution. Derrida's analysis of this dialogue does not tell us that Plato's pharmacy dispenses exclusively to mortals, and that only in the face of incurable death does the word *pharmakon* justify its ambiguity as both medicine and poison. For the *kouros*, the tragic inevitability of death is no less pronounced. After a discourse on eternal being, the goddess returns the youth to the world of life and death, no matter how illogical and foreign such a cosmos may be to her way of thinking. Parmenides himself, although a "healer" of great repute,[10] and well versed in ritualistic and medicinal healing, ultimately delivers the same verdict: death is incurable.

It would be trivial, although still tragic, if these dialogues simply stated "these are mortals, and as such they are condemned to die." What lifts these works to philosophical heights is puzzlement: even as mortals, we have, through *logos* (and perhaps through *erōs* in the case of the *Phaedrus*), some access to immortality. Language is "divine" and, if not eternal, then at least atemporal. Metaphysics is not an achievement of language: it is its essential nature. The philosophical problem that these two thinkers wrestle with is: how do we speak/write about the finite, fragile, irreplaceable, incarnate fate of specific mortals, when language is, in some sense, outside of time? Parmenides and Plato negotiate this predicament by charting a path between the two realms, one mortal and precious and the other immortal and unchanging. The motif of journey describes the transition from one realm to the other. Several other themes form a constellation around this theme of unavoidable but incomprehensible mortality. I have mentioned the motif of journey, but there are others: exclusion from the city, contrast with "other mortals," specificity (the initiated, the beloved), desire, temporary experiences of immortality, especially through *logos*, and philosophy as a therapy that is equally curative and poisonous.

I will close this introduction by clarifying my aim: to illuminate common themes in *Peri Phuseōs* and *Phaedrus*. The *Phaedrus* is not an exegesis of Parmenides' poem, but it takes up ideas from Parmenides and translates them into a Platonic outlook.

Early Attempts at Comparing Parmenides and the *Phaedrus*

The first part of Parmenides' work, the proem, survives in an extensive quote by Sextus (*Adversus Mathematicos* VII.111). Sextus adds an interpretation, where he reads the journey of the *kouros* allegorically. His interpretation is colored by a later version of a chariot ride, the famous journey of the soul in Plato's *Phaedrus*. Sextus is not alone; indeed, during his time, it had become fashionable to read Parmenides' proem with the myth of Plato's *Phaedrus* in mind.[11] The issue of Parmenides' Platonism is an anachronism, deserving no further comment. However, scholars are divided on the question of Plato's debt to Parmenides. Among those who see Parmenides' influence on the chariot journey of the *Phaedrus* are Natorp (*Platons Ideenlehre*)[12] and Frutiger (*Les mythes de Platon*).[13] There are those who do not see any connection between the Parmenidean journey and Plato's description of the soul's itinerary. To this group belong Robin (*Phèdre*)[14] and Hackforth (*Plato's Phaedrus*).[15] I quote Hackforth to illustrate this point of view:

> Scholars have speculated as to the resemblance between Plato's chariot and that in which Parmenides made his journey to an unnamed goddess, passing the gates of Night and Day, and guided by the daughters of the Sun: equally doubtful is any allusion to the chariot of Empedocles, of which we hear a single obscure line; neither of these poets suggests any comparison to the soul. But surely the representation of the ruling part of the soul as a chariot-eer is so obvious and natural, especially in view of the common metaphorical use of *heniokseuein* and its cognates, that we need look no further than to the *Republic* itself for that simile.[16]

Taran is convinced by Hackforth's point of view: "While in Parmenides nothing suggests the comparison of the chariot with the soul, in the *Phaedrus* (246 a 4–7) it is explicitly stated that the myth is such a comparison."[17] Taran adds more points of contrast between the two great journeys of ancient Greek philosophy, such as the winged charioteer, mortal and immortal horses, and so on, which are peculiar to Plato's version.

It seems to me that scholars note two general points of disparity: Plato explicitly relates the chariot ride to the soul, and his imagery is different. The latter point is trivial and may, therefore, be ignored: there is no reason to expect Plato to copy the specifics of Parmenides' vision. However, the first point—that the journey is undertaken by the soul in Plato, but by a living mortal in Parmenides—is a serious one. Did Plato have Parmenides' description of the chariot ride in mind when he wrote the *Phaedrus?*

My answer is yes: there are thematic resonances to Parmenides throughout Plato, including the *Phaedrus*. Nevertheless, it is not always reasonable to expect Plato to acknowledge his debt. Even when he does, "No one is going to say that the dialogue titled *Parmenides* is an historical document of the Eleatic's own thoughts. Plato himself is explicitly apologetic about the liberties that he takes with Parmenides' thought, and speaks playfully of having to commit parricide. But the irresistible effulgence of Platonic thought causes Parmenides to be lost, so to speak, in it. He becomes hardly identifiable as an independent thinker."[18] Indeed, it is in such a state of immersion in Plato that later readers receive Parmenides' philosophy, and the proem in particular. We have to sharpen our vision to see Parmenides' shadow behind Plato's brilliant reflections.

Parmenides' proem provides other parallels, however. Scholars have generally dismissed the proem, and Plato's dialogue with his Eleatic predecessor has been viewed solely through the lens of his ontology and methodology, focusing almost entirely on the *alētheia* speech.[19] Scholars claim that the proem is "not an allegory," but is merely a "literary device."[20] When we compare Parmenides' journey with the highly philosophical allegory that we take Plato's chariot ride of the soul to be, we see the difference between them is exaggerated. To see the essential connection between the two journeys, we have to restore the philo-sophical core of the proem, its own relationship to the "soul." In the first line of the proem, Parmenides uses a "soul-word" to define the journey: its trajectory is determined by the *thumos*. This and other parallels, which I demonstrate in the following sections of this chapter, will bring Parmenides and Plato close together in a deeper sense than any comparison of metaphors and language could.

Journey

The motif of journey is central to both Parmenides' poem and Plato's *Phaedrus*. Even if we consider Plato's *Phaedrus* on its own, it is difficult to isolate the chariot ride as the sole motif of journey in that dialogue. The dialogue itself begins with a journey, taking Socrates beyond the walls of Athens. I have explored the significance of the relationship between the journey metaphor and philosophy elsewhere. Here I would like to draw attention to Socrates' journey outside the city walls.

The entire dialogue occurs outside the city, and Socrates and Phaedrus travel many realms—both in landscape and in *logos*. An affinity between philosophy and the image of journey is powerfully present in Plato, as it is in Parmenides, but remains largely hidden both in the proem and in the dialogue. Perhaps this concealment is intentional on the part of the two thinkers, or perhaps it is due to our prejudices concerning what we are willing to regard as philosophy. We have discarded the existential significance of the journey because we refuse to recognize its philosophical significance.

Before I expand on the temporal dimension the metaphor of journey introduces into philosophy, I wish to mark a further point of similarity between Plato and Parmenides in relation to the city. Socrates' walk escorted by Phaedrus and Parmenides' journey to the goddess leave behind a certain kind of knowledge that is linked to the city. On their way out, Phaedrus points out how out of place (*atopōtatos*) Socrates seems outside the walls of the city. Socrates supplies the answer: he is a lover of wisdom (*philomathēs eimi*) and, unlike the countryside and the trees, people in the city (*astei anthropoi*) have something to teach him (*didaskein*, 230d). In the very next line he confesses that Phaedrus has found the potion (*pharmakon*) to lead him out of the city. It is clear that Socrates leaves behind the city (*astu*; cf. *Peri phuseōs* 1.3), men (*anthropoi*), and a certain kind of knowledge taught in the city (*didaskein*). The new landscape he enters (*topos*) is one where he essentially does not belong, where he is out of place (*atopōtatos tis*).

Parmenides describes the journey of the *kouros* in similar terms. The boy clearly leaves the everyday domain to reach the goddess, a place "far from the step of mortals (*anthropōn ektos patou*)." The road that he follows leads him out of all cities (*pant'aste*). That he is a knowing man (*eidota phōta*), can only mean that he has the knowledge of the cities and knows its limits, which he overcomes by entering a realm where he does not belong: the realm of the goddess. Parmenides has found the *pharmakon* for a visit to the immortals.[21]

Introduction to a Reading of Plato's *Phaedrus*

Platonic dialogues are not philosophical treatises artificially enclosed in dialogue for stylistic reasons. The dialogue cannot be translated into a philosophical dialectic, independent of considerations such as setting and historical context. Scholars now regard the dialogue as an artistic unity,[22] in which the nature of the speakers as well as the circumstances in which they find themselves form an integral part of Plato's philosophy. Rosen calls this method of approaching the dialogue, taking into account its form and its dramatic content, the "dramatic perspective."[23]

Plato's work is available to us only in dramatic form. Plato himself says that he wrote no separate books on his philosophy (*Letter VII*). Within the dialogues, Plato never speaks *in propria persona*. If we want to access his philosophy, our only option is a careful reading of the conversation. Plato eschews the unambiguous rationalist, positivist voice of the physician, historian, or lawgiver. The *Phaedrus* combines the erotic speech of Socrates with the charismatic nature of Phaedrus. The *showing* of how philosophy is done together with the philosophy itself is of great pedagogical importance. The how, why, and what of philosophy is inseparable in Plato from his philosophical conclusions, and this is achieved through the dramatic form. In many, if not all, his dialogues (especially those that bear the protagonist's name), Plato pays special attention to the identity and individuality of his characters. He does not simply put words into their mouths. The specific individuality of each character lends a "voice" to the lines of argument.

No individual is more lovingly, respectfully, or critically portrayed in Plato's dialogues than Socrates. Scholars have approached the individual Socrates in two ways: they search either for the historical person, or for the immortal philosopher. In either case, we lose Plato's efforts to capture the tragic individuality of his teacher. I call this individuality the mortal soul. By individuality, I do not mean a simple psychological entity or autonomous subject—concepts that dominate modern philosophy. By individuality, I mean most emphatically "mortality," the life-trajectory of an individual from birth to death. Philosophy often searches for timeless truths, which obscure the fragility, irreversibility, and finality of an individual life. Written texts have the danger of exacerbating this artificial sense of fixedness, a problem that Plato thematizes in the *Phaedrus*.

Both philosophy and the individual Socrates are inescapably mortal. My reading restores the mortal dimension, by accepting the death of Socrates as a philosophically worthy topic. Socrates died for philosophy, one could argue; but, traditionally, his philosophy has been thought to consist of a search for timeless truths or immortality. Many think that Plato pioneers the denial of a mortal Socrates. I argue against this view: Plato's writings attempt not only to capture Socrates' utterances, but the living breathing man himself—an individual, I argue, who cannot be excluded from philosophy, least of all from Platonic philosophy. As Benardete notes, "The longest series of [Platonic] dialogues . . . is connected in order to time through an external event, the trial and death of Socrates: *Theaetetus, Euthyphro, Sophist, Statesman, Apology of Socrates, Crito* and *Phaedo*."[24] The philosophy for which Socrates gave up his life is in need of rejuvenation that only mortality can provide. Philosophy cannot separate the man and his ideas. Philosophical ideas (such as those propounded by Plato or sometimes by the Platonic Socrates) have developed into a theology of sorts, but can we restore Socratic philosophy as *anthropo*logy, that is, as an account of the *anthropos*, the mortal singular?

In this reading, I argue for a plurality of persons, voices, and philosophical positions contained in the dialogue. From the complete generality and universality of the Forms, to the most specific event of his death, Socrates the individual is on a journey. The plurality of the dialogue I mentioned earlier, and this particular fate of Socrates, together provide an account of the life-journey of Socrates and the world in which he remains.

Plato uses various techniques to preserve Socrates' individuality in the dialogue *Phaedrus*. This dialogue comments on several intellectual disciplines and themes: history, medicine, law, myth, dialectic, love, writing, the possibility of immortality, and others. I will argue that Plato's criticism of each arises from his allegiance to Socrates and a denial of universal accounts that many of these disciplines provide for mortals. For example, the famous evaluation of writing versus speaking raises the question: does each preserve or kill the individual life? Just a glance at the history of scholarship reveals how little emotional involvement we invest in Socrates the human. His unique mortal existence should make his unique philosophical contribution comprehensible.

Plato preserves Socrates as a *totality*, as the phenomenal *singular* individual. Thus Socrates' views about the world need to be presented in the context of his being in the world. This gives us the crucial question of the Platonic project: "what does it mean to be a finite, singular, ephemeral mortal whose mortality cannot be preserved, but whose *logoi* can be?" The dialogues disclose the cross-roads between the "way of mortality" and the "way of words, ideas and Forms."

To anticipate my conclusions: myth and dialectic prove to be especially suitable for Plato's difficult task. They best capture the finite and ephemeral nature of mortal life, by resisting the generalities of positivist thinking.

In this chapter, I want to emphasize that by "individuality" I do not mean a thinking ego, or a transcendental ego, or any variation of it: this is not only anachronous, but also, in my view, useless. I have a strictly temporal identity in view: a being, which comes to be, thrives, and perishes in time. This view of individuality emphasizes the particular, singular, irreversible, asymmetrical against the divine, monistic, universal, symmetrical, harmonious, ordered, and eternal being. As such, my view of individuality is not only not psychological, but it is also not comprehensible in those terms. Embodiment is the primary requirement for such individuality, which, consequently, is lost upon a person's physical death. By individual, I do not mean anything "interior" except as a property of a person: if anything it is a being in the phenomenal world "outside." Among the words for the "self" in Ancient Greek, the word *thumos* comes closest to my meaning of individuality, although *psukhē* and *nous* are not problematic in themselves, as long as the reader does not think of them either as disembodied, non-temporal entities or as strictly rational, universal entities. I use "self," "self-knowledge," "mortal," "individual," and sometimes "person" in this specifically temporal, phenomenal sense. I do not imply any substance or objectification or hypostatization or essences.

Recipe for Individuality: Dialogue and Myth

Plato's dialogues are myths from beginning to end, from the first word to the last. This relies on a radical understanding of "myth." We cannot confine "myth" to a few pieces within the dialogues, such as the myth of Er or the myth of the soul as a chariot. What do I mean by myth? Myth is narrative that surpasses factual, positivistic thought. It rejects allegory and is unbounded by logic. Myth presents phenomena more fundamentally and more comprehensively, prior to their ordering by a ratiocinative calculus. Myth stands midway between chaos and cosmos (order). Whereas chaos dissolves phenomena, cosmological order abstracts from them. The cosmos stands under the sign of *anangkē* (necessity),[25] while myth stands under the sign of *tuchē* (chance). Myth is prescientific in this fundamental way: it discloses a world. Probability, not the necessity of reason, governs the relationship between phenomena in the mythic world. Within this world, however, we can raise epistemological and moral questions and develop the various sciences. Myth therefore allows us to understand the Platonic dialogue in a more contextual way. Plato presents more than verifiable arguments: he captures the phenomenon of Socrates himself. By describing existing individuals and their philosophical journeys, Plato avoids both the desire to abstract away from reality (philosophical *anangkē*) and to succumb to Cratylian flux. He incorporates both mortal individuality and phenomena (philosophical probability, *tuchē*).

Myth thus mediates between Forms and phenomena, or between Parmenidian being and Heraclitean flux—to apply the traditional rubrics. The dialogues as myths *are* Platonic philosophy.

Current scholars debate the status of speakers in Platonic dialogues. The "anti-mouthpiece" interpretation argues that no character is a mouthpiece for Plato.[26] This means that the arguments of the interlocutors do not represent Plato's own views. Scholars holding this view have a literary appreciation for Plato's dramatic narrative. They think that Plato's views emerge through the dialectic embodied in the dramatic narrative of the dialogues. The anti-mouthpiece view is not so problematic when we consider a character like Thrasymachus, but the dramatic Socrates poses greater problems. Diogenes Laertius tells us that five characters, namely, Socrates, Parmenides, the Eleatic Stranger, Timaeus, and the Athenian Stranger, speak for Plato. This "mouthpiece" argument has survived in one form or another ever since Diogenes. The mouthpiece and anti-mouthpiece interpretations share a common feature. They both separate "argument" from dramatic context. The mouthpiece interpreters ignore the dramatic elements, while the other camp argues that the independence and importance of the dramatic form is greater than any individual statement it contains.

If we think of dialogues as spoken by mouthpieces, we lose the Platonic dialogue altogether, and Plato's dialogic form degenerates into "style." On this reading, these mouthpieces are *all* Plato, and thus strictly speaking there is no dialogue, or even conversation. The anti-mouthpiece reading, which values the intellectual autonomy of the characters, is a better reading; however, the characters still fall under Plato's authority. Although I agree with the "anti-mouthpiece" interpretation, I wish to go a step beyond it. I claim that Plato not only preserves the "views" of his "characters," but even more, he gives testimony to their existence—albeit mythically, rather than historically. I am arguing for the existential *person*-hood of Plato's characters: their reality as singulars, with existences and points of view that will not yield to a literary program. In short, I wish to clarify that the characters maintain their "fictional" status as "merely fictional."

Like myths, Platonic dialogues transcend the possibilities of both "literature, understood as fiction" and "history, understood as facts with evidence." They relate to the ways of being: being in the world, and being mortal.

These writings are not "orphaned," waiting to be completed by a reader.[27] It would be misleading to privilege the reader over the characters, and assume that Plato is more interested in the reader than in his characters. The dialogues require that we understand myth as a primordial account, within which all other types of specialized accounts, including philosophy, can occur. Lysias mistakes the primacy of myth with its generality, and thus his speech remains a rhetorical exercise, cut off from Phaedrus' life and fate. As an alternative to generality, myth allows us to give an account of specific, singular individuals, together with the most universal shapes of being and becoming in the world.

Many Journeys and Various Voices

In the opening line of the dialogue, Socrates asks Phaedrus, "Where are you going and where are you coming from?" (227a).[28] This line suggests an odyssey, which includes not only Phaedrus' excursion outside the city of Athens (as he explains to Socrates), but also the movement of his soul from rhetoric to philosophy, a movement prompted and guided by Socrates (cf. 278b).[29] Socrates himself, we can say, evolves through revising his position on love in the various stages of his "seduction" of Phaedrus away from Lysias and what he represents. Each revision, as we will see, is a move from scientific generalization to concrete individualism.

The dialogue in the *Phaedrus* occurs outside the city, and Socrates and Phaedrus traverse a great deal of ground. Journey is not a mere metaphor or image for philosophy; philosophy *is* a journey. Every journey includes finite and temporal aspects. Life itself is, fundamentally, a journey from birth to death. Philosophy, generally to its detriment, seeks to explain life without reference to passing time. We shut out the existential significance of the journey because we do not wish to address our finitude and mortality.

Socrates portrays his own life as a journey of discovery. Scholars have usually sought to distinguish between the itinerant Socrates of the *agora* and the Academic Plato.[30] Socrates, on this view, represents the very model of the endlessly seeking thinker who refuses to admit any unexamined view or perhaps, in fact, any conclusions at all. This Socrates, commentators feel, is depicted in the "aporetic" or unresolved Platonic dialogues. Plato, on the other hand, has become a symbol of dogmatism. Settled in the Academy, it is as if he uses Socrates as a mere heuristic.

I wish to propose another view of the fundamental relationship between Socrates and Plato, one not based on the usual dichotomies (*agora*/Academy, itinerant/fixed, and oral/written). Plato himself, in *every* dialogue, imitates the wandering Socrates. He follows Socrates on his journey. A Platonic dialogue is not an autopsy (in the modern sense of dissection) of Socrates carried out in the Academy. Plato accompanies Socrates on his journeys through philosophy and life (these two things, for Socrates, being inseparable), bearing faithful witness. The dialogue is an autopsy in the Greek sense: seeing something with one's own eyes.[31] Although Plato was not always physically present at the dialogues he relates,[32] through his authorial presence he memorializes a moving image of the living Socrates. He is not an omniscient narrator, not a director or an editor (to use a modern idiom from the cinema), but a co-traveler. He preserves Socrates within his own mortal lifetime, while often focusing, even to the point of obsession, on the circumstances of his death. The dialogues restore a mortal Socrates rather than resurrect Socrates as an immortal philosopher. All Plato's work consists of a search for this Socrates. Even writing, he says in the *Phaedrus* (278c–e), must always yield to things "more important" than what is written.

Besides these personal itineraries, Plato attempts to capture the journey of philosophy over history. One way he expresses this is by problematizing the transition from an oral tradition to a written one. Although the pre-Socratics did write down their cosmologies, the art of writing philosophy was a recent phenomenon. Plato's own mentor, Socrates, favored speaking over writing, and conducted his philosophical inquiries orally. The "Oral Tradition" itself was the repository of myth rather than philosophy, as we know it. The dialogue attempts to examine the journey of thought from imaginative myth to self-conscious philosophy. It is more rewarding to read the dialogue with the background of this mythic tradition in view.

The transformation of the dominant mode of thinking from myth to philosophy is closely related, perhaps even causally related, to the replacement of oral traditions by a new world dominated by prose writing (as Plato conceived it).[33] Vernant writes: "Prose composition—medical treatises, historical accounts, the speeches of orators, and the dissertations of the philosophers—represents not only a different mode of expression from that of the oral tradition and poetic composition but also a new form of thought."[34] It is simplistic to say that a close study of the language in its oral or written form is sufficient to understand either myth or philosophy. However, the demand for a new type of expression has a conceivable effect on thinking itself.[35] Whatever the actual causes of such a change, the transition from oral expression to specialized forms of written expression is linked to the transition between the decline of myth and the beginning of philosophy as the dominant mode of thinking. Plato creates a play between the art of writing on the one hand and Phaedrus' philosophical education on the other, bringing to light the various aspects of this transition.

Among the different disciplines that adopted writing at that time were medicine and history (or historiography). Medical treatises strive for exhaustiveness and clarity, and are usually catalogues of a patient's symptoms (as the Hippocratic writings were), with a view to finding a cure. It does not engage in dialectic with the patient. Since it treats physical conditions rather than the soul, it does not rely on *logos* in the relations between physicians and patients. Whereas the body may respond to medical remedies (*pharmaka* in Greek), the soul requires something more for its growth, as Plato understood, such as beauty, rhetoric, dialectic, or philosophy.

Phaedrus is aware of both his physical and spiritual needs: following the suggestion of the physician Acumenus (227a),[36] he is taking a walk outside the city, directly after an indulgence in a speech composed by the orator Lysias. The reference to Acumenus in conjunction with the *logographer* Lysias raises the question: what are their respective modes of expressing themselves, that is, their voices (as I will call them)? Answering this question will offer us another approach to issues of *logos*, of speech versus writing, which the *Phaedrus*, prompted by Lysias' speech, raises.

Moreover, mention of Acumenus refers us back to the *Symposium* where his son, Eryximachus, engages in a twofold enterprise: he cures Aristophanes of his hiccups (185d–e) and makes a speech on love (186a–188e). He applies a physical remedy to hiccups, but then makes the mistake of applying a similar approach to *erōs*: he explains it physically. This impossibility shows that the physician too must address separate domains, developing two voices, as it were. In the *Symposium*, these two methods fuse in the person of this particular physician. In the *Phaedrus*, these two functions, the physical and the spiritual, separate into two: the physician (Acumenus) tends to Phaedrus' body, whereas Phaedrus' soul turns to Lysias first and then to Socrates.

Writing and speaking serve different purposes with respect to the body and the soul. The *Phaedrus* problematizes the usefulness of writing for serving the needs of the soul. Medicine, as written down, is a theoretical endeavor with a practical application. Philosophy, in contrast, especially as practiced by Socrates in the *Phaedrus*, does not permit a distinction whereby theory can be abstracted from *praxis*. Socratic philosophy requires dialectic between living persons in a concrete philosophical encounter. This is Socratic *praxis*. The theoretical component of Socratic philosophy (that is, the search for truth and knowledge), on the other hand, might lead Socrates out of the city into mythical realms or into *aporia*. Socratic theory is thus secondary to Socratic *praxis*. This is what Socrates means by his comment on "self-knowledge" being more important to him than the task of demythologization (*Phaedrus* 229e–230a). Among the various voices taken from different disciplines, Socrates struggles to find the appropriate voice for Phaedrus' soul.

Plato is equally suspicious of historical voices as of medical prescriptions. That this dialogue probably could not have occurred historically[37] shows the irrelevance of historical facticity to philosophy. Evidently, Plato is not concerned with historical accuracy, which is the domain of the historian rather than the philosopher. Historical voice is not the same as philosophical voice: the former is not adequate for philosophy. This is why Socrates is not interested in investigating, using clever contemporary methods, the "real meaning" of the story of Boreas' rape of Oreithuia (229c–e). In this, we might contrast Socrates with historians such as Thucydides.[38]

Continuing on the journey with Phaedrus and Socrates: Socrates learns that Phaedrus was present at a feast of speeches by Lysias and others at Epicrates' house, a house that formerly belonged to Morychus the *bon vivant* (*Phaedrus*, 227b). The reference to Morychus evokes a speech-making banquet quite different from the spontaneous gaiety of the *Symposium*, more *salon* than philosophical-gathering.[39] This suggests artificiality, which is precisely Socrates' criticism of Lysias' speech when he hears of it from Phaedrus. The setting thus gives us a clue to the condition of Phaedrus' soul; Socrates makes it his task to tend to his soul. Socrates is eager to listen to this speech, but adopts the voice of the poet Pindar in answering Phaedrus with the words "more important than business" (227b). Socrates' earnestness is closer to the voice of the poet than to the orator's. Earnestness dwells more in poetry than in a *logos* such as Lysias', which adopts an artificial stance. Poets, poetry, and the Muses are always a part of Socrates' speeches in the *Phaedrus*.

Lysias' speech, a written copy of which Phaedrus delivers to Socrates, concerns *erōs*. This again recalls the *Symposium* with its speeches on love: in both works, Socrates is depicted as especially interested in *erōs* (*Phaedrus* 227c, 257a). In his speech, Lysias writes that a beautiful youth "should gratify the one who does not love rather than one who does" (227c). Socrates points out the general and impersonal nature of this speech by replying that Lysias ought to include the old and the poor as well among criteria a youth should look for before he gratifies a man. Lysias' speech could be addressed to any Athenian youth, whereas the speeches on love given later by Socrates take Phaedrus' soul into account, that is, his individual nature. Socrates, who claims to be interested in "self-knowledge," also says that he "knows" Phaedrus' soul (228a). Socrates mocks the formulaic nature of Lysias' speech by saying that with his revisions, such a speech would be more "beneficial to the general public" (227c–d). The association between utility and generality contrasts with the individuating nature of *erōs* and Socrates' philosophy. Lysias' voice resembles the impersonal voice of the physician.[40]

The setting of the dialogue outside the city walls is significant for the themes of both *erōs* and *logos*. Outside the city walls, *erōs* is free to be manic. In the *Symposium*, whose setting is a private drinking-party, to which only a small group of select individuals are invited, *erōs* is no longer a god, but a daemon facilitating communication. In the *Republic*, which occurs in a more civic setting,[41] *erōs*, identified with tyranny, is chastised and subdued by mathematics.[42] Thus, the setting of each dialogue determines the function of *erōs*. Socrates never adopts a single unified voice. Released from the night and the inebriety of the *Symposium*, as well as the chastising city of the *Republic, erōs* emerges most resplendently in the noonday riparian landscape of the *Phaedrus.*

The setting of the *Phaedrus* outside the city wall also influences the voice of the speakers. Once outside the *polis,* Socrates chooses a mythic voice, presenting us a vision of the Forms through myth. *The Republic* presents us with a journey of a different sort: Socrates walks down to Piraeus, to witness the festivities in honor of Bendis, but he never crosses the city wall. The journey never leaves the city, and it remains political. Within the city, poetry is banished together with *erōs.* There (on the road from Piraeus to Athens), philosophy must speak to the public in the unambiguous voice of mathematics. When it comes to law, myth must withdraw its poetic, ambiguous voice, as it must also do when the voice of history and medicine dominates. The *Phaedrus,* by contrast, as a journey and as a voice, strives to preserve the individuality of Socrates and Phaedrus.

Faulty Memory

Plato finds many of the voices we encounter in the *Phaedrus* unsuitable for philosophy. His criticism, ironically, is that they overgeneralize, abstracting away from the individual. This critique of mythic voices is followed by a critique of writing in the second half of the dialogue. In each case Plato bemoans the loss of individuality and interpersonal discourse. "Memory" provides Plato with a starting-point from which to launch this criticism.

Plato calls attention to the relationship between written speech and memory by depicting Phaedrus at a loss: he is unable to recite Lysias' speech from memory. Plato already explored the question of memory in his *Theaetetus,* where he probes the question of knowledge. Eucleides recounts from memory the conversation between Socrates and Theaetetus, as recounted to him by Socrates himself. Eucleides admits that he cannot remember the dialogue entirely, and returns to Socrates a few times for correction. In the *Phaedrus,* an admission of faulty memory precedes the reading of an erotic speech, whereas in the *Theaetetus* an admission of faulty memory precedes a reading of an epistemic narrative. This is no coincidence, because the *Phaedrus* and the *Theaetetus* describe complementary poles of Plato's conception of philosophy. I follow Rosen in identifying these two aspects as the *poetic* and the *mathematical.*[43] The *Phaedrus* explores the former aspect, while the *Theaetetus,* in which Socrates converses with a brilliant student of mathematics,[44] explores the latter.[45] Why does Plato raise the issue of memory in each of these dialogues? To answer this question, we need to relate memory to Plato's theory of knowledge.

Memory is linked to Plato's theory of knowledge (in both works) through a term he uses for knowing: *anamnēsis* (or recollection). It is crucial to remember the two senses of memory: a memory that transcends historical time and facticity (*anamnēsis*), and a memory that obsesses over factual accuracy of past events (history). Plato wishes his dialogues to illustrate the former philosophical function.[46] Thus, the dialogues recover the philosophical journey of Socrates (in the first sense), while, crucially, preserving his individuality—rather than presenting a mere historical account. The kind of memory that presents inert facts and organizes events into a static sequence is the kind that Plato devalues in his critique of writing. This type of writing replaces myth with history, and Plato casts a negative light upon it by depicting the weakness of (faulty) memory in both the *Theaetetus* and the *Phaedrus*.

Phaedrus reveals his nature by saying that he would rather be able to remember Lysias' speech than come into a large sum of money. Phaedrus is not a materialist, in other words. He resembles the philosopher in valuing memory more than money.[47] However, unlike the philosopher, he loves speeches that do not take either the individual (Phaedrus) or the universal (*erōs*) into account; he thinks they are still of use to the general public, as evidenced by his infatuation with Lysias' style. Further, the kind of memory valued by Phaedrus is the non-philosophical kind—useful, perhaps, for history, but of little help in attaining self-knowledge.

Phaedrus' desire to memorize Lysias' speech as well as his admission that he finds it impressive (228a, 227c) reveal that Phaedrus is in love with the speech. This undermines the message of the speech, which praises the non-lover, because its existence depends on its reception by a loving reader, such as Phaedrus. Phaedrus, since he is a lover (of speeches), cannot take seriously the speech's praise of the non-lover. Later, Phaedrus will praise the speech for its exhaustiveness and style, rather than for its content.

Socrates, unlike Lysias, fashions his speeches in accordance with his audience. He responds to Phaedrus' claim that he does not remember the speech by fostering a different kind of talent: the philosophical pursuit of self-knowledge. This task requires a different kind of memory—not the dogmatic memorization of written texts. Socrates invokes his most fundamental philosophical imperative: "know thyself." With the words, "Oh Phaedrus! If I don't know my Phaedrus, I have forgotten myself, yet neither of these things is true" (228a), Socrates begins Phaedrus' *paideia*.

Historical memory does not appear favorably in this section on self-knowledge. Memory is crucial for positivistic thinking and the retention of facts. The Thaumus myth tells us, however, that memory must go beyond facts to the most universal perspective on being: the Forms. Memory is unhelpful if it does not aid in self-knowledge. By contrast, Socrates' myth of the soul *memorializes* individuals: mortal, distinct, and unable to abide in the atemporality of the Forms.

Socratic Identity and the Beginning of Philosophy

In the *Symposium*, Alkibiades interrupts speeches on the theory of love. This disruption of the discussion marks the end of the speeches that try to address *erōs* in general terms. This end is not so much a conclusion as a failure. An inquiry into the nature of *erōs* continues in the *Phaedrus*, where *erōs* is closely associated with *mania* and philosophy. In the *Symposium, erōs* is at best practical, a daemon of communication. The "universalizing" that Diotima advocates loses track of the individual, and the arrival of Alkibiades with his highly personal account of his love for Socrates is a welcome return to mortal existence. Appropriately, Alkibiades' speech on love revolves around the question, "who is Socrates?"

In the early part of the *Phaedrus*, Socrates declares his true interest, namely, answering the question "What type of a being am I?" in accordance with the directive of the Delphic Oracle (230a). Indeed, the erotic speeches of the *Phaedrus* are rife with questions of identity. How can Socrates profess knowledge of Phaedrus as well as his identity with Phaedrus (as he implies) while simultaneously maintaining that he does not know who he is?

We have to remember that Socratic ignorance is not the same as the ignorance contained in the following sentence: "I am ignorant of the technical terms my physician uses." The difference is this: Socratic ignorance is not ignorance of an object, a thing; it is the philosophical state of wonder. By wondering whether he is like the mythic beast Typhon, a symbol of chaos, he brings to his ignorance and his quest a sense of fear and wonder, which in the *Theaetetus* he describes as the fundamental philosophical attitude (155c–d). In Greek myth, Typhon (also called Typhoeus) shook up the ordered universe and threatened Zeus' rule. Being like Typhon would mean that Socrates would shake the foundations of Athens. His self-knowledge could prove to be a transgression and could lead to his condemnation.

The question of Socrates' identity is raised explicitly in the *Theaetetus*. Socrates' interest in the future of Athens and the intellectual potential of its youth is related to the question of how Socrates appears to Athenians. Should he wear a sophistic mask over his Typhonian self? In that work, Socratic identity is unable to appear as the Silenus figure described by an erotically inspired Alkibiades in the *Symposium*. In the *Theaetetus*, only the grotesque exterior of Socrates is available to the mathematician Theodorus.

We have three representations of Socrates. Socrates is compared to a technical artifact, a statue of Silenus, which when opened reveals the god-like image of Socrates to Alkibiades. This is, as the dramatic setting shows, a private and privileged vision. Secondly, there is the public vision, which is mathematical, and does not penetrate his grotesque exterior. Midway between these two representations stands the vision of Socrates the mortal, who in the *Phaedrus* is a lover of speeches, a mentor, a lover, a poet, a mythmaker, a seer of Forms, and a mantic.

What is common to all these representations? The quest for identity is always undertaken as a comparison with an other. Nowhere does Socrates say "Let me examine my innermost structure as a subject and see who I am." There are no Cartesian meditations here to empty the mind of all extraneous material. Socratic doubt is the opposite of Cartesian doubt.

What do we mean by identity through comparison? Our habit of referring to the objects of the world around us, by means of concrete nouns, is based on an act of comparison.[48] For example, a horse is a concept derived from our comparison of several specimens; a comparison with donkeys and zebras gives us the concrete noun "ungulate" and so on, until we arrive at higher and higher genera. Plato uses this method in his definitions: a definition of a particular being includes both the common class it belongs to and the specific differentiae that distinguish it from other members of the class. Plato self-consciously describes this method in the *Sophist,* together with its shortcomings. It is no accident that here again, in this dialogue, the driving question of who Socrates is plays a pivotal role, namely, whether he is a genuine philosopher or a sophist.

Who is Socrates? Part 2: From Artifact to Individuality

Socrates and Phaedrus both love speeches, but they hesitate to make speeches of their own. Even when Socrates soliloquizes, he often disclaims authorship or recants at a later point. Phaedrus elicits speeches from Lysias and Socrates, and Socrates is overcome with *mania* (238c–d). He characterizes his speeches as a gift of the Muses or the myth of a poet (cf. Stesichorus, 244a). Certainly, neither Phaedrus nor Socrates is a writer. Socrates takes pains to demonstrate his sympathy toward the mythical voice from the beginning. Even as he stresses the philosophical nature of his conversation with Phaedrus, he hints at the mythical voice he will eventually adopt. Phaedrus plays an important role in Socrates' path to self-knowledge, both by reminding Socrates of himself and by goading him into making better *logoi.*

As Socrates points out, Phaedrus wishes to practice his memory with Socrates. The written word engenders this inferior form of memory (as the myth of Thamus illustrates), because, it turns out, Phaedrus has memorized a written copy of Lysias' speech. Phaedrus, under the spell of the written word, cannot address reality, the reality of Socratic pedagogic love. Socrates, seeing through Phaedrus' ploy, frustrates the non-philosophical task of memorization of the written word. He invokes a higher kind of memory: the knowledge of the soul, to recollect the reality of Phaedrus' soul and its desires. Phaedrus attempts one more time to test his recall of Lysias' speech. Socrates asks Phaedrus to produce the speech itself, thereby turning the Phaedran project away from memorization to reading. This shift seems important to Plato, and he repeats it in the *Theaetetus*: Eucleides' memory is weak, and finally a slave boy reads the dialogue.

It is our task to inquire into the shift from memorization to reading. This shift in presentation emphasizes an important purpose served by writing: preserving memory. "Though of course I am your friend," says Socrates, "if Lysias himself is here . . ." (228e). Writing conceals the presence of the author, he becomes an object at hand, ready to speak at the reader's whim. It becomes an object of *tekhnē*. Socrates identifies himself with Phaedrus and Lysias with his written speech. Lysias' utilitarianism renders him as dead as an artifact. In the *Symposium*, Alkibiades compared Socrates to an artifact. The Silenus figure with a grotesque exterior and a divine content is reversed here: Lysias' speech is a grotesque sentiment framed within a beautiful speech.[49] Plato, in his ongoing attempt to answer the question "Who is Socrates?," had invoked the image of the drunken Alkibiades. Nonetheless, Alkibiades' love for Socrates retains the divine interior within the artifact. Then, in the *Phaedrus*, Plato, in an attempt to overcome the comparison of Socrates to an artifact, inverts the image of the artifact. This new artifact is compelling on the outside, but the interior[50] is now occupied by the obscene image of the non-lover. By rendering the artifact ugly, Plato overcomes the inadequacy of using an artifact to define Socrates' self-knowledge. Moving beyond the artifact, Socrates is attracted to the beautiful Phaedrus, while Lysias himself remains fixed in the artifact of the written copy of his speech.

Who is Socrates? Part 3: *Erōs* and *Eidōlon*

1.   Within the city, Socrates cannot reveal who he really is. The *Theaetetus*, the *Sophist*, and the *Statesman* form a trilogy of dialogues that reveal the absence of another dialogue, the *Philosopher*. This is especially striking, because Socrates asks the Eleatic stranger explicitly about the philosopher. The absence of a work about the philosopher is due to the fact that, within the city, philosophers are mistaken for statesmen, sophists, or simply mad people (*Sophist* 217d). We may expect, therefore, Socrates to reveal his identity as a philosopher outside the city walls.

2.   Socrates reveals himself not only as a philosopher, but also as a pedagogue and a lover. The excursion outside the city is reminiscent, albeit inversely, of the social ritual of abduction of the *eromenos* by an older *erastēs*. Plato is at pains to defend this type of homosexual relationship: "Its aim is to educate" (*Symposium* 209c). The sexual connotations of this type of relationship have hindered commentators from seeing its pedagogical aspects. The setting of *Phaedrus* recalls the passage in Strabo,[51] which describes the "abduction" and consequent initiation of boys into the *andreion*. The powerful mentorship contained in the erotic speeches of Socrates, whereby Phaedrus is allowed to see the Forms themselves, is an occurrence alien to us. Mentorship and erotic love both address themselves to individuals in their specific individuality. Thus although one of Socrates' teachings is a study or vision of the Forms, it is nevertheless counterbalanced by self-knowledge. In the erotic interaction

between Socrates and Phaedrus, we see references to Socrates' quest for self-knowledge, as well as his addressing Phaedrus in his singularity. Lysias, by contrast, writes "general" speeches. For Socrates, dialectic meant philosophizing *with* and philosophizing *by* an individual—criteria the written word cannot satisfy. Hence Socrates' critique of writing as leading to the loss of the philosophically valuable individual.

It is important to bear in mind that Phaedrus is not only a symbol of philosophical apprenticeship; perhaps his beauty inspires Socrates to philosophy and Lysias to rhetoric. In fact, Socrates' speeches and discourses, with which he attempts to outdo Lysias, may be seen as an erotic *agōn* for Phaedrus' affections. In the background lies Plato's own seduction by Socrates, memorialized in all his writings. Socrates uses philosophy to seduce Phaedrus, while at the same time both Socrates and Phaedrus succumb (ultimately) to the seduction of philosophy itself. However, Socrates' seduction of Phaedrus to philosophy is not free of danger. Might it turn into another path of perdition, just as Boreas' abduction of Oreithuia resulted in her death? The Athenians tried and executed Socrates on the twin charges of impiety and of corrupting the Athenian youth. In a morbid reversal of roles, as compared with Boreas' mythical seduction of Oreithuia, Socrates' flirtation with Phaedrus proved deadly to him. The *Phaedrus* examines various healing spells against mortality, among which the leading candidates are love, rhetoric, myth, writing, philosophy, and dialectic. Perhaps in some of these cases the proposed cure proved to be a poison.[52] Did Socrates die for philosophy, or did philosophy kill him?

3.   At this stage, the similarity between Socrates and Phaedrus is questioned. Plato achieves this by having Phaedrus comment that he is fortuitously unshod on this walk, while Socrates always is (229a). Comparison with Phaedrus is still inadequate at this stage, and requires the myth of erotic descent to complete a full account of individuality in terms of mortality.

Philosophy is consolation for mortals in general, but Phaedrus, alone, offers consolation to Socrates in his mortality. The strongest elements of consolation are *erōs*, friendship (both preserved in playful dialectic—this dialogue is one of the few true conversations in Plato's works), and *sophrosunē*. Phaedrus is Socrates' pedagogue, even more than Diotima in the *Symposium*. In this dialogue, Socrates leaves behind his "usual role" in the city, and in the Platonic dialogue. Phaedrus offers Socrates self-knowledge—as an *eidōlon* ("if I did not know my Phaedrus, I would not know myself"). Phaedrus, interestingly, is more maieutic here than Socrates. He suggests he will seduce Socrates, joking about throwing him to the ground, wrestling him, and forcing him to speak. He is Socrates' friend outside the city; he is Socrates' teacher. He is able to perform the ultimate task: he makes him fertile. He is also able to lead Socrates (as though dangling a carrot before a horse) out of the city, and he has erotic power over Socrates in a way even Alkibiades does not. It is no coincidence that Phaedrus is the first speaker on love in the *Symposium*.

In that dialogue, Socrates' account of Diotima's teaching as an erotic teaching is interrupted by Alkibiades' dramatic entry and his claim to "know Socrates." The *Phaedrus* works out the implications of combining self-knowledge with *erōs*, a philosophic task Diotima is unequal to. Moreover, her speech is in poor taste because she cannot see the full glory of Erōs,[53] the highest of the gods, as Phaedrus insists at the beginning of the *Symposium*. Even more than Lysias, Diotima presents a false account of Erōs, which Socrates errs by repeating. Phaedrus instructs Socrates in his error. Socrates returns to the specific nature of love they were discussing: homosexual love. In his second speech (discussed below), Socrates recants Diotima's and Lysias' general accounts of love. As the author of the Socratic dialogues, Plato performs the same functions for Socrates as Phaedrus does. He is a companion on Socrates' mortal journey, preserving his individuality between the twin abstractions of the Forms on one hand and the city on the other.

To drive home the question of Socrates' individuality and his professed quest for self-knowledge, Plato introduces myth. Once myth arrives on the scene, Socrates no longer compares himself with Phaedrus, instead framing the question of his identity in mythical terms. At this stage, the distance between Socrates and Phaedrus becomes a yawning gulf, and Socrates appears to Phaedrus to be a stranger and out of place (230d).

The erotic interplay of the persons in the dialogue enables Socrates' quest for self-knowledge in two ways:

1. Overcoming generality by refuting speeches that do not address specific individuals, but only general issues.
2. The "dead" nature of written speeches is also overcome by a corresponding interest in living individuals. Thus the artifact (*eidōlon*) ceases to be a satisfactory description of Socrates.

Who is Socrates? Part 4: From Individuality to Mortality

The Greek word *pharmakon* appears several times in the *Phaedrus*.[54] Derrida in his seminal essay "Plato's Pharmacy" points out the importance of the word in unraveling the *Phaedrus*, and in showing it to be a unified and well executed work.[55] In recounting the myth of Boreas' abduction of Oreithuia, Socrates mentions that she was playing with a playmate named Pharmakeia (229c). *Pharmakeia* is a noun suggesting the application of a *pharmakon*. The word *pharmakon* is usually translated as medicine or drug. However, this is an inadequate interpretation, as Derrida demonstrates. The word has several meanings, including the antithetical senses of "cure" and "poison." Plato exploits the polysemy of the word *pharmakon* and its cognates, by using them as keys to each of his themes:

1.   Political transgression: Socrates admits that Phaedrus has discovered a *pharmakon* for leading him out of the city (*dokeis moi tēs exodou to pharmakon heurēkenai*, 230d5–6).

2.   Erotic writing: In a playful sexual allusion, Socrates asks Phaedrus to show him what he has concealed under his cloak (228d). This turns out to be Lysias' erotic speech. This speech is the *pharmakon* that leads Socrates out on a walk with Phaedrus. Socrates reinforces the phallic metaphor and clarifies its association with writing. The *pharmakon* is both a written speech (*en bibliois*, 228d) and a dangling carrot which Socrates follows like a hungry animal.

3.   Erotic transgression: Oreithuia succumbs to Boreas' deadly erotic seduction while playing with Pharmakeia (*sun Pharmakei paixousan*, 229c).

4.   Mortality: Pharmakeia does not cure our mortality, and neither does *erōs*. The erotic seizure of Oreithuia by an immortal does not result in her escape from mortality, as in the case of Ganymede, whom Zeus carries off. Socrates mentions this love, in another context, speaking of the way desire gives us wings (255d). Neither her lover's immortal nature nor his "flood of passion" (255d) gave Oreithuia wings; her erotic encounter leads to her fatal descent into mortality.

5.   Writing versus speaking: Socrates presents writing as a *pharmakon* in an Egyptian myth. Theuth, in presenting the gift of writing (*grammata*), to king Thaumus, says of it: "This discipline (*to mathēma*), my king, will make the Egyptians wiser and will improve their memories (*sophōterous kai mnēmonikōterous*): my invention is a *pharmakon*" (274e).

6.   Enchantment, bewitchment, magic: *Pharmakeus*, a word that does not appear in the *Phaedrus*, is nevertheless relevant here, as Derrida demonstrates. Diotima calls Erōs himself a sorcerer, which Derrida interprets as one of Socrates' masks. He writes, "Socrates in the dialogues of Plato often has the face of a *pharmakeus*. That is the name given by Diotima to Eros. But behind the portrait of Eros, one cannot fail to recognize the features of Socrates as though Diotima, in looking at him, were proposing to Socrates the portrait of Socrates (*Symposium*, 203c, d, e)."[56]

We can see how the words *pharmakon, pharmakeia, pharmakeus* link the most important themes of the *Phaedrus*. I agree with Derrida in his analysis of this word and its relevance to the dialogue, but I disagree with him in his conclusions. Derrida ignores the erotic speeches completely, and focuses exclusively on the theme of writing. Even within writing, he ignores the erotic relationship between two individuals as lovers, and stresses a hierarchical power-relationship of the commanding father-king and subordinate. In short, Derrida's Socrates is less like a lover and more like the father, king, judge Thaumus, whose pronouncements convict writing precisely because of its ambiguous qualities.

Derrida also downplays the dichotomy of life and death from mortals to modes of expression, by stressing the second half of the dialogue at the expense of the first. Oreithuia's death is no longer the fate of every mortal, but a special effect of Pharmakeia/writing. "Through her games" he writes, ignoring the role Boreas plays in Oreithuia's death, "Pharmacia has dragged down to death a virginal purity and an unpenetrated interior."[57] I read the passage differently: the fact Oreithuia succumbs to an erotic rush and suffers a mortal fall shows that Pharmakeia's games are a pointless play against the surge of *erōs* and death. Like *erōs*, death chooses each individual as an individual, and not only can Pharmakeia not provide an antidote to the erotic and deadly aspects of mortal fate, she also cannot be a substitute.

Derrida's interpretation thus ignores mortality, *erotics*, individuality, the quest for self-knowledge and Socrates' accusation of writing from the point of view of our mortality. These are crucial concerns of the dialogue, and ignoring them would violently reconstruct the dialogue. As a remedy, I propose that we shift our obsession away from "writing," which itself is not as simple as marks on paper. I will discuss the polyvalent nature of writing, and its complicated relationship to speaking in a later section. Here I want to shift the focus from *biblia* back to beings, mortal and erotic, such as Socrates. The remedy that cures us of our textual fetish is an understanding of Socrates himself as the *pharmakos*, the scapegoat or mortal victim condemned to die.

The missing link, which nevertheless is present as *un vouloir-dire*, is Socrates as a *pharmakos*, the ritual scapegoat of Athenian politics. Jane Harrison writes: "That the leading out of the *pharmakos* was a part of the festival of the Thargelia we know from Harpocration. He comments on the word: 'At Athens they led out two men to be purifications for the city; it was at Thargelia, one for the men and the other for the women'. These men, these *pharmakoi*, whose function it was to purify the city, were, it will later be seen, in all probability put to death . . . The ceremony of expulsion took place, it is again practically certain, on the 6th day of Thargelion, a day not lightly to be forgotten, for it was the birthday of Socrates."[58]

Derrida is not unaware of this text; he footnotes this exact passage. However, Derrida succumbs to the oldest of metaphysical tricks: he excludes time, and thus he reads death allegorically. Socrates had warned him, along with the demythologizers, that one ought not to rush into allegorical interpretation (229d). In place of this boorish kind of expertise (*sophiai khromenos*, 229d), he recommends a worthier model for philosophy: the non-metaphysical endeavor of seeking "self-knowledge." As his metaphor for what kind of person he is, Socrates mentions Typhon, who shook up Zeus' hierarchical order. For this anti-foundational move, Zeus punished Typhon, even as Athens punished Socrates for positing self-knowledge as an alternative to the city's "written" laws and to its concerns. Socrates, in Schürmann's words, rejects the task of being a "functionary" of the city and its laws.[59] The Socratic quest for self-knowledge is anarchic, because the unsubsumable individual, as mortal, cannot provide stable foundations for the city in a way the written laws can. Writing is therapeutic to the city, while mortality threatens it by turning citizens into individuals. Therefore, metaphysics is a useful tool, which suppresses the disruptive thirst for self-knowledge by holding up Forms, Laws, History, Logic, Argumentation, Writing, and Sciences . . . in short all generalizations and atemporalizations . . . over the mortal individual and his fate. Seen from the city's point of view, Socrates was nothing short of a traitor. His philosophy, by following the implications of mortality, and by exposing the city's metaphysical program and banishing it into an unreal *topos noētos*, betrays the city. By condemning Socrates, the city purifies itself of his mortal and erotic subversions designed to create individuals rather than citizens. He needed to be utterly destroyed, and then silenced through the subsequent institutionalization of his teaching.

Harrison writes, "This necessity for utter destruction [of the *pharmakos*] comes out very clearly in an account of the way the Egyptians treated their scapegoats. Plutarch in his discourse on Isis and Osiris says, on the authority of Manetho, that in the dog days they used to burn men alive whom they called Typhonias . . ."[60] The word Typhon used in the context of Socrates' exodus from the city alludes phonetically (*phōnē*) to the Typhonians and thus again to scapegoating (*phonos*, murder) and city-sponsored execution. Unwittingly, Derrida takes his stance against Socrates, and in describing Socrates as a *pharmakeus* and an authority figure who condemns writing, binds to Socrates' head "moral business, not his own."[61] Derrida neutralizes Socrates' erotic playfulness and mortal instability by firmly reestablishing a hierarchical model (father/king). From this atemporal metaphysical *topos*, a place where the foundations of the city rest, he sentences Socrates.

One final point on the *pharmakon*: is it relevant and appropriate to use this metaphor for fifth-century Athens? Let us refer to Lysias' own testimony. In a separate speech, composed against Andokides, he writes as follows. "We needs must hold that in avenging ourselves and ridding ourselves of Andokides we purify the city and perform apotropaic ceremonies, and solemnly expel a *pharmakos* and rid ourselves of a criminal; for of this sort the fellow is."[62]

At the end of the dialogue, Socrates prays to Pan, the scapegoat god. Theocritus' poem describing the fate of that divine *pharmakos* is preserved for us as follows:

Dear Pan, if this my prayer may granted be
Then never shall the boys of Arcady
Flog thee on back and flank with leeks that sting

When scanty meat is left for offering;
If not, thy skin with nails be flayed and torn
And amid nettles mayst thou couch till morn.[63]

Harrison writes, "Pan is beaten because . . . he has failed to do his business. It is sometimes said that Pan is beaten, and the *pharmakoi* are beaten, in order to 'stimulate their powers of fertility'."[64] Socrates, by remaining sterile, is no longer in the service of the city; he fails to do his business in providing "evidential moorage" for founding the city. The city expects this business of the philosopher. Thus, in the *Apology*, Socrates asks for meals at the city's expense, because by failing the city as a philosopher, he will instead perform his civic duty as a *pharmakon*.[65]

This detailed description of the *pharmakos* was necessary to balance Derrida's displacement of the trial of Socrates by the trial of writing. I retain his insight that *pharmakon* and its cognates are central to understanding the dialogue, but I add the *pharmakos* (the scapegoat) as another important dimension in addition to the six meanings traced above. The Socrates who emerges in this tragic landscape is different from the Socrates as rational philosopher, for whom philosophizing means asking questions and examining life means a fidelity to reason. The Plato who likewise emerges is not interested in a mere doctrine; for Plato, writing philosophy means giving testimony to the life of the Socrates, and retaining his individuality.

The dialogue itself undergoes a transformation. It is no longer a conversation between Plato and the reader, where the dialogue is a technical apparatus made up of conversing viewpoints.[66] The dialogue opens a dangerous space, where Socrates and Plato retain their individuality and converse with each other through a complex technique of immortalizing their mortality, their existence in this world as mortals. Entering the dialogue means acknowledging our mortal nature and the irreversibility of time. It means accepting that Plato and Socrates are, beyond their words, dead, and will never have a conversation with us. When we enter the Platonic dialogue, we encounter not only the theory of Forms, as *pharmakeia*, but also its inability to aid us in our upcoming death. Like Socrates, we wander, without *topos*, displaced between the Forms and the city, and their illusory denial of our temporal natures.

Socrates' Second Speech: From Love to Individuality

Socrates makes a second speech recanting his previous speech, which, like Lysias' speech, was blatantly impious. This palinode has the purifying function of washing away the first speech. It challenges the generality that a beloved should prudently favor the non-lover. Such a theory, beyond being profane and materialistic, also lacks an account of self-knowledge, something Socrates indicates he is interested in. Socrates therefore introduces individuality through a discussion of *erōs* in its relationship to the soul. This account, fittingly, begins with a banquet in heaven, and follows the soul's descent (not ascent!)[67] into the world. The soul descends from generality in the realm of Forms to the human world of individuality through love. *Erōs* functions in the space between mortal individuals and immortal Forms. The cosmos is depicted in highly individual terms, and the gods themselves typify the individual nuances of love. The speech ends in a prayer and a confession: Socrates is a divinely talented lover, and he prays to Erōs to spare his talents. Further, the prayer beautifully recapitulates the different fates of individuals: Socrates, Phaedrus, and Lysias.

My reading of the dialogue exposes the twin themes of a descent into the cosmos and the embodiment and individualization of the soul. The Socratic quest for self-knowledge always requires this element of individuation. Elements such as time, nourishment and growth, reward, punishment and ultimately death are essential to understanding individuals (although not to understanding unchanging reality). Socrates' quest for self-knowledge takes him on a journey into this world, and enables him to reclaim his basic identity as one fully conscious of himself as a mortal. This means understanding himself as a mortal in all its consequences. Parallels with Parmenides' poem (discussed below) allow us to see that both works raise the question of the founding of stable knowledge while keeping the problem of human mortality and its ultimate inescapability in view. The tragic insight of these philosophers that *logos* transcends time while we remain inescapably mortal is crucial to understanding their philosophical program. This insight, I argue below, "solves" the problem of *doxa* or mortal opinions in Parmenides' poem and the "problem" of writing in Plato's dialogue.

The palinode begins with a set of deliberate misunderstandings cleverly framed to demonstrate the state of self-knowledge Lysias' speech has brought the speakers into. Socrates declares that whereas the first speech was by Phaedrus, the second, the palinode, is by Stesichorus. Socrates' use of patronymics and demotics to identify Phaedrus and Stesichorus fully, while incorrectly attributing works to them, only underlines the irony of the situation. Strictly speaking, Phaedrus had only read out a speech written by Lysias, while Stesichorus (author of the paradigmatic palinode to Helen) only provides a model for Socrates' palinode. Neither Phaedrus nor Stesichorus composed these speeches. At the end of this purifying speech, Socrates' prayer assigns these works correctly to their individual authors. Individuality, in addition to a genealogical description of persons (given by patronymics or in myths such as Hesiod's), requires a psychology, which in turn requires a cosmology (in the pre-Socratic sense), as Socrates proceeds to demonstrate. Socrates does not, in fact, leave behind his youthful interest in physics, when he explored epistemology and the theory of Forms (*Phaedo* 96a–98a); his quest for self-knowledge embodies a descent from the Forms to the mortal universe.

The contrast between the non-lover and the lover is straightforward: the former is sound of mind (*sophronei*) and the latter is mad (*mainetai*). But the enormity of this difference is realized when we compare the dialogue to Parmenides' poem. The goddess is sober in her *elengkhos,* her speech on truth, while the second part of her speech describes mortals as the very opposite of sober: theirs is a wandering *nous* (6.6). Socrates' palinode has all the elements of the backward turning (*palintropos,* 6.9) *logos* of the mortals in Parmenides' poem. As the goddess demonstrates, the mortal account describes a cosmos steered by a goddess (12.3): she devises Erōs as the first of all (13) and presides over the union and painful birth of beings (12.4) that receive nourishment and perish. Plato complements Parmenides' poem with his dialogue; Socrates' palinode and Parmenides' palintropic cosmology are recantations which atone for the loss of individuality in the preceding speeches, marked by the sobriety of the goddess' and Lysias' generic, impersonal, formal arguments. Standing outside the metaphysical realm of the goddess and the rationalistic walls of the city, the twin realms that console mortals by excluding time, Socrates in his radical individuality necessarily appears displaced (*atopōtatos*) and mad.

Sober argument, in the style of Lysias and the goddess, is good for achieving generality and universality, but not individuality. Madness, on the other hand, enables Delphic prophetesses and the priestesses of Dodona to profit not only states (*dēmosiai*) but also individuals (*idiai*). Individuals are important to Socrates from the very beginning of the palinode. The palinode is addressed very specifically to the "boy I was talking to . . . he must listen" (243e). In contrast, Lysias' speech is general, like that of the politicians whose forms of address, such as "*edoxe . . . tēi boulēi ē tōi dēmōi*" ("resolved by the council . . . or by the people," 258a) betray a certain erasure of specific individuality.

Socrates chooses to defend madness, rather than reconcile it with sobriety. He lists four kinds of madness: prophecy, purification (prayer), poetry, and the erotic madness of the lover. Socrates comprehensively practices all these forms of madness. Gods send the first three forms of madness. Of the fourth kind, Griswold writes: "Divine erotic madness is not so much sent from gods external to the individual as sparked from a source within him, as is suggested by its association with *anamnēsis* [recollection]."[68] Socrates' quest for his individuality depends not so much on a theory he espouses or a philosophical doctrine he defends, but on his being a lover, filled with all sorts of madness, especially erotic love. Such a radical individuality also marks the Parmenidean *kouros'* quest, whose journey is an extension of his *thumos* (1.1), a word rich in connotations of individuality. Beyond the gates of Dikē, he enters the atemporal realm of the goddess (where the question of whether he is dead is moot). His return to the mortal cosmos, by contrast, requires an unflinching description of mortality. Mortality and individuality together constitute the core of both the Socratic quest for knowledge and the Parmenidean journey.

However, a middle term between the immortal realm of the goddess (which is one and inviolate, *hen*) and a mortal cosmos (*polu: plural* and discrete) is missing in Parmenides. Thus, the goddess' *logoi* on eternal being and the phenomenal world of becoming seem disconnected, even contradictory. Little wonder, then, that in the history of philosophy Parmenides came to symbolize eternal being, thanks to the seductive power of the goddess' articulation of the immortal viewpoint. Socrates' *apodexis* defending erotic madness clarifies both the limits of the goddess' speech, as well as the inevitability of a descent, a return into the mortal cosmos. Socrates' account of the soul forms a middle term between the immortal realm and our mortal one, the causes and effects of whose descent he takes pains to explicate. We need a mortal *thumos* (desire to overcome death) to reach the logical realm of immortality, but paradoxically, we need to view the immortal soul in order to be able to return ourselves as mortals and individuals, that is, to be able to arrive at a genuine appreciation and acceptance of our mortal condition. Philosophy is "preparation to die" (*Phaedo* 64a) in this strong sense, that it allows us to reclaim our mortality *after* a vision. We may argue, in light of this, that, considering both Socrates' theory of Forms and his desire to know himself, only the latter is properly philosophy.

Socrates begins his demonstration with the words "all soul is immortal (*athanatos*), for that which is perpetually in motion (*aeikinēton*) is immortal." With these words, the Parmenidean goddess' realm is shattered. There, what was eternal was always at rest. Whereas there being was one (*hen*), here it is all (*psukhē pāsa*).[69] *Psukhē pāsa* (245c6) forms the bridge between the Parmenidean *hen* and *polu*, standing between inviolate unity and unsubsumable plurality. *Psukhē* is to be understood not so much as mortal afterlife, but as an after-death of the most virulent form of immortality: the description of being according to the Eleatic's goddess. If the goddess' being ceased to be exclusively one, gave up rest in favor of motion, merged with the phenomenal cosmos, became capable of embodiment, only then would immortal being (ungenerated and imperishable, but nevertheless acting and being acted upon, changing) be acceptable to Socrates. Moreover, he would no longer call it being—he would call it soul. Such a dispersion of being from the chains of necessity into a cosmos of phenomenal change and movement ruptures theoretical being and allows the *kouros* (in Parmenides' poem) to reenter the cosmos.

Notice that Socrates is not manic at this point: he becomes more poetic toward the very end of the second speech, where he accepts his gift of erotic love in the prayer following the palinode. The dismantling of the one being, the first part of his speech, is done in the most *sophrōn* of voices. As his account of the soul becomes more individual and phenomenal, it becomes increasingly poetic and manic. Breaking away from the metaphysical realm of immortal being is the second condition for individuality and its attendant madness after leaving the walls of the city. Once these two conditions are fulfilled, Socrates becomes properly manic, and composes a mythical description of the soul in its cosmological setting.

The word cosmological describes a hyperuranian, sublunar being; philosophically speaking, we may term such being *phenomenal* being. As he leaves behind sterile monism and enters this pluralistic universe, Socrates understandably discards the principles operative there. Socrates trades a true account for a likely account and describes resemblance rather than true being. For the metaphysical question "what the soul really is" (246a), which he says can be properly answered only by a god, he substitutes the question "what is the soul like." An account of true being is only possible for immortals (such an account is *theias*, 246a4) whereas a likely account (*hoi de eoiken*, 246a5) is within mortal reach (*anthropinēs*, 246a5). Likeness replaces true being, just as the description of the cosmos in Parmenides is declared to appear likely (*diakosmon eoikota*, 8.60). With these words, Socrates follows Parmenides out of metaphysics into a mortal cosmos, into physics.

Before we follow the soul's journey, we should note that just as the account of the immortal soul is an image (*eikōn*) for us mortals, and our mortal bodies an image for the gods, so too are the gods' immortal bodies an image for us. Socrates clarifies this point (246c) in his explanation of why living beings are separated into the mortal and immortal. When gods and men lose their eternity, they become temporal in different ways. Once being loses the shackles of necessity and truth, it falls to the earth and is embodied in mortal individuals as their soul.

The interpretation of Socrates' myth of the soul as a descent of Parmenidean being, via motion, into temporality is important for understanding the Socratic quest for self-knowledge. I will call this interpretation, for lack of a better term, an "ontological" explanation, provided "ontology" is not understood in theological or logical terms, but in terms of a primary showing of being as phenomenal beings. This ontological interpretation is meant to replace a "moral" interpretation of the myth, which seems to presuppose a certain individuality and immortality of the soul. Socrates proceeds to describe the attainment of individuality, and thus it is incorrect to attribute it to him as an assumption. Socrates introduces immortality of the soul in relation to motion, and not to individuality, a phenomenon he is yet to account for. Failure to see that there is no individuality at the beginning of Socrates' myth leads to problems. I will describe two such problems.

Robinson writes "It is not even clear whether 'soul' here is meant to refer to soul collectively or to individual souls."[70] Some have interpreted this neoplatonically (A. F. Festugière, *Platon et l'Orient*)[71] by subsuming the unified nature of the soul under the name World Soul. Others, assuming that the soul here to be individual, become entangled in the anachronistic issue of whether the fall of the soul described here is an original fall or the soul was previously earth-bound.[72] The soul's fall would now require an explanation of what exactly the fall consists in—the clever answer to this inappropriate question is "embodiment."

More problems follow from presupposing the individuality of the soul at the beginning of Socrates' exposition. Vlastos, interpreting the soul as if it were an ego,[73] claims that Platonic *erōs* is egotistical, because a lover loves his beloved merely as a stand-in for the much more desirable Forms. We can spin out any number of equally uncompelling explanations: the evil horse (in the myth of the soul) as selfish sexual gratification, the good horse as appropriately restrained sexuality, and so on. The former, we might add, is corporeal, the latter spiritual. We thus inflate our sexual life to cosmological proportions.

The ontological interpretation, on the other hand, is not morally prescriptive but descriptive of phenomena, especially our mortal and individual nature, despite our ability to transcend both in thinking and in *logos*. Even more emphatically, thinking always produces this transcendence; the world of thought is always "up there," an ascent. The descent, which Socrates pursues, is tantamount to a complete reversal of the fanciful flight of thinking; Socrates returns thinking, through thinking, to its original state and context: embodiment in a mortal individual. This "turn" in thinking yields "Socrates" and not the "Forms." Socrates' philosophical journey of self-knowledge consists in his tragic descent from the immortal *logos* of the Delphic oracle to his death in Athens. Or, in the case of the palinode we are discussing, the descent delivers Socrates from the immortal soul that views the Forms, to the prayerful mortal lover striving to win the esteem of a beautiful boy. Armed with self-knowledge, these two individuals emerge self-consciously mortal as Socrates and Phaedrus. The ontological interpretation is a study in self-knowledge as mortality.

The myth of the soul, appropriately enough, begins in heaven and ends on earth. Or, it begins in the realm of the Eleatic's goddess and ends within our world. In the goddess' realm, there is no individuality; soul is as comprehensive and as abstract as the goddess' description of being. Socrates, however, has already effected the dispersal of this being by adding motion. Thus the textual problem of whether to read the soul's movement as *aeikinētos* or, favoring the Oxyrhynchus fragment, as *autokinētos*[74] is an academic rather than philosophical concern. After the dispersal of this being by motion, we enter the phenomenal cosmos, where mortals and immortals are distinguished, and images emerge as descriptions. Socrates adjusts his description of the soul appropriately to reflect this stage: he gives us the image of a team of winged steeds and their winged charioteer, with radical differences between the souls of mortals and immortals. Plurality and enantiomorphism, two of the Parmenidean goddesses' worst nightmares, are introduced, along with the non-being that characterizes the nature of images.

'Eleatic' being (which had existed only theoretically in the logical realm), now moves, as the soul, into heaven—now populated by the souls of mortals and immortals—now firmly located within our cosmos. A plurality of gods travel here; the heavens themselves are described cartographically as having "many spectacles of bliss upon the highways whereupon the blessed gods pass back and forth" (247a). Journeys define the heavens. Hestia, who alone remains home, suggests the stationary goddess of the Parmenidian poem. In this form, she is constrained from even a passing vision of the metaphysical being, now plural, around her. Her being, seen from a viewpoint within our cosmos, is unable to maintain the theoretical unity she argued for, and splinters into many Forms.

Writing versus Speaking

In this section I discuss the other central concern of the *Phaedrus*, writing versus speaking. I discuss the temporal nature of this distinction, and how memory can be an enrichment of mortal life, rather than an immunity to time. Finally, I argue, against Derrida, that "writing" is not the *pharmakon*: Socrates is. In the first half of the dialogue, Socrates is an erotic individual; in the second part, dealing with writing, he emerges as a mortal individual.

The *Phaedrus* presents us with some apparent paradoxes. The first half of the dialogue contains a series of speeches united by the theme of *erōs*. The second half contains a critique of writing. Even upon closer examination, it is difficult to see the unity of these two halves. There is a long tradition of criticism, extending from Diogenes Laertius to Schleiermacher, which maintains that the dialogue is not one of Plato's best, and that its overall quality reflects Plato's immaturity or senility. If we wish to defend the dialogue, we must provide a unifying theme that relates the speeches on *erōs* to the criticism of writing. Derrida, in his influential essay, "Plato's Pharmacy," attempts such a defense. His careful reading, he claims, "unites a whole *symplokē* [of] patiently interlacing arguments . . . That entire hearing of the *trial of writing* should some day cease to appear as an extraneous mythological fantasy, an appendix the organism could easily, with no loss, have done without. In truth, it is rigorously called for from one end of the *Phaedrus* to the other."[75] The "more secret organization of themes, of names, of words," which Derrida meticulously uncovers, reveals the "trial of writing" as the unifying program of the dialogue.

The "trial of writing" issues a complex verdict: writing embodies the ambiguous properties of a *pharmakon*, simultaneously a poison and a cure. *Qua* cure, Derrida argues, writing is indispensable to Plato. *Qua* poison, writing embodies some very problematic qualities—qualities Socrates himself articulates. "What is magisterial about the demonstration affirms itself and effaces itself at once, with suppleness, irony, and discretion."[76] Thus Plato writes with a pen in one hand, as it were, and an eraser in the other. The erasure is an overt criticism of writing, which Plato pens into the dialogue. Thus, Derrida suggests, Plato attempts to overcome the negative effects of writing, and employs it merely as a second-rate substitute for orality.

There are a few problems with this view. Derrida does not gather into his unifying theme the speeches on love. In fact, he skips the speeches on love and rushes to the criticism of writing, pausing very briefly at the myths (those of Oreithuia and Thaumus) while ignoring the central myth of the soul. In the "trial of writing," myths serve as evidence, which further complicates his strategy: it is not clear whether these myths are "written" by Plato or "uttered" by Socrates. Like the dialogues themselves, myths are not univocal: they display aspects of both writing and speaking. The distinction between speaking and writing is not as clear-cut as Derrida presents it. The "trial of writing" demands a proper identification of the accused; Derrida must first show what "writing" means in the Platonic context. The trivial identification of writing with making marks on paper instead of articulating sounds is inadequate in this case. To be sure, Derrida admits that there is some convergence, as Socrates, for example, speaks in metaphors derived from writing. However, nowhere does Derrida admit that this "convergence" is vital enough to frustrate the supposedly clean division of speaking and writing. Instead, rather than supporting his case, these points deconstruct the dialogue, where the glaring opposition of speaking and writing is underlined.

Derrida's writing neglects not only the erotic speeches, but all individual characters of the dialogue. Thus very little is made of Socrates' journey outside the city walls, Phaedrus' background and education, or the erotic interplay between Lysias, Phaedrus, and Socrates. Derrida stresses only those characters that occur within the "mythologemes," mostly the relationship between Thaumus and Theuth. Even within the myths, Derrida takes pains to erase erotic elements. Oreithuia is no longer the victim of Boreas' erotic abduction. Derrida distorts the myth thus: "Through her games, Pharmacia has dragged down to death a virginal purity and an unpenetrated interior."[77] Individuality, as I have argued before, is a central theme of this dialogue, and it is surprising to see it completely neglected in Derrida's account. In the *Phaedrus*, the *writer* Lysias takes up the cause of the non-lover, disparaging *erōs*. In a similar move, the commentator, Derrida, defending *writing*, replaces *erōs* with an obsessive meditation on another non-erotic relationship: that of the father and son and the murderous relationship that links them.

The suppression of *erōs* as a guiding theme allows Derrida to displace Socrates as the *pharmakon* with writing. Here, *pharmakon* means scapegoat, as I discussed above. The emphasis on writing as the dominant character in Derrida's interpretation resembles the view Lysias advocates: both speak without any reference to actual individuals. Derrida's commentary exemplifies the crucial criticism Socrates raises against writing: the neglect of persons. Indeed, such an "erasure" of individuals is endemic to an entire tradition of Plato commentators, beginning with Diogenes Laertius. Diogenes points out the unreal nature of Plato's characters, all of whom are dead at the time of writing. He believes that five characters in particular are mouthpieces for Plato (Socrates, Parmenides, the Eleatic Stranger, Timaeus, and the Athenian Stranger);[78] thus, he denies them their individuality. The persons of Plato's dialogues are typically read as if they were "characters"; the drama of persons becomes a drama of characters. This means that Plato either invented these "characters" or used existing persons as stand-ins for "points of view" (his own or others'). On this reading, the dialogue degenerates into a flimsy framework for the "more real" philosophical issues. Derrida belongs to this tradition: for him too, the dialogues are not descriptions of a community of real persons; they are Plato's "voices" on philosophical issues, in this instance the "trial of writing."

The case I am arguing is decidedly against a reading of Plato's characters as mouthpieces. I am arguing for something more radical: that the characters have a life of their own, beyond the views they proclaim in the dialogues. Their "background" does not merely provide a framework for the views they espouse; their biographies are not contexts for their viewpoints. The stronger, reverse case is true: the characterizations preserve the individual through a portrayal of his ideas. This means the dialogue not only aims to use Socrates as a proponent of a certain point of view, but attempts to preserve Socrates himself in his mortality.

To illustrate my point more clearly, consider the parallels with the poem by Parmenides. The goddess' grammar, in her speech on monism (fr. 8) illustrates the dangers of following language in its making an altogether different turn (*per*version) away from actions to structures. This is what language does: phenomenal reality, which consists of actions such as appearing and disappearing, is converted into stable structures. These structures are at once syntactical relations and relations between stable nouns. The poem illustrates not only the way in which action is replaced by structure, but also verbs by nouns. We search helplessly for a noun in this passage (a subject for *estin*). In fact, Proclus corrects the oddity of this situation, when he misreads Parmenides, "wrongly" taking this fragment as evidence that Parmenides understood a "plurality in the intelligible world" (*In Parmenides* I.708).[79]

In short, the issue is more complicated than Derrida admits. "Writing" is not an orphaned "son" of a living "speech." Viewed from the mortal standpoint, which is temporal at its very core, *language, both in its written and spoken forms, is itself brought to trial*. To complicate matters, Socrates analyzes "writing" and "speaking" in relation to two communicating persons, and in terms of "living or dead." This means not only language, but certain disciplines as well, such as history, are more "written" in character, while certain other disciplines, such as myth, retain their verbal and oral character even when written down. The distinction between writing and speaking, far from being as superficial as the contrast between eardrums and papyri, goes back to a discovery the goddess in Parmenides' poem fully exploits. Socrates' criticism cuts through both Derrida's obsession with the form of writing, as well as the "orality-literacy" debate found in modern classical studies. In one simple grammatical move, the goddess turned language into logic, from which all time (and the experience of human mortality) is excluded. Socrates' complicated myth of the soul makes this cosmos less of a "writing" (atemporal text) and more "spoken" (temporal process, life). The trial of language, which Derrida misconstrues as the trial of writing, and several commentators misconstrue as a trial of rhetoric, is more than that. It is a trial of our irresponsibility, the evasion of our mortal nature through language, and the atemporal science it engenders.

Conclusion

Socrates and Plato, like the pre-Socratics, wish to give an account of being in *logos*. Parmenides, more than any other pre-Socratic, provides a model for the philosophical journey. This journey is curiously schizophrenic: as a lived life, no one would contest the finite directionality of life. As a journey in the vehicle of language, these same philosophers argue about immortality, and, in a shocking move, even question the reality of the first sense of journey. Language is not simply "divine" in the sense that it cannot account for anything mortal. The *logos*-induced atemporality answers the call of our deepest desire (cf. *thumos*, 1.1). The metaphysics it engenders is actually a consolation, a palliative to our fearful mortality and our helplessness in the *phusis* of our cosmos. Thus Parmenides, in the third portion of his poem, provides an account of this mortal universe, to which the *kouros*, having explored the goddess' logic of immortality, must return.

Socrates is aware of the awesome seduction of the goddess' logic. I have argued that his quest for "self-knowledge" reverses the flight of thinking to language and brings him back to the phenomenal world. The split in the "journey" must be reconciled in language, and somehow language must have both mortal and immortal aspects. As with writing, Plato is not suspicious of history, medicine, or metaphysics in themselves, nor does he doubt their usefulness. He questions the philosophical value of their obsession with facts; those addicted to "information rather than instruction" will become "wise in their own conceit" (*Theaetetus* 274). The point is neither that facts are useless nor that philosophy operates "beyond" facts. We might make the point more strongly: while facts are indispensable, they suffer the following shortcomings:

1. They stand in the way of unpredictable coming-into-being, and thus mask the presencing of being.

2. They confer a "stability, permanence" to things past, which confuses being as a phenomenon with being as a steady presence, emphasizing in a dishonest way the reified illusions of our thought.

3. Facts are the instruments of domination par excellence. The "disambiguation" they promise participates in a tyranny of human will and language over unconquerable time. Thus the philosophical task is not to demolish facts, but to establish them as fiction. A certain violence to facts is inseparable from all philosophy, drawing an absolute boundary between love of wisdom and the vampiric love of facts. One might object: what about facts like the Holocaust? What will happen if history becomes mere fiction? My answer: the philosophical task is independent of history. No one should read philosophy with a view to explaining history, or to establish regimes, an attempt that has proven disastrous time and again from Plato to Heidegger. History remains positivistic,

and thus needs to be subjected to a critical examination. Historians and politicians should note this, and avoid a naïve "philosophical" justification of their writings and actions.

Although Socrates explicitly criticizes previous poets near the end of the work (278b–e), it needs to be spelled out that the criticism is not of poetry itself, but of a certain kind of poetry. For Socrates, poets are not "live" enough in that they adopt an artificial stance or present incomplete views. By saying "not live" I mean that poetry seeks to supply stable *arkhai*, give *aitiai*, or even lay down the law. "Cross-examination" and "live defense" (*Phaedrus*, 275e) are not about "truth" in the modern moral factual sense, but about "what is likely" (ibid., 273a), in the sense in which a Lysias would understand this expression. It is for this reason that Socrates demands that the *logos* be available for interrogation in turn (ibid., 275e). Rather than epistemological or moral criteria, these criteria preserve the "encounter" between individuals, which in turn requires temporality. An encounter, as seen in the Platonic dialogue, is an abiding in mortal time. Nowhere does Socrates transcend the phenomenal world, except mythically—and these myths are composed for and delivered to real individuals.

Thus there are two poles to the dialogue: one eternal and one mortal. The theory of Forms is the complete exposition of the former, and the quest for self-knowledge is exemplified by the latter. Again, both rational *logoi* and *mūthoi* can either enable the erasure of time or preserve time, depending upon whether we stress their "nominal" and "verbal" poles, as Parmenides' goddess illustrates. The search for self-knowledge and dialectic are verbal activities: as verbal, they occur within mortal time, and Socrates calls them "living" speeches. Poetry, inasmuch as it excludes mortals, that is, provides accounts of the universe or of humans or of the past as static, joins epistemology in rousing the ire of the philosophical pair (Socrates and Plato).

Erōs and death, in making being comprehensible as unique, finite, and generating motion, provides a suitable paradigm for understanding both immortals and ourselves as mortals. In love, I recognize the singularity of my lover, while in death, his loss brings home his singularity with exceptional force to me. Apart from these two instances, where I recognize what is utterly unique, inexpressible, and irreplaceable about a person, everything I know about someone relates to characteristics that can be grasped by language, that is, expressed in linguistic categories and, as such, relate to him as a particular rather than a singular.

Part IV

Forewording

Conclusion

Returning to Parmenides

Heidegger's history of being and of Western metaphysics, the problem of historicism, Nietzsche's rejection of metaphysics, Hannah Arendt's notion of singularity, and the relationship of philosophy to theology in the twentieth century have been implicit throughout in this work. I would like to conclude by explicitly returning to this twentieth-century state of affairs.

Heidegger gives us a narrative in which Parmenides plays an important role: his *Seinsgeschichte* begins with Parmenides and other pre-Socratics and ends with Nietzsche; this career of being is also the story of the rise and fall of metaphysics. At the end of metaphysics, Heidegger returns to Parmenides and that understanding of being which he claims was incipient in pre-Socratic thought and later lost through Plato's "metaphysics."[1]

However, as we have seen in the previous chapters, Parmenides' understanding of being is ultimately linked to his understanding of mortality. Hence, the return to Parmenides' thought cannot take place via either the question of the meaning of being, that is, the *Seinsfrage*, or that of the truth of being, or even of the *topos* of being—three ways in which Heidegger attempts to circumscribe being.[2] Rather, it must take place, as I have argued here, via the mortal singular. Beyond Heidegger's *Seinsgeschichte*, which cannot account for the mortal singular, I have outlined a philosophy here that accounts for not only beings in the world and the being of beings but also, in addition, for the mortal singular. Therefore, we must return to Parmenides again but through *Plato* rather than Heidegger, as I have argued. Without singularity, being, even if it is being-toward-death, remains conceptual rather than concretely human.

In this concluding chapter, I engage with Heidegger, in the hope of clarifying Parmenides and defending Plato's reception of Parmenides.

Return to Mortals versus Return to Pre-Socratics

Parmenides' poem, I have argued, links metaphysics to the liminal experience of the *thumos*, that is, death. Parmenides thus links philosophy to the individual's ultimate concern rather than to any tradition. Metaphysics is one response to this play of life and death.

In contrast, Heidegger's return to the pre-Socratics occurs explicitly under the impulse of a historical problem: how to think now at the end of metaphysics? How to respond to the withdrawal of being that, as he claims, has been ongoing since Plato and reaches its culmination in Nietzsche? How to think in this particular situation of global technological domination? For Heidegger, then, the question of being and the question of metaphysics must provide some salvation on a historical level or, to put it differently, the return to the question of being must engender a saving *topos* within history. I first elaborate on Heidegger's thesis of the "end of metaphysics" before illustrating how Heidegger's historical thinking of the end differs from my thought of mortality.

Heidegger's thesis of the end of metaphysics is succinctly defined by Joan Stambaugh as follows:

What does metaphysics, which Heidegger defines as the separation of essence and existence that began with Plato, have to do with the ontological difference of Being and beings? One might say that the tradition, particularly the medieval tradition, would equate these two distinctions. Being (*esse*) is the essence of beings, of what exists (*essentia*), the essence in the sense of the universal One which unifies everything. For Heidegger, the distinction essence-existence actually belongs in the tradition on the side of Being, but the *difference* between Being and beings, although constantly presupposed in all metaphysics, was never thought. Only when metaphysics reaches its completion does the possibility arise of transforming the ontological difference, of thinking it from the unthought presupposition of all metaphysics back to its essential origin in Appropriation.[3]

The end of metaphysics, according to Heidegger, occurs historically at the moment when Nietzsche inverts the traditional priority of *esse* over *existentia*: as Heidegger notes, Nietzsche himself describes his philosophy as "inverted Platonism."[4] Heidegger asserts that this reversal of Platonism in Nietzsche merely signifies the end of metaphysics, when it fulfills all its possibilities, without being able to inaugurate a true break, an overcoming (*Überwindung*) of metaphysics. For Heidegger, such overcoming requires a reaching back even further beyond Plato to the beginnings of Western thought in the pre-Socratics.[5] Such thinking is no longer "metaphysics," because it precedes the distinction of being into being and existence in Plato and, later, in Aristotle. However, even this return is ambiguous in that Heidegger specifically critiques Parmenides for naively interpreting being according to its most immediate visible aspect, that is, in terms of sheer presence. Thus in *Being and Time*, he writes:

Legein itself, or *noein* – the simple apprehension of something objectively present in its pure objective presence [*Vorhandenheit*], which Parmenides already used as a guide for interpreting being – has the temporal structure of a pure "making present" of something. Beings, which show themselves in and for this making present and which are understood as genuine beings, are accordingly interpreted with regard to the present; that is to say, they are conceived as presence (*ousia*).

However, this Greek interpretation of beings comes about without any explicit knowledge of the guideline functioning in it, without taking cognizance of or understanding the fundamental ontological function of time, without insight into the ground of the possibility of this function.[6]

Critically, what remains unthought in the history of Western metaphysics, according to Heidegger, is the difference between being and beings which expresses itself in the human's understanding of being. Consequently, being itself is taken as a being, whether as the *summum ens* of medieval Scholasticism or as the *analogia entis* of Aristotelian philosophy. Thus, Heidegger explicitly conceives of his project as a destruction of the history of traditional ontology, in which the unique relation of the finitude of human existence to being becomes the guiding-line (*Leitfaden*) for carrying out this deconstructive project.

Heidegger is correct in his intuition about death and the manner in which it discloses *Dasein* but this is a philosophically stylized cogitation. It has nothing to do with Ivan Ilych or myself or Reiner or other singulars. Following Schürmann, I would say that it is only in the singular (more precisely, in the tragic condition in which the singular is handed over to the contrary phenomenological traits of *Gebürtigkeit* and *Sterblichkeit*, as Arendt and Schürmann have shown) that the "other" of metaphysical conceptual thought reveals itself. Hence, I have argued throughout that Plato is heedful to Parmenides in this recovery and retention and recapitulation of the singular and mortal and for the necessity of returning to Parmenides via Plato rather than Heidegger.

"Mares which carry me as far as *thumos* might reach" (1.1)—with these words, Parmenides sets the limits of that which is properly human. The philosophical depth of these words differs from Heidegger's analysis of death in *Being and Time*. Though aware that death is disclosive of human being and as well as of being in the form of "care," Heidegger's analysis of death does not belong to any concretely existent individual. Thus the existential condition of being that it always is as some specific being in this world given over to its own unavoidable death is an insight Heidegger does not develop further. Mortality is forgotten in Heidegger's thought and when it returns in his later works, it is merely as one of the fourfold.[7] The abandonment of the mortal criterion in the destruction of metaphysics is surprisingly set aside as Heidegger progressively becomes historical. Thus history gains priority over death.

It would be easy to misread Heidegger's choice as undertaken in the shadow of National Socialism (or even, as some have argued, undertaken for its sake). However, there is more to the story. Heidegger insists upon history in order to preserve a Lutheran experience whereby the individual self is saved and death overcome in history. And thus in the very attempt to escape metaphysics *qua* history of philosophy, Heidegger succumbs to metaphysics *qua* theology. Heidegger allows for a metaphysics that, within this historicity, still exceeds the *aiōn*. I reject this overspilling: the mortal life must be understood from out of its own mortal span and not reduced to a particular within the horizon of a history. As I have argued in this work, everything which exceeds the *thumos* is metaphysical; history, which is precisely beyond the *thumos*,[8] is thus essentially metaphysical even if it is "essential history," as Heidegger claims. That is why Plato does not give us a history of the Greeks like Thucydides or Herodotus but a very specific presentation of Socrates as *memento mori*. For all his talk of authenticity, Heidegger never talks about the self in the Greek sense of *autos*. Thus his use of death as mortality leads to authenticity as a disclosure of being, but not authenticity in the sense of that which is proper to the self (*ta autos* = the things of the self). In order to return to Parmenides, then, we must first set aside Heidegger and his Lutheran project, as I have done in my work so far. In the penultimate section, I wish to explore some of the consequences of Heidegger's appropriation of Luther before turning back to Parmenides.

Singularity versus *Jeweiligkeit*

Why does Heidegger insist upon this radical finitude, if it does not lead him back to the mortal singular? To understand the role the emphasis on finitude plays in Heidegger's critique of the philosophical tradition beginning with Plato, one must turn back to his early writings from the 1920s, specifically to his interest in Luther's reading of Paul's *Letter to the Thessalonians*. As I have argued in a recent paper, Heidegger's deconstruction of metaphysics is ultimately a theologically motivated rejection of ancient Greek thought rooted in Luther's destruction of the *theologia gloriae* by the *theologia crucis*.[9] Hence, Heidegger's critique of "metaphysics" and his thesis of the end of metaphysics cannot be understood without understanding the role a *specific conception of the human life-span, that is, of human mortality, and its need for a specific kind of salvation* plays in this conception. Drawing upon his reading of Luther in the 1920s,[10] Heidegger articulates a radical demand for a philosophy rooted in the "facticity" (*Faktizität*) of human existence. Heidegger opposes this philosophy of immanent being to the ontological speculations of Greek philosophy and, critically, to the post-Aristotelian Scholasticism founded upon Greek ontology.

The key concept Heidegger employs in articulating this critique is that of the "Jeweiligkeit" (which can be translated as "at the present while," "the particular while," "being its while") of human existence. Specifically, he opposes a conception of time as *jeweilig*, that is, as always particular, unrepeatable, and as unique to a specific person, to Aristotle's conception of time as based upon a series of identical and interchangeable "nows."[11] Although the importance of the concept of *Jeweiligkeit* in Heidegger's thought has been noted by scholars such as Perrotta and Kisiel,[12] to my knowledge no one has analyzed the concept of *Jeweiligkeit* in relation to its specific function of *a critical appropriation of Aristotelian time*. In *Being and Time*, Heidegger argues that Aristotle's "treatise on time" "can be taken as a way of discerning the basis and limits of the ancient science of being." Indeed, he claims that "[t]he Aristotelian treatise on time is the first detailed interpretation of this phenomenon that has come down to us,"[13] completely overlooking both Parmenides and Plato's interpretations of time. Yet, why does Heidegger turn to Aristotle as his definitive predecessor (and indeed, of Western thinking as a whole) as regards time? Heidegger's exclusion of the pre-Aristotelian tradition is extraordinary considering that explicit speculations on time can be found in both Plato and the pre-Socratics. I suggest that Heidegger's complicated relation to Aristotle's theory of time is best understood out of Aristotle's unique position in relation to Plato. By rejecting Plato's doctrine of transmigration, Aristotle prepares the way for a different kind of eschatology by defining time as linear.[14] Thus *contra* Parmenides and Plato, who both have a clear notion of return and of imperishable being, Aristotle is the first to consider change and movement as *real*, that is, as being more than mere appearances. By his own admission, Aristotle is the first to introduce qualified non-being in order to explain change. But it is only once non-being is granted existence, that a specific experience of loss or of perishing becomes possible— and with it, a specific experience of time. Indeed, as I have argued elsewhere, the Aristotelian interpretation of time originally enables Heidegger to exclude cyclical temporality, whether thought of as transmigration of the soul (Plato) or as eternal recurrence (Nietzsche).[15] It is this aspect above all, I believe, that best explains Heidegger's early fascination with Aristotle. But while Heidegger draws upon the Aristotelian analysis of time as linear, he also critiques Aristotle for thinking time as infinite.[16] Thus, what Heidegger is specifically interested in is an experience of time as linear *and* finite. This is precisely the understanding of time that is experienced in the awaiting of the *parousia*.

Thus, in addition to the distinction between the rejection of metaphysics (anachronistically) in Parmenides and the theological destruction of metaphysics in Heidegger, I also wish to distinguish mortal knowledge in Parmenides (with its emphasis on the *kouros* and his return to the mortal cosmos of singulars) from Heidegger's emphasis on facticity. In the next and concluding section, I argue that Heidegger's interest in an experience of time that originates in the Christian experience of the *parousia* prevents him from fully understanding or appreciating the Greek experience of time in its twofold aspect of fluxing becoming and eternal being and thus leads him to dissolve the temporal *aporia*.[17] In this valorization of individual temporality, Heidegger loses precisely that aspect of being which is paramount in Parmenides: its Janus-faced nature paradigmatically expressed in the goddess' two speeches.[18]

Deconstruction versus Initiation

Once one rejects the thesis of time as finite or as *jeweilig*, it seems one must necessarily also lose the emphasis upon individuality. Indeed, it seems as though Heidegger is correct when he, following Kierkegaard,[19] suggests it is only through the experience of oneself as radically *jeweilig* and finite and thus in need of salvation[20] that true individuality becomes possible.[21] But, as I have argued in the better part of this work, this is not so. Indeed, I have attempted to show how richly aware ancient thinkers such as Parmenides and Plato were of the need to preserve mortal singularity and that they were more sensitive to the complex issues at stake in articulating individuality than we moderns are.[22] For us, the question of this radical individuality becomes merely a question of *persona*—it is either the subject within or the identity without.[23]

I would therefore like to close this concluding section by opposing "deconstruction" as a methodological response to the problem of individuality with "initiation" as a model for preserving singularity. In singularity, I not only find a more radical deconstruction of metaphysics *qua* metaphysics, but also a deconstruction that is truer to the mortal condition.

Recent researches by Burkert and Kingsley have shown that the initiatory model pervasively structures ancient thought. In fact, Burkert has argued that Parmenides' poem can only be understood when one sees the journey as replicating a *katabasis*.[24] Further, Burkert argues for a "religious" experience at the heart of Parmenides' poem,[25] an experience at once deceptively close and utterly distant from the *theologia crucis* of Heidegger.[26] Parmenides and Plato explicate the ultimate concern of mortals by using the language of mysteries at the core of their philosophical experience. I believe that the initiatory model better preserves the aspects of individuality than Heidegger's theologically motivated valorization of *Jeweiligkeit*. But more than that, I would like to claim that the ancient analysis—what I have referred to here as the "crossing of mortals and immortals"—provides us a better avenue for thinking about a possible *non-metaphysical* transcendence.

In contrast, Heidegger's *Seinsgeschichte* leaves us with only two possibilities:

1. An inauthentic "metaphysical" transcendence (exemplified by the Platonic Forms, Christian heaven, etc.).
2. The rejection of every form of transcendence in favor of the experience of "lived temporality," which Heidegger considers characteristic of Early Christianity[27] and finds exemplified in Scotus.[28]

Thus beyond Heidegger and his emphasis on facticity and rejection of metaphysics, Parmenides' thought remains curiously ahead of us. Heidegger's deconstruction of metaphysics is useful in recovering the *theologia crucis*, but Plato and Parmenides have a different approach to questions of ultimate concern. They *begin* with the mortal condition and not with textuality, as I showed in my *Phaedrus* commentary. Thus, the focus is not on deconstructing a tradition, but on making the ultimate concern of the philosophical adept— whether the *kouros* or Phaedrus—primary. Here, both Plato and Parmenides give an answer that deserves a genuine philosophical explication. My analysis has taken the form of a "return" from the transcendence of metaphysics, texts, and traditions.[29] But, from this 'purified' state, is another form of transcendence possible for the mortal singular? But that is a subject for another work; here, I end the "purification" portion of Parmenides, that is, our traditional reception. A philosophical investigation whereby Parmenides provides a positive response to the ultimate concerns of the mortal reader constitutes the next step.

Appendix

Translation and Textual Notes
of Parmenides' *Peri Phuseōs*

Section I: The Journey

I (i): Translation of Fragment 1 (Lines 1–21)

1 Mares which carry me, as far as *thumos* might reach,
  were sending me, when, leading, they set me onto the much-famed road
  of the deity, which bears the knowing man through all cities*;
  there I was borne; for there the much-discerning* mares bore me,
5 straining the chariot, and maidens were leading the way.*
  The axle in the hubs was emitting the sound of a pipe,*
  Blazing,* for it was driven by two whirling
  Wheels at either side, when they were hastening to send (me),
  the maidens, daughters of the Sun, leaving behind the houses of Night,*
10 into the light, having pushed away with hands their veils* from their heads.[1]
  There are the gates of the paths of Night and Day,*
  And them a lintel and a stone threshold hold on either side;
  these ethereal (gates) are filled with great doors,
  and of them much-avenging* Justice holds the corresponding keys.
15 Her (Justice) the maidens appeasing with soft words
  Persuaded wisely that for them the bolted bar*
  She push away swiftly from the gates; and, spreading open,
  they made of the doors a yawning gap, turning the much-bronzed
  posts in their sockets in turn,
20 fitted with pegs and pins; then there straight through them
  the maidens guided along the carriage-road the chariot and horses.

I (ii): Textual Notes on the Translation of Fragment 1 (Lines 1–21)

1.3. "through all cities": the text of this line is corrupt. The MS is nonsensical: *kata pant' atē, astē,* "cities," is a traditional conjecture (Diels-Kranz, etc.). However, recent editors move away from this reading of Parmenides' line: Gallop[2] (48) prints *asinē*, "unscathed" (modifying "man"); Coxon[3] (45) adopts Heyne's conjecture, *antēn*, and translates "through every stage." I argue in Chapter 6 that Plato's *Phaedrus* 230d5, in which Socrates journeys away from *hoi d' en te astei anthropoi*, "the men in the city," resonates back to Parmenides and thus provides evidence for reading *astē* here. "Cities" also resonates back to Homer, *Odyssey* i.3: *pollōn d'anthrōpōn iden astea kai noon egnō*. Cities, there, represent the sum of mortal achievement.

1.4. "much-discerning": following Taran[4] (see 12–13). The verb *phrazō* also suggests intelligent speaking (cf. the related compounds of *phrazō*, *poluphrades*; *LSJ*, s.vv.). This verb or its compounds appear frequently. See 1.16 *epiphradeos* of the *kourai*, 2.6 *phrazō* of the goddess, 2.8 *phrasais* of the youth. See also 6.2 note.

"a pipe": syrinx. This is not a flute, it is a reed instrument which is closer to an oboe or a bag-pipe than a flute. It produces a squealing sound. Kingsley[5] discusses (esp. 131–5) the role of this instrument in certain ritual contexts. The same word "sockets" recurs at 1.19.

1.7. *aithomenos*: this appears to be the first metaphoric use of the word (see *LSJ*, s.v.). Literally, it means burning, blazing.

1.9. The direction of the journey is clear: from darkness toward light. Kingsley, on the other hand, envisages a journey *into* darkness; he holds that the maidens return with the *kouros* to the house of Night. He follows Burkert's influential view of a *katabasis* (i.e., a descent into the underworld).[6]

kaluptras, "veils": this word is related to *kaluptō*, "conceal," a key concept in Heidegger's notion of truth.

This is Gallop's translation of this line. His and other translations have been of great help to me, but I have not been able to note down all places where they have influenced my phrasing.

1.14. *polupoinos*: this is a very interesting epithet, especially in the context of Parmenides. On the one hand, it seems to be an expectable epithet of Dikē, but, given the relationship the *kouros* might hope to develop with her, a shift in meaning might be worth considering. So while *poinē* is often synonymous with *dikē*, meaning requital, vengeance, and so on, in Pindar, it appears to have the sense of "release, redemption" (P.IV.63).

1.16. "the bolted bar": I adopt the words of Gallop (51). O'Brien (6) interpolates even more specifically, translating: "the bolt fitted with its pin."

1.18. *chasm' achanes*: a *lusus etymologicus* or a phrase that highlights the common etymology of the component words.

Section II: The Goddess

II (i): Translation of Fragment 1 (Lines 22–32) and Fragments 2–8 (Lines 1–50)

Fragment 1, continued: Lines 22–32

22 and a goddess received me kindly,* and she took my right hand
    In her hand, and thus she uttered a speech and addressed me:
    O youth (*kouros*), companion of immortal charioteers,
25 With mares who carry you reaching* as far as our house,
    Welcome, since no evil fate (*moira kakē*) sent you forth to travel*
    This road (*hodon*), for indeed far outside the stepping-path (*patou*) of men
       it is (*estin*),*
    But [rather] Themis (Right) and Dikē (Justice) [sent you forth]. You should
       learn all things,
    both the untrembling heart of persuasive* truth (*alēthēs*)
30 and the opinions of mortals (*brotōn doxas*) in which there is no true trust
       (*pistis alēthēs*).
    But all the same this too you will learn, how it was inevitable for things
       seeming to be (*ta dokounta**)
    to be (*einai*) assuredly (*dokimos*), ranging throughout all things completely.*

Fragment 2

    Come on, I shall tell, and you listen and keep well (*komisai**) the narrative
       (*mūthon*),
    What the only roads of inquiry there are to conceive (*noesai**):
    The [first] one, that it is and that it is not possible for it not to be,
    Is the path of persuasion, for it accompanies truth (*alētheia**);
5   The other [second road] that it is not and that it ought (*khreōn**) not be,
    This I declare to you to be an entirely unlearnable (*panapeuthea**) path;
    For you would not know the non-being, for it is not possible,
    Nor could you declare it.

Fragment 3

    For it is the same thing to conceive (*noein**) and to be.

Fragment 4

    Gaze upon things, absent though* they be, as steadfastly present to the mind;
    For you will not sever being (*to eon*) from holding fast (*echesthai**) to being
       (*tou eontos*),

Neither [being] scattering everywhere in every way throughout the universe
(*kata kosmon**),
Nor coming together.

Fragment 5

All the same to me it is
From where I begin, for to that place I shall return* again.

Fragment 6

One ought (*khrē*) to say and to conceive (*noein*) that being (*eon*) is, for it is
    possible to be;*
And nothing is not possible [to be]: I bid you consider* these things.
For from this first road of inquiry I restrain you,
But then from this one (the road), on which mortals, knowing nothing,
5 Wander two-headed (*dikranoi*), for helplessness in their
Breasts guides their wandering thought (*nous*), and they are carried,
Deaf and blind equally, bewildered, undiscerning (*akrita**) tribes,
For whom to be (*to pelein*) and not to be are thought* the same
And not the same, and the path of all is back-turning.

Fragment 7

For never shall this be forced,* that things that are not *are*,
But do you restrain your thought (*noēma*) from this road of inquiry.
Nor let habit, much-experienced, force you along this road,
To ply an unseeing eye and an echoing hearing
5 And tongue, but judge by reason (*logos*) the strife-ridden refutation
Spoken by me.

Fragment 8

Yet one narrative (*mūthos*) of a road
Is left, that it is (*estin*); on this road there are very many
Signs,* that being (*eon**) is unborn and unperishing (it),
Whole, one-of-a-kind (*mounogenēs*), untrembling (*atremos**) and without end
    (*ateleston**);
5 Nor ever was, nor will be, since now (*nun*) is, all together (*homou pān*),
One, continuous; for what birth of it will you inquire?
How and whence grown (*auxēthen*)? Neither from non-being (*mē eontos*) will
    I allow
You to speak nor to conceive (*noein*); for not sayable nor conceivable (*noēton*)
Is it, that it is not. And what necessity (*khreos*) urged it,

10 Later or earlier, having begun from nothing, to come into being (*phūn*)?
Thus, it is necessary (*khreōn*) for it either to exist all-in-all (*pampan*),
   or not.
Nor ever will the strength of trust (*pistis*) allow something from non-being*
To be born (*gignesthai*) besides it; for this reason, neither to be born (*genesthai*)
Nor to perish did Dikē (Justice), loosening her shackles, allow,
15 But she holds fast; and the discernment (*krisis*) about these things is in this:
Is it or is it not? But now it has been decided (*kekritai*), just as necessary
   (*anangkē*),
To allow that the one road is inconceivable (*anoēton*), unnamed (*anōnumon**),
   for not of truth
is it the road, but [to allow about] the other road that it is, and is true.
How could what-is (*to eon*) be in the future (*epeita*)? And how could it
come into being?
20 For if it came into being, it is not, nor if it is ever going to be.
Thus birth (*genesis*) is extinguished and perishing unheard-of (*apustos*).
Nor is (it) divisible, since (it) is all same*.
Nor (is it) in any way more in some place, which would restrain it from
   holding together,
Nor (is it) in any way less, but (it) is all full of being.
25 Therefore (it) is all continuous; for being approaches to being.*
But unmoved in the limits of great bonds
(it) is, without beginning (*anarkhon*) and unceasing, since birth and perishing
have been driven* very far away, and true trust (*pistis alēthēs*) thrust (them)
   away.
Remaining the same in the same* it lies by itself
30 And thus will remain there securely; for powerful necessity (*anangkē*)
Holds (it) in (the) bonds of a limit, which restrains it all around;
Therefore it is not lawful (*themis*) for what-is (*to eon*) to be without an end;
For it is not lacking; for if it were,* it would lack everything.
And the same thing is (it) to think (*noein*) and wherefore there is thought
   (*noēma*);
35 For not without what-is, in what has been stated,*
Will you find thinking (*to noein*); for nothing else either is or will be
Apart from what-is (*tou eontos*), since Moira (Fate) shackled it at least
To be whole and unmoved; wherefore all things have been named
As many as mortals (*brotoi*) have established, trusting (*pepoithotes*) to be true;
40 To come into being and to perish; to be and not,
And to change place and to exchange shining complexion.*
But since (there is) an ultimate limit, it [i.e., what-is] is perfect,
Everywhere like the bulk of a well-rounded sphere,
From its center equally balanced everywhere; for it is necessary for it
45 To be neither in any way greater nor in any way lesser here or there;
For neither is there not-being, which would stop it from approaching

To [its] like, nor is being such that there would be
More of being here or less there, since it all is inviolate*;
For everywhere equal to itself, uniformly it falls* in limits.

II (ii): Textual Notes on the Translation of Fragment 1 (Lines 22–32) and Fragments 2–8 (Lines 1–50)

Fragment 1, continued: Lines 22–32

1.22. "kindly": the word *prophrōn* etymologically means "with forward (*pro-*) mind."

1.25. *hikanōn*: the verb *hikanō* recalls line 1, where the *thumos* "reaches"; here, however, the goddess attributes the *kouros'* arrival at her house to the mares (25), omitting any reference to his *thumos* which propels him (1). I argue in this study that *thumos* is the "mortal soul." The goddess therefore ignores the mortal component of his journey.

1.26. *neesthai*: it is worth considering whether the verb *neomai* carries some Homeric and Pindaric baggage here: with respect to the former, one cannot help but think of *nostos* (for this *kouros*, is this journey a return home? Is this journey/revelation actually a return to a primordial state?); with respect to the latter, it is used for traveling the path of song (P.IV.427; also see *Hymn to Hermes* 451 for the *oimos aoidēs*).

1.27. In this line, notice that words such as *hodon* and *patou* represent the journey in spatial terms. The word *estin*, "it is," occurs at the end of the line as a copula; later, the goddess will focus exclusively on *estin*, rather than journey, in describing motionless being.

1.28. "learn": the verb is *punthanomai* which means "enquire about." But it is equivalent to *manthanō* in 1.31. Enquiring and learning are the same thing in philosophical activity.

1.29. "persuasive" (Sextus Empiricus): instead of this adjective Simplicius reads, and some editors adopt, *eukukleos*, "well-rounded"; see, for example, Gallop (52–3). 2.4 may support Sextus.

1.31, 32. Lines 31 and 32 are obscure lines, but rich in resonances of key terms.
   dokimōs: this word means "assuredly," "certainly." It seems as if it is formed from the same root as *doxa*, the mortal "opinion" the goddess mentions in line 30 and criticizes in much of her speech. Yet, *dokimōs* comes from *dekhomai* "to accept" and *dokimazō* which means "to test," "to assay," "to scrutinize." (*LSJ*, s.vv.) Even more, what here exist "assuredly" are "things seeming to be," *ta dokounta*, a participle formed from the verb *dokeō*. Clearly, the philosophical problem for

Parmenides here is not merely textual. Things that exist spatio-temporally do exist in a certain way, although not as fully as being.

1.32. For the very difficult second half of this line, I have adopted wording from both Gallop and Coxon. Gallop (53): "how the things which seem / Had to have genuine existence, permeating all things completely." Coxon (48): "how it was necessary that the things that are believed to be should have their being in general acceptance, ranging through all things from end to end." Curd[7] (21): "how it was right that the things that seem be reliably, being indeed, the whole of things." Curd's translation ignores the force of *khrēn*, "it was necessary." O'Brien's (8) might be the most syntactically appropriate and clear translation: "how the things that appear would have to have real existence, passing the whole way through all things."[8] There are three different forms of necessity: logical necessity, circumstantial necessity, and external compulsion. Death is the best example of circumstantial inevitability: given birth, death is inevitable.

Fragment 2

This is Coxon's fragment 3.

2.1. Compare page 44 (text and footnote) for discussion of the possibilities for *komisai.*

2.2. "inquiry": *dizēsis* also occurs at 6.3, 8.6, 7.2.

2.2. *noēsai* (or *noein*): I translate "conceive" (as Coxon does). K. von Fritz writes: "The fundamental meaning of the word *noein* in Homer is 'to realize or to understand a situation.' . . . [Parmenides'] work marks the most decisive turning-point in the history of the terms *nous, noein,* and so on; for he was the first consciously to include logical reasoning in the functions of the *nous.*"[9] By using the word "conceive," I wish to stress the notion of "grasping," etymo- logically present in the word "conception" from Latin *concipio* or *cum + capio.* I do not mean a purely mental representation. In fact, I see it as the passive reception of a situation by the mind; "conceive" should be understood as a grasping of phenomena, provided we remember this means a passive grasping, not an act of will. Schürmann translates forms of *noein* by "heeding," in accordance with Heidegger; this also has the advantage of having a passive, receptive emphasis.

2.4. Some editors emend one word to make this line read: "for it (persuasion) attends upon truth." So Gallop (54–5) and Coxon (53). However, the text reads *alētheia* (nominative, making "truth" the subject; see Sider and Johnstone, 12).[10]

2.5. *khreōn:* unlike the previous usage of this word (line 28), she means here a *logical necessity*, as opposed to a conditional or ontological necessity.

2.6. *panapeuthea*, "entirely unlearnable," contains a form of the verb *punthano-mai*, used already at 1.28 (*puthesthai*). There, the goddess said it was necessary for the *kouros* to know both truth and *doxai*. Hence, the unlearnable road of what-is-not, here, refers not to mortal *doxai* but to non-being. But in 8.21, the related word *apustos* describes destruction and death. Hence, in a different way, death and birth also cannot be learned, and a *logos* cannot be provided for singulars. It is interesting to interpret "truth" as used in John in this Greek sense (individual, singular) rather than the Hebrew sense (fidelity). *Alētheia*, as I have argued throughout this work, is not exclusively the domain of logical concepts and argumentation (*logos*), but is established on the existence of concrete singulars. Jesus himself is *logos* in this concrete, non-conceptual sense. Jesus, when asked by Pilate questions related to his identity and to "Truth" (John 18) remains silent. Singulars can only be pointed to.

Fragment 3

3.1. For *noein*, see note on line 2.2 above.

Fragment 4

4.1. "Gaze upon": suggested by Coxon (56). *Homōs* can be used to delimit single words.

4.2. *echesthai*, "to hold fast," reappears at 8.6 (*hen suneches*, "[being is] one, continuous"), 8.23 (*sunechesthai*, "[being is not more or less here or there, which would keep it from] holding together"), 8.25 (*xuneches*, "continuous").

4.3. *kata kosmon*: this phrase embodies a pun. It means both "in due order" (a Homeric phrase) and "throughout the universe" (since *kosmos* refers to the ordered universe). Also, Matt Newman suggests the following regarding the translation here: "Perhaps it is something more like 'neither that which is being scattered throughout the universe, nor that which is coming together.' This is rather troublesome, but I get the sense that the goddess is saying that no matter the movement of *to eon*, diffusion or concentration, it is always integral."[11]

Fragment 5

5.2. "Return" here translates *palin hixomai*; literally, "I will come back." "Return" for the goddess cannot mean the same as it would for the mortal *kouros*. She employs the image of journey, but only in her language and only referring to her speech. She is stationary, her ontology is one of stasis, and her metaphor for being is a sphere. Therefore her circular *logos* cannot know the unidirectional finitude of mortals preserved in the latter's life, journey, and narrative.

Fragment 6

6.1. Heidegger misunderstands this line, wrongly reading *t' eon*, that is, *t(e) eon*, as *to on* (being); Schürmann repeats this.[12] There is no doubt about the Greek here; the elided vowel must be epsilon, not omicron, and the phrase *legein te noein t(e)* demands a second *te* (a correlative, "and"). This said, the line remains difficult and somewhat obscure. What interests me now is the goddess' description of her subject matter, being, in terms of speaking and conceiving, what I call "*logos*."

6.2. *phrazesthai*: the verb *phrazō* carries root meanings of "show, tell." The middle form, found in this line, and meaning, "consider (to yourself)," implies that the listener (the *kouros*) internalizes the words of the goddess. I point this out because of the interest of various words for "thinking" and related activities. Here, thought is fashioned from *logos* rather than from phenomena or sensation.

6.7. *akrita*, "undiscerning": the verb *krino* also appears in 7.5 (*krinai de logō*, "judge by reason"), 8.15 (*krisis peri toutōn*, "the judgement about these things") and 8.16 (*kekritai*, "it has been decided").

6.8. *nenomistai*: apparently the goddess puns on this verb, *nomizō*, and the word *onoma* ("name"), since later she describes mortals' going astray in naming things as a defining characteristic of the mortal *kosmos* of division, plurality, and contrariness.

Fragment 7

7.1. "be forced": borrowed from Taran (73) and Sider and Johnstone (15). Newman comments that, if this is passive (which it seems), it is not future, but aorist subjunctive, perhaps volitive given the following line's imperative: "let this never be proven."

Fragment 8

8.2. *epi' sēmat' easi*: the goddess refers to two different kinds of signs: those of the way of being, and others which names the birth-death trajectories of beings. See also 8.55 with the note there.

8.3. *Eon* is of great interest here. Whether it is the grammatical subject of the Greek sentence is somewhat ambiguous, especially lacking the definite article *to*. The word, the Ionic form of *on*, is the neuter singular present participle of the verb *einai*, "to be" (of which the third-person singular is *estin*, "he/she/it is"). As a participle or verbal adjective, it means "being." My reading is closest to that of Barnes. He takes *eon* as a circumstantial participle: "that, being, it is ungenerated and undestroyed."[13] However, most scholars take the participle as a verbal *noun* (a gerund), "being." Thus: "what-is" (Mourelatos, 94;[14] Gallop, 65), "Being" (Taran, 85; Coxon, 60). This takes Parmenides' usage as anticipating Aristotle's use of *to on* for "being" (see also the note on 6.1, above). Indeed, we know this fragment 8 from Simplicius' *Commentary on Aristotle's Physics*. However, we must first inquire whether Parmenides does in fact use *eon* (= *on*) as a verbal noun (gerund). Although in 6.1 he does not use the definite article, in 8.19 he uses the article. In 8.46 and 8.47, he uses *eon* as a participle, and thus without an article.

Parmenides uses being with the definite article in several passages, for example, *tou eontos* (4.2, 8.35), *to pelein* (6.8). The articular infinitive does not occur in Homer. It is of some philosophical significance to my thesis that articular infinitives allow us to think about mortal actions in an abstract way. Parmenides uses articular infinitives elsewhere, such as 6.1 (*to legein*) and 8.36 (*to noein*). The first speech on truth, understandably, contains all occurrences of the articular infinitives in the surviving fragments.

8.4. The word *atremes* also occurs in 1.29 where it qualifies the heart of *alētheia*, "truth," and here, being. Variant emendations exist for the ending of this line; however, *ēd' ateleston* is the reading of Simplicius, who is the unique source (see Coxon, 61, n. 4).

8.6. *suneches* describes being in 4.2, 8.23, and 8.25.

8.12. Instead of *ek mē eontos* ("from non-being"), Taran and Gallop accept Karsten and Reinhardt's emendation *ek tou eontos*, "from being." But this cannot be; the line would then mean, "nothing comes from being besides itself," but being does not come from itself; this would be a banal and a tautological argument, perhaps even requiring infinite regress. I have translated the manuscript reading (Gallop, 66) with Diels, Sider, and Johnstone and Coxon; it means, "nothing can come from non-being."

8.15–16. See note 6.7 for usage of *krisis* and related terms.

8.17. Naming is a significant feature of mortal activity. See 8.38 where all things are named by mortals (*onom' estai*).

8.22. This line can be, and has been, read in two different ways. Gallop (16) argues, following Owen, that *homoion* is adverbial, and he translates "since [it] all alike is." (That is: "since it all exists equally/in a like way.") He argues that the argument demands this. (His reading requires accenting the verb *estin* with an acute accent on the penult.) But a natural reading of the line would be to take *homoion* as a predicate adjective: "[it] is all same." I follow Mourelatos (111, n. 30).

8.25. Compare Plato, *Symposium* 195b: *homoion homoioi aei pelazei*, "like always draws near to like." Mourelatos (111, n. 30) points out the "obvious echo" in

Parmenides (and then Plato) of Homer's line, [*hōs*] *aiei ton homoion agei theos hōs ton homoion*, "god always leads like to like" (*Odyssey* xvii.218). Parmenides' line contains the same suggestion of movement, although scholarly translators have been uncomfortable with this notion: as Gallop writes (16), "the goddess does not, presumably, mean to recognize two or more discrete entities adjacent to one another." Taran translates (85): "Being is in contact with Being." Gallop (69): "for what-is is in contact with what-is." Coxon (66): "for Being is adjacent to Being." By using the verb "is," they suppress the idea of being "approaching" being; but that is the clear meaning of *pelazō* (as Sider and Johnstone point out, 17). Note the fracture in Parmenides' One, as the goddess recounts it. Even the translations quoted, while denying the hint of movement, nevertheless suggest a multiplicity in being. Parmenides' doctrine of the "One," contrary to first impressions, is in fact very fragile, and upon closer examination, reveals many fractures and joinings. The One seems to be an ultimate principle, but a precarious one.

   In fact, this line already introduces, and requires, principles of the cosmology with (for example) the two cohering forces of *erōs* and "mixing."

8.28. *eplakhthēsan*, "have been driven," inevitably recalls the second line of Homer's *Odyssey*: Odysseus "*mala polla / plangkhthē*" (*Odyssey* P.1–2). In accordance with this, I translate as a passive verb, adopting Gallop's (69) "driven . . . off" rather than Coxon's (68) "have strayed." Thematically, Parmenides reverses the point of the *Odyssey*. In being driven far from home, Odysseus encounters the goddesses Circe and Kalypso and lives with each of them for a time, but rather than stay with Kalypso and accept her offer of immortality, Odysseus longs for home and his mortal life. In Parmenides' account of the goddess' speech, the opposite: mortality is thrust away. If we are to understand that there is, in fact, some Homer in Parmenides' use of *neesthai*, discussed above, one may wonder whether the goddess has somehow tried to obviate or fulfill the need to "go home" at 1.26.

8.29. Presumably, "remaining the same in the same (place)." Kirk-Raven-Schofield (KRS) translate this line as "remaining on its own."

8.33. "for if it were": I understand, bracketing *mē* (with KRS, Diels-Kranz (DK)) *eon d' an* as "(it) being [so]," but I am uncertain about this half-line.

8.35–36. These lines may mean that thinking is dependent upon being (see Sider and Johnstone, 18).

8.41. *khroa*: both Gallop (71), and Sider and Johnstone (19), translate "color." Not really. *Khrōs* means "flesh," "skin," or "surface of the body," that is, of the human body exclusively or (even in Homer) its complexion. Parmenides here refers to something like "surface appearance," but it is significant that he uses a word referring to human bodies. Coxon (74) elaborates on the notion of "exchange": "(to) alter their bright aspect to dark and from dark to bright." Although a free translation, he brings out the implied meaning well.

8.48. *asulon*: "inviolable," apparently the first occurrence of this word in extant Greek literature (Taran, 147). In ancient Greece, this word refers to the institution called (in English) *asylum*, the right of protection in a sanctuary. An individual who clung to a statue of a deity was protected from seizure or arrest. Here Parmenides subtly invokes the authority of the goddess for the truth of being: it is under her oversight. This line says that being (metaphysics) takes refuge under a divinity—from death.

8.49. *kurei*: this verb, "fall," also contains a suggestion of motion.

Further note on this section

Some texts print another fragment, the so-called Cornford's Fragment (= Sider and Johnstone's fr. 20). I have chosen to exclude this fragment because it is incoherent and untranslatable by itself. The language echoes 8.38.

Section III: The *Kosmos*

III (i): Translation of Fragment 8 (Lines 50–61) and Fragments 9–19

Fragment 8

50 Here to you I stop (my) trustworthy speech (*logon*) and thought (*noēma*)
    about truth; from this point mortal opinions
    learn, listening to the deceitful ordering (*kosmon*) of my words,
    for to name shapes they (mortals) established (*katethento*) two knowings (*gnōmas*),*
    of one which it is not right (*khreōn*) to name*; in this they have wandered stray,
55 and they distinguished things opposite in body and established signs (*ethento sēmata*)*
    apart from each other: on the one hand, the aetherial (*aitherion**) fire of flame,
    being mild, immensely light, everywhere the same to itself
    but not the same as the other; and (on the other hand) this (other), in accordance with itself,
    the opposites, obscure night, thick in body* and dense.
60 I declare to you that this ordering (*diakosmon*) is entirely (*panta*) likely (*eoikota**),
    So that never any knowing (*gnōmē*) of mortals might outstrip you.

Fragment 9

But since all things have been named light and night,
And the (names*) [have been given] in accordance with their powers
   (*dunameis*) to these things and to those,
All (*pān*) is full of light and obscure (*aphantou*) night together,
Of both equally, since in neither does nothing have a share.

Fragment 10

And you shall know both the nature (*phusin*) of the *aithēr** and all the signs
In the *aithēr* and the obscuring works of the pure brilliant sun's
torch, and whence they came to be, and you will learn the wandering
works of the round-eyed (*kuklopos*) moon,
and its nature, and you shall know also the sky (*ouranon*) all about,
whence it came into being (*ephu*) and how Necessity, leading (it), bound it
to hold the limits of the stars.

Fragment 11

. . . how earth and sun and moon
and common air (*aithēr*) and the Milky Way and
furthest Olympus and hot strength of stars were set in motion
to come into being.

Fragment 12

For the narrower* ones [i.e., rings] are filled with unmixed (*akrētoio*) fire,
And those (next) to these with night, and a portion (*aisa**) of flame radiates
   forth
And in the middle of these a daimoness,* who steers all things;
For she rules* over hateful birth and mixing (*mixios*) of all* things,
5 Sending female to mix (*migēn*) with male and again the opposite (*to enantion*),
Male with female.

Fragment 13

First, on the one hand, of all the gods she devised Love (Erōs)

Fragment 14 [of the moon]

Night-lighting,* astray around earth, a foreign* light

Fragment 15 [of the moon]

always searching* out the rays of the sun

Fragment 15a [of the earth]

rooted-in-water

Fragment 16

For as each* (man) has a mixing (*krasin*) of much-wandering* limbs,
So mind (*nous*) is present in men; for the nature (*phusis*) of the limbs for men
Is the same thing which thinks (*phroneei*),*
For each and every one (man); for it is mostly thought (*noēma*).

Fragment 17

on the right [sides] young men (*kourous*), on the left [sides] young females
    (*kouras*)*

Fragment 18

When woman and man together mix (*miscent*) the seeds of Venus (love)
in the veins, from the diverse blood a shaping power (*virtus*)
maintaining proper proportion fashions well-made bodies.
For if the powers (*virtutes**) war with each other when the seed is mixed,
5   And do not make a unity in the body resulting from the mixture, (then,)
        terribly
They will vex the growing sex with (i.e., through) the double seed.

Fragment 19

In this* way, for you, according to opinion (*doxan*), these things emerged (*ephu*)
    and now are,
And henceforth, from now on, having been nourished,* they will perish.
And men established a signifying (*episēmon**) name for each one.

III (ii): Textual Notes on the Translation of Fragment 8 (Lines 50–61) and Fragments 9–19

Fragment 8

8.53. Mortals establish names for things, not the phenomena themselves (*morphas*). "Forms" (*morphas*) should be understood as physical-phenomenal shapes or forms—not Platonic Forms (*idea, eidos*). Coxon translates "Forms," ambiguously (76), without making a commitment to the physical reality of things. Of course, both *morphē* and *eidos* can be used pejoratively, "in appearance rather than in reality." This use is found both in Homer and in Hesiod.

katethento, "established": the verb often implies, "lay up for the future" (*LSJ*, s.v. II.4, "deposit," "lay up"; II.6, "lay up in memory or as a memorial"): as in *Theognis* 717, with the object *gnōmēn* (a word I translate as "knowing" in Parmenides)—the closest verbal parallel to the current line. Memory plays a crucial role in mortal thought. The goddess excludes time; by insisting on the now, she excludes both the future and the past and thus, memory and anticipation of death: precisely what define mortality. She also uses *katethento* at 8.39, in conjunction with mortals (*brotoi*) and their naming (8.38–9); and likewise, see 19.3: "And men established a signifying name for each one."

katethento . . . gnōmas I have taken as "decided" (*LSJ*, s.v. *gnōmē* IIIa). The standard reading separates *duo* from *gnōmas*. This is possible, as closing the phrase before the caesura. This problem has led some editors to prefer the emendation *gnōmais*, adopted by Gallop: "For they established two forms in their mind for naming." Alternately, *gnōmas* can be read as a synonym for *doxa*, which is not my argument here. Many translate 8.53 as "for they decided (*katethento gnōmas*) to name two forms"

8.54. Following O'Brien and others, Taran translates *mian* as "a unity" ("for they decided to name two forms, a unity of which is not necessary"; 86), misleadingly in my opinion. This is an unnatural translation of *mian*.

8.55. *demas* echoes *morphas* in line 53; it refers to a physical, living body; see also the note on the word *khrōs*, in 8.41, in Section II. Kirk, Raven, and Schofield translate *demas* as "appearance." I disagree, because *demas* means frame or structure; for example, in Homer, the human body. *Demas* is also used in 8.59, where it is used of the dense physicality of Night.

sēmata: this word, "signs," was also used at 8.2, where the goddess says there are many signs pointing to the true road. Again, notice the frequency and variety of polysemic vocabulary in the poem: the "many signs" now hint at a new, mortal discourse taught by the goddess (see 10.1–2 note).

8.56. *aitherion*: see discussion in the notes to fragment 10.

8.59. Gallop, Coxon, and O'Brien take *demas* as a noun in apposition to *nukta*.

8.60. Sider and Johnstone (20) translate *eoikota panta* as attributive adjectives with *diakosmon*. My translation reads these words as in predicate position in indirect discourse.

Fragment 9

This is Coxon's fragment 11. In other words, the ordering of these fragments remains uncertain. Simplicius places these lines "a few verses" later than 8.59 (Coxon, 232).

9.1–2. These are difficult lines, engendering confusing translations. Coxon makes "all names" the main point of lines 1 and 2, and thus removes light and night from line 2 (84). The apparent difficulty is the plural in the second line *toisi* and *tois*.

9.2. *ta*: literally "the things." Sider and Johnstone interpret this as equivalent to *tauta*, light and night. I have taken this more broadly, to refer to things other than light and night. Kirk-Raven-Schofield take *epi tois te kai tois* to refer to night and light, translating "to each." But the plurals must be broader, referring to two categories of things. Plutarch (Kirk, Raven, Schofield, fr. 304) understands Parmenides as assigning all phenomena to light or night, or a mixture.

Fragment 10

This is Coxon's fragment 9.

10.1–2. Bicknell suggests that fragment 10 should follow the proem, that is, he places it after 1.32. Gallop approves of this idea (79) because "It can be read as part of a synopsis of topics that the goddess promises to cover in the second part of her discourse." This may indeed be a good idea. If so, it is important to note that the goddess' discourse on the "Way of Seeming" would (then) begin with the *aithēr*.

For the meaning of *aithēr* as "air" before the fourth century BCE, see Kingsley:[15] "In the earliest surviving Greek literature, and in poetic tradition down to the fourth century BCE, *aithēr* was the basic term for what we call air. *Aēr*, on the other hand, was originally only a very isolated example of air: obscure mist or cloud . . . [and, he goes on, referring to Parmenides,] . . . it makes immediate and obvious sense when, as in the case of all other sixth- and fifth-century writers, *aithēr* is accepted as referring to the 'upper and lower regions of the air . . . evidently thought of as a continuum extending from the earth's surface to the stars or beyond.' "

We have already seen that the gates Parmenides passes through, as he enters the realm of the goddess, are described as *aitheriai* (1.13). There, the *kouros* passed from the mortal cosmos to the limits of the *aithēr*. Now, after the goddess has completed her discourse on immortal being, she charts an opposite path. Having reached the limits of this being of hers, she crosses over, in her speech to the *kouros*, into the mortal realm, by reentering *aithēr*. "*The* kouros, *in this way, reenters* aithēr, *that is, our mortal universe*." This represents his return, if only in discourse, to the cosmos.

"all the signs in the *aithēr*": Taran (242) says that these can only be stars. Perhaps he connects the *sēmata* to *astrōn* in 10.7. But, "signs," used also in 8.55 (. . . established signs) and 19.3 (a function of naming . . .), induce mortals to differentiate all things (see notes *ad loc*).

10.5–6. *phusin*, "nature," is significant in describing the *aithēr*; this characterizes it as mortal (cf. 10.1–2 note). *Ephu*, in line 6, is the verb cognate with *phusis*. "Nature," as a translation of *phusin*, should not be understood to mean "essence."

The Greek word implies growth in the natural world, the life-process of coming-into-being and passing-away. Coxon translates "origin" (80), to convey the idea of coming-into-being.

10.6–7. Necessity shackles the mortal cosmos, just as Moira (Fate) binds being (8.37–8). We might expect this to be the other way around. *Moira*, "fate", referred earlier to death (1.26). We might expect Fate to apply to the human realm, and necessity to being.

Fragment 12

12.1. "narrower" is a feminine adjective, *steinoterai*, whose noun has to be supplied. *Stephanai*, "crowns" or "crowning rings," is supplied by Testimonium A 37 (from Aetius; conveniently printed in Gallop, 116; see also Gallop, 83).

12.2. *aisa* of flame: *aisa* means portion or fate (i.e., one's allotted portion). *Aisa*, like *moira* (see preceding note), can refer to death. Here, it refers to fire ejected into night. Here in the cosmos, the opposites come together, which the goddess cannot keep separate.

    meta . . . hietai: the reading of *meta* has been variously understood: "injected" (Guthrie, 61; that is, "of fire and darkness mixed," 62); Coxon (86), "in which moves a proportion of flame." Grammatically, they take *meta* either as an adverb ("among") or as a preposition with an implied dative (*meta* + dative = "within"). I take the two words as an example of tmesis.

    I understand the arrangement of the cosmos, here, in this way. Fire and night are two contiguous concentric rings. Night is thicker (not only less "narrow" in circumference compared with the ring of fire). This is because night is denser than light. From the inner infernal ring, flames are sent forth into the adjacent portions of the ring of night. Thus, a mixing of fire and night is found in this region. Beyond extends the remainder of the ring of night into which the flames of fire do not project. This accords with the testimonium of Aetius, 37, which speaks both of pure bands (both of rare, and of dense) and of mixed (light and darkness).

12.3. These words refer to a second goddess whom we may call *Thea Physica*, a *daimoness* (specified as feminine by the feminine relative pronoun) who steers all things.

12.4. Reading *pantōn* with Gallop (82). Others read *pantē*, *pantēi*, "everywhere." Some conjecture is necessary as most MSS read *panta* ("all things") which is impossible.

    arkhei can mean both "rules over" (governing the genitive case, as here) or "makes begin," "initiates." This latter, implied, sense of the word would suggest a relation of this generative goddess with nature (*phusis*). Parmenides probably puns on the possibilities in this word. The verb is related closely to the noun *arkhē*, "rule" or "beginning."

Fragment 14

nuktiphaes: this unusual word also occurs in *Orphic Hymn* 54.10.[16]

allotrion phōs (*phōs* being contracted *phaos*): Parmenides here puns on the Homeric phrase, *allotrios phōs*, "foreign man."[17]

Fragment 15

paptainousa: the verb has the sense of "look about one with a sharp, searching glance" and "look round for, look after" (*LSJ*, s.v.). Sider and Johnstone write (22): "As examples of this verb in Homer show, the moon here is not 'looking *at*' but 'looking *for*' the light of the sun." Gallop translates "looking towards," which does not capture the full nuance of this verb.

Fragment 16

16.1. Instead of *hekastos*, some editors read *hekastot'* (Kirk-Raven-Schofield, Sider and Johnstone), meaning "at any moment" (KRS, 261). The subject of the line would then be *krasis* (reading the nominative instead of the accusative *krasin*), with *ekhei* meaning "is."

poluplangkton: an interesting parallel occurs in a Greek inscription from Rome: *poluplangktoi prapides*, "much-erring wits" (*IG* 14.1424; *LSJ*, s.vv. *poluplangktos* and *prapides*; *prapides* is synonymous with *phrenes*).[18] Newman pointed out to me that, in this inscription, *IGUR* 1163 in Moretti's collection, Zeus (whose identity is possibly both pagan and Judeo-Christian in this inscription) "once offered to the *poluplangktoi prapides* of men a deathless and ageless *psukhē*." The inscription as a whole speaks to an extremely odd description of the deceased's death—it seems to describe a multicultic ritual suicide and perhaps a deathlessness possibly achieved by, among other means, completion of an unqualified *oimos*. See note on 1.26 for possible characteristics of journeys in Parmenides, here, and in Greek poetry.[19]

16.2–3. Translators do not seem to understand this line. They have trouble with both the grammar and the sense. Gallop: "for it [*nous*] is the same thing / Which the constitution of the limbs thinks." Coxon: "for it [*nous*] is the same as the awareness belonging to the nature of the body." O'Brien's take is somewhat different: "For what the limbs think of is just the same for all men and for every ‹man›."

Fragment 17

Gallop supplies as subject "She placed . . ." explaining: "the subject of this line will be the goddess, referred to at 12.3 as presiding over birth" (89). However, the testimonia mostly describe the sperm deposited by the male in the womb; see Testimonia A53 and 54 (DK; conveniently printed in Gallop, 122–3).

Fragment 18

This translation is from Latin, since this fragment is preserved only in the Latin translation by Caelius Aurelianus (a medical writer of the fifth century CE). Caelius himself took it as an explanation of homosexuality (Gallop accepts Caelius, see 103). Taran explains it that way (263–5), as referring, in his unfortunate words, to "abnormal sex" (265, n. 99). This imports more than the fragment warrants. Caelius, in explaining this passage, talks about "desire" as a psychosexual function of the individual. This notion is foreign to Parmenides. The passage does seem to refer to a mixture in the offspring of qualities from its father and its mother (see Taran, 264), but we should not go further than that.

18.4. *virtutes*: Diels and Kranz relate this to *dunameis* (9.2).

Fragment 19

This is Coxon's fragment 20.

19.1. *houtō*: *LSJ*, 507. In addition to the common meaning of "in this way, in this manner" this word also is used with a qualifying power: "so, only so, simply, no more than." Here, I read the opening of this line as possibly meaning "only for you" as opposed to herself, the goddess. *Toi* = *soi* = "to you" (Sider and Johnstone suggest "for you, in your eyes"; 23). Thus, *toi* applies to the *kouros* whom she is addressing. Since her saying is *kata doxan*, she implies that the *kouros* is also a representative of the mortals whose speech belongs to the realm of mortal opinion (*doxas broteias*, 8.51). We might take *houtō* closely with *toi* to mean "thus (only) to you [a mortal]." Earlier in the proem, she had taken him by his right hand and had said that he had come far from the path of mortals. Now, in the description of the mortal cosmos, the *kouros* returns home to his own kind, the mortals, with the goddess' speeches still ringing in his ears.

19.2. *traphenta*: see Sider and Johnstone (23): an aorist passive participle from the verb *trephō*, "nourish." Coxon translates it as "having received their sustenance" (92). This verb in the passive has two basic meanings: to grow and thrive as well as to receive nourishment. O'Brien adopts the former in his translation, and by rendering it finite he elicits the sense, against translations that maintain it as participial and circumstantial of death, that growth is simply coordinate to it (and birth, and present being) in accounting for temporal whole of mortal existence. The word can also mean "to thicken," "to become firm," "to curdle," "to congeal" (*LSJ*, s.v. I). Observe how concrete the overtones of this word are.

Also compare this word with *auxēthen* (8.7) which means "grown," "increased," and so on. In addition, nourishment is closely linked to *thumos* (on which, see my discussion of the proem as a journey).

19.3. *episēmon*: *LSJ*, s.v., defines as: "distinguishing mark, device, badge; . . . device on a coin; . . . serial number; . . . generally, mark, imprint." A related noun, *episēma*, can mean "grave-marker" (*LSJ*, Supplement, s.v.). *Sēma*, "tomb," is part of the famous Orphic catch-phrase, *sōma sēma*, "the body (is) a tomb [i.e., for them, of the soul]." The point here is that the terminology used by the goddess also has allusions to mortality and not merely logical and semantic connotations. See also passages 8.55, 10.2.

Fragment 20

I have chosen to omit fragment 20 here; Sider and Johnstone (23) explain that many scholars regard it as "a restatement of 8.38."

Notes

Introduction: Parmenides and Renewing
the Beginning

[1] Reiner Schürmann, "Tragic Differing: The Law of the One and the Law of Contraries in Parmenides," *Graduate Faculty Philosophy Journal* 13.1 (1988): 5.

[2] Martin Heidegger, "Moira" in *Early Greek Thinking*, trans. David Farrell Krell and F. A. Capuzzi (San Francisco: Harper, 1975), 100–1.

[3] W. K. C. Guthrie, *A History of Greek Philosophy*, vol. 2 (Cambridge: Cambridge University Press, 1965), 1.

[4] Schürmann, "Tragic Differing," 5.

[5] The tragic reading I articulate for here is by no means a 'soft' reading of Greek philosophy. Tragedy, as I understand it and as I use it here, is not an illustration of either a fine philosophical point or a moral lesson or an extreme situation in life. In any of these situations, tragedy is not to be construed as a loss of meaning or a problematization of our positivistic philosophies. Tragedy is the very nature of being, especially being as described by the pre-Socratics: coming-to-be, flourishing, and passing-away. Only in such an understanding of being is tragedy even possible. Even more, tragedy is possible because our experience of being is at its core tragic. What is tragedy? Why is it tragic? Terry Eagleton's explanation is elegant and succinct: "The richness that dies along with a single human being is beyond our fathoming, though tragedy may furnish a hint of it." Terry Eagleton, *Sweet Violence: The Idea of the Tragic* (Malden, MA: Blackwell, 2003), 27.

[6] Schürmann, "Tragic Differing," 3.

[7] "In essential history the beginning comes last." Martin Heidegger, *Parmenides*, trans. A. Schuwer and R. Rojcewicz (Bloomington, IN: Indiana University Press, 1992), 1.

[8] I use the terms bibliography and biography in the following senses: By "bibliography" I refer to decontextualized "ideas," *logoi* disembodied from their mortal source (the speaker, but most often the writer) and retained in a static, retrievable medium. It corresponds to my understanding of *psukhē* as opposed to *thumos*. I argue in this study that Plato's criticism of writing in *Phaedrus* and in *Letter VII* (341c–e) refers to the erasure of this human, mortal temporality. "Biography," in contrast, embodies the human dimension of *logos*, giving blood to the temporal sterility of lifeless "bibliography." It corresponds to *thumos*. It is not just a matter of writing versus orality (as Derrida would have it), but an issue of mortality. Thus, the Platonic dialogue retains the mortal Socrates as a central theme (I argue). Plato through his biographical writing immortalizes the mortality of

his dead teacher. Other works of this nature include Augustine's *Confessions*, Nietzsche's *Thus Spoke Zarathustra*, and Homer's poems. Moreover, it is also possible to read Hegel's *Phenomenology of Spirit* in this way—counter to the traditional interpretation—as the *mūthos* of his (singular) consciousness.

9 See also my articles "Derrida, Textuality, and Sacrifice," *Southwest Philosophical Studies*, vol. 29 (Spring 2007): 9–19, and "The Perils of Textual Transmission: Decapitation and Recapitulation," *Seminar*, no. 608, special issue titled *The Enduring Epic: A Symposium on Some Concerns Raised in the Mahābhārata* (April 2010): 48–54.

10 Reiner Schürmann, "Ultimate Double Binds," *Graduate Faculty Philosophy Journal* 14.2–15.1 (1991): 224.

11 Plato later takes up the same theme for investigation in the *Theaetetus*, where he examines the question of Heraclitean flux. Plato's treatment, however, is discursive; I wish to underscore the existential aspects of *phusis*.

12 See, for example, Taran, who writes, "To be sure, his [Parmenides'] purpose was to show that the identity of what is precludes the characteristics of the phenomenal world and, since the theories of his predecessors were meant to explain this world, they are all refuted. They are all refuted because Parmenides denied the reality of the phenomenal world." Leonardo Taran, *Parmenides: A Text with Translation, Commentary, and Critical Essays* (Princeton: Princeton University Press, 1965), 109.

13 One of Socrates' central claims in the Platonic dialogues is that philosophy is a special sort of *praxis*: a purification which has as its ultimate concern the inescapable fact of our death (see *Phaedo* 69c, 80e, 82c–d, 83a–b, 84a–b, 114c, *Republic* 618c, 619c, *Phaedrus* 249a–c, *Gorgias* 526c–e). Hence, what I call the mortal reading of Plato/Socrates is not merely restricted to one of his so-called erotic dialogues, but is distributed across both his political and epistemological dialogues.

14 Whereas Parmenides preserves mortal temporality by inscribing it into unchanging being and thus also preserves the basic paradox of fluxing time, Heidegger's valorization of finite, ecstatic time leads to a dissolution of the temporal *aporia*. In doing so, Heidegger reduces the human condition to an awaiting of the eschatological event of the *parousia* (thought of as the event of one's death rather than Christ's arrival) in which there is no place for the tragic mortal condition. See also Reiner Schürmann, *Heidegger on Being and Acting: From Principles to Anarchy*, trans. Christine-Marie Gros (Bloomington, IN: Indiana University Press, 1990).

15 Although there are already many excellent Parmenides translations such as those of Denis O' Brien, David Sider, Coxon, Taran, Gallop, which I have referred to extensively in my own translation, I have nonetheless provided my own translation in order to provide further evidence of Parmenides' poem as "mortal philosophy." By analyzing Parmenides' vocabulary for its wealth of mortal resonances, this philosophical translation highlights specific aspects of his work that are often only diffusely present in other translations. Thus, while I do not claim that my translation is definitive, it is integral to justifying my claim that the motif of mortality runs through Parmenides' thought as a constant theme.

16 Nietzsche declares "God is dead" twice in *The Gay Science* (1882) and repeats the claim later in *Thus Spoke Zarathustra* (1885).

17 See Heidegger's "Das Ding," in *Vorträge und Aufsätze* (Pfullingen: Neske, 1954); Heidegger writes: "The mortals are the humans. They are called the mortals,

because they are capable of dying. To die means: to be capable of death as death" (177, cf. also 150; my translation).

18 Reiner Schürmann, *Broken Hegemonies*, trans. Reginald Lilly (Bloomington, IN: Indiana University Press, 2003).

Chapter 1: Radical Individuality: Time, Mortal Soul, and Journey

1 In the Platonic sense of the expression.

2 In *The Death of Ivan Ilych*, Tolstoy succeeds brilliantly in portraying this very problem, when he shows Ilych grappling with the syllogism "Caius is a man, men are mortal, therefore Caius is mortal." Through Ilych's existential confusion, Tolstoy demonstrates the limits of adopting a syllogistic approach to the death of singulars: only in a *mūthos* such as Tolstoy's own story, is the fact of our death brought home to us—in a way that is neither abstract nor limited to the particular.

3 That is, as coming-to-be and passing-away of the totality of beings.

4 Augustine, *The Confessions of St. Augustine*, trans. J. K. Ryan (New York: Image Books, 1960), 287.

5 Kant's views of death are implicitly contained in his comments on the value of life and the nature of the body. In the *Critique of Judgement* § 83, Kant repudiates a life whose aim is happiness and posits rationality or some other goal utterly independent of nature. In fact, the very existence of nature ought to be subject to such a goal, which Kant claims ought to be "imposed" or sought outside all life (§ 29). His explanation of life is presented in relation to pleasure and pain, especially *Gemüt*. The body itself is seen by Kant as an artifact of nature, whose organization, he says in § 75, "another Newton" might one day explain in terms of natural laws. While the experience of the body is central to Kant's ethics and aesthetics, the *Critique of Judgement* does not make any room for an existential understanding of death. Finitude, for Kant, is thus ultimately linked to either knowledge or to space. Conceptually, Kant is more interested in the relationship of the body to space (see his *Metaphysical Foundations of Natural Science*) and Descartes' mind-body dualism (see the Paralogisms of Pure Reason in the *Critique of Pure Reason*).

6 See Newton's *Philosophiae Naturalis Principia Mathematica* Third edition (1726) with variant readings (in two volumes), Alexandre Koyré et al., ed. (Cambridge, MA: Harvard University Press, 1972). Also see Howard Stein, "Newtonian Space-Time," in *The Annus Mirabilis of Sir Isaac Newton 1666–1966*, ed. Robert Palter (Cambridge, MA: MIT Press, 1967).

7 On *phusis*, see Pierre Chantraine, *Dictionnaire étymologique de la langue grecque: Histoire des mots* (Paris: Klincksieck, 1968), s.v. See also Heidel's useful study "*Peri phuseōs*: A Study of the Conception of Nature among the Pre-Socratics," *Proceedings of the American Academy of Arts and Sciences*, 45 (1910): 79–133 as well as Dietrich Mannsperger, *Physis bei Platon* (Berlin: de Gruyter, 1969). Mannsperger's study is, however, highly influenced by Heidegger's reading of Aristotle.

8 According to Heidegger, this latter aspect comes especially to the fore in the Greek translation of *phusis* by *natura*, thence leading to the modern concept of

"nature" as objective reality or as pure presence; see his "On the Essence and Concept of Φύσις," in *Pathmarks*, ed. William McNeill (Cambridge: Cambridge University Press, 1999) as well as his "The Question Concerning Technology," in *Basic Writings*, ed. David Farrell Krell (San Francisco: Harper Collins, 1993). Schürmann provides a useful summary of Heidegger's thesis as follows: "The Greeks used the term *phusis* to refer to all that is, insofar as it is. Today we translate this word as "nature," from the Latin *nasci*, to be born. The Greek word comes from *phuein*: . . . opening out, which is also the root of the word *phainesthai*, to enlighten, to shed light on. In a rough distinction, Latin thinking attends to the generation of things, and Greek thinking attends to their appearance or emergence into light. Nature according to what the Greek word states is the whole of that which shows itself to us, it is showing itself . . . The origin of all things, according to this vocabulary, lets itself be thought as the presence of that which is present: a presence which is prior to any human intention, and which makes it possible. The origin of all things is their appearing in presence." Reiner Schürmann, "Symbolic Difference," *Graduate Faculty Philosophy Journal* 19.2–20.1 (1997): 23.

⁹ See Hannah Arendt, *The Human Condition* (Chicago: University of Chicago Press, 1958), 18. Arendt writes, "The Greek's concern with immortality grew out of their experience of an immortal nature and immortal gods which together surrounded the individual lives of mortal men. Embedded in a cosmos where everything was immortal, mortality became the hallmark of human existence. Men are 'the mortals,' the only mortal beings in existence, because unlike animals they do not exist only as members of a species whose immortal life is guaranteed through procreation. [Arendt cites Aristotle *Economics*, 1343b24: Nature guarantees to the species their being forever through recurrence (*periodos*), but cannot guarantee such being forever to the individual.] The mortality of men lies in the fact that individual life, with a recognizable life-story from birth to death, rises out of biological life. This individual life is distinguished from all other things by the rectilinear course of its movement, which, so to speak, cuts through the circular movement of biological life. This is mortality: to move along a rectilinear line in a universe where everything, if it moves at all, moves in a cyclical order."

I am obviously indebted to Arendt for the identification of a life-story from birth to death and its rectilinearity as phenomenological traits. I would add that rectilinearity also implies individuality, finitude, and irreversibility. It also means inability to control, arrest, or hasten this "movement." I differ significantly from Arendt in considering "mortality" to be the fundamental sense of temporality, and the universe with its eternal and immortal objects appear so only from this mortal point of view. Biological immortality, achieved through circularity, is an excessively Aristotelian feature underlining *entelechia*. I argue that the pre Socratic view of time as coming-to-be and perishing preserves the sense of individuality and thus rectilinearity throughout the cosmos, and to us also through biological life. Thus Parmenides' cosmology is a mortal cosmology, and circularity is reserved for the goddess' argument for eternal being (fr. 5). Mortality is not only essential to understanding the mortal cosmos, but also that which is not mortal, be it eternal or immortal, and thus mortality is the fundamental phenomenological trait. Within the epistemological sphere, I argue that human mortality, with its individuality, finitude, and singularity, as well as its uncontrollability, is fundamental to the epistemological project.

¹⁰ M. Merleau-Ponty writes: "The feeling of eternity is a hypocritical one, for eternity feeds on time. The fountain retains its identity only because of the continuous pressure of water. Eternity is the time that belongs to dreaming, and the dream refers back to waking life, from which it borrows all its structures. Of what nature, then, is that waking time in which eternity takes root?" As quoted by Charles M. Sherover, *The Human Experience of Time* (New York: New York University Press, 1975), ii. The original citation is from M. Merleau-Ponty, *Phenomenology of Perception*, trans. Colin Smith (London: Routledge & Kegan Paul, 1962), 377.

¹¹ Socrates may allude to his own mortality at another point. He expresses a wish for philosophical students and successors (143d–e). Benardete asks, "Is Socrates, then looking for his own successor?" Seth Benardete, *Plato's Theaetetus* (Chicago: University of Chicago Press, 1986), 88.

¹² F. M. Cornford, *Plato's Theory of Knowledge* (New York: Humanities Press, 1935), 101–2.

¹³ *Theaetetus* 183e, trans. Cornford; emphasis added. The phrase "one being" is a nice pun in the Greek on Eleatic monism, well preserved in Cornford's translation (as noted by Cornford, ibid., 101, n. 1). With this pun, Socrates challenges and replaces the one being of Eleatic monism (*hen on*), the most extreme foundation for stable knowledge, with the most ephemeral, individual reality (*hena onta Parmeniden*). In my readings of both Parmenides and Plato's *Phaedrus*, in subsequent chapters, I will show that the temporality of radical individuality provides an inescapable challenge to stable knowledge—a fact Socrates, in my view, was clearly aware of.

¹⁴ Traditionally, the "parricide" has been equated with the overturning of Parmenides' monistic doctrine. On a deeper level, however, applying the doctrine to the man makes it impossible for him to have existed. This is the sense in which I take "parricide": erasure of the mortal man, rather than his doctrine. For an example of the latter, that is, parricide as overturning Parmenides' doctrine, see Kenneth Sayre, *Plato's Late Ontology: A Riddle Resolved* (Princeton: Princeton University Press, 1983); second edition with a new introduction and the essay, "Excess and deficiency at Statesman 283C–285C" (Las Vegas: Parmenides Publishing, 2005). "Before Plato is ready to attempt an integration of his accounts of becoming and of being into a coherent theory of participation, however, another important problem from the *Theaetetus* must be resolved. Although λόγος is made possible by the weaving together of Forms (*Sophist* 259E5–6), not every case of λόγος is a case of knowledge. It is just the difference between true and false discourse, in fact, that ultimately marks the difference between philosophy and sophistry. To complete the 'official' mission of the *Sophist*, which is to make the nature of the latter clear, the distinction between truth and falsity in judgment must be firmly established. To complete its account of being, in turn, which is the more substantial purpose of the dialogue, is to show how the objects of knowledge (the Forms) must be related to make the distinction between true and false judgment possible. To this end Plato develops an account of not-being (of what is not) that remains among his more impressive accomplishments of the intermediate period. The sophist is a producer of semblance in discourse, which means that he influences our minds 'to think things that are not' (240D9). What we thus understand him as doing, however, is precisely what Parmenides had proclaimed not to be understandable at all. 'That it is not,' he said, 'is not to be said or thought' (Kirk and Raven, 1995, fr. 347.8–9)

rather, 'all that can be thought is the thought that it is' (ibid, fr. 352.1). Thus to complete his definition of the sophist's art, the Stranger must engage in a form of parricide (241d3), and show that 'what is not' can be thought after all" (228–9).

[15] I use the term "mortal cosmology" here to refer to the goddess' second speech, in which she describes the entire cosmos as coming-to-be and perishing and as ruled over by a goddess of "hateful birth and mixing" (*stugeroio tokou kai mixios*, fr. 12; my translation). A "mortal cosmology," as I define it, is one that pays attention to the aspect of the cosmos' participation in change, and hence, in mortality. The thought of a mortal cosmos, however, is not unique to Parmenides; the idea can also be found in Empedocles and in Heraclitus. On Heraclitus, see my paper "Heraclitus on *Thanatos*," in *Abstracts of the 136th Annual Meeting of the American Philological Association*, Philadelphia 2005.

[16] See, for example, Plato's *Theaetetus* 152e–153, 160d, 179e for the relationship between sophistry and Heracliteanism. See also Walter Pater, who writes, "sophistry is a reproduction of the Heraclitean flux. The old Heraclitean physical theory presents itself as a natural basis for the moral, social dissolution, which the sophistical movement promotes." Walter Pater, *Plato and Platonism* (Whitefish, MT: Kessinger Publishing, 2004), 68.

[17] The phrase "aporia of time" comes from Ned Lukacher, who refers to "the enigmatic character of the question of time . . . that which is neither becoming nor eternity and yet both of them at once . . . Rigorously speaking, we cannot say whether time is finite or infinite, or if there is an infinite series of finite universes that rise and fall, or whether creation is sequentially singular or simultaneously multiple (i.e., 'the multiverse'). We can, however, consider what has been said, what arguments, concepts, words, and images have been used to indicate the persistent aporia of time and/or to conceal, evade, or simply ignore it." *Time-Fetishes: The Secret History of Eternal Recurrence* (Durham, NC: Duke University Press, 1998), 4–5.

[18] The paradox of time is only apparently resolved by Aristotelian substance ontology, for it postulates an uncanny and unknown "x" (Aristotle's "substance" or *hupokeimenon*) as the bearer of all changes.

[19] Contrast, however, Aristotle's view: for him, the essence of tragedy lies in its thematization of *hamartia* or human error (cf. Aristotle, *Poetics* 1453a). In the *New Testament*, two broad categories of sin are described. The first category is *hamartia*, roughly translated as "sin" (see Matthew 1.21, 3.6, 9.2 for examples). The second category is *parabasis* ("transgression"), referred to in Romans 2.23, 4.15, 5.14.

[20] See, for example, Marcel Détienne, *The Daily Life of the Greek Gods* (Stanford: Stanford University Press, 2000) and R. B. Onians, *The Origins of European Thought* (Cambridge: Cambridge University Press, 1951).

[21] Indeed, this is the meaning of his famous Copernican revolution where he proposes that objects must conform to our knowledge (B XVI). Knowledge for Kant is essentially experience containing two components: a sensory and a rational, subjective component. Further, sense intuition is always spatial and temporal because space and time are forms of sense-perception.

[22] Martin Heidegger, *On Time and Being*, trans. J. Stambaugh (New York: Harper & Row, 1972), 6–9.

[23] Martin Heidegger, *An Introduction to Metaphysics*, trans. Ralph Manheim (New Haven and London: Yale University Press, 1959).

24 Cf. Martin Heidegger, *Early Greek Thinking*, trans. David Farrell Krell and Frank A. Capuzzi (San Francisco: Harper, 1984).

25 Cf. Schürmann, *Heidegger on Being and Acting*.

26 "Being-in-the-world" should be read here in its full Heideggerian resonances of denoting, not only our factical, worldly being, but also its "being-toward-death." In this sense, it maintains a sense of our mortal temporality in contrast to the intrinsically human urge to overcome this temporality through metaphysics. However, the notion of mortal singularity for which I argue here differs in one key aspect from Heidegger's "being-in-the-world": Heidegger's notion has specific theological and Lutheran resonances, which I reject (see the concluding chapter of this work).

27 Thus the natural sciences, epistemology, and logic are all metaphysical.

28 There are, to be sure, different kinds of *logos*, such as biography which, in contrast to bibliography, maintains the temporal and personal dimensions of human existence. See also the section on myth "Recipe for Individuality: Dialogue and Myth" on pages 99–101.

29 Friedrich Nietzsche, *The Twilight of the Idols* (Cambridge: Cambridge University Press, 2005), s.v. "How the True World Became a Fable."

30 Heidegger, "The Question Concerning Technology," 307–41.

31 While this idea of a unique, unidirectional, non-reversible temporality may seem to have much in common with Heidegger's notion of "Jeweiligkeit" (translated by Theodor Kisiel as "the particular while" or "temporal particularity" and with the meaning of *being* one's respective time, having a limited time, etc.), there are important differences between my notion of temporal singularity and Heidegger's *Jeweiligkeit*. As I argue in the conclusion to this work, Heidegger's notion of the uniqueness of human being is intrinsically related to his reappropration of Luther's project of a destruction of the *theologia gloriae* by a *theologia crucis*; thus what he seeks to recover with the notion of *Jeweiligkeit* is a specifically Christian and Pauline experience of time as open to the arrival of Christ in the *parousia*, that is, as the time of *awaiting*. Even when the theological notion of arrival is replaced by the "phenomenological" event of death, the basic motif remains the same: Heidegger's time is radically eschatological. Heidegger's appropriation of Luther is thus characterized by its emphasis on *Diesmaligkeit* (this-time-liness) or *Diesseitigkeit* (immanence, this-world-liness), which leads to a corresponding devaluation of transcendence. Heidegger thus separates the experience of the here and now (Heidegger's "facticity" or "being-in-the-world") from the experience of enduring being (the subject of Parmenides' goddess' first speech). In other words, Heidegger's notion of *Jeweiligkeit* precisely undoes what I have here called "the crossing of mortals and immortals," the attempt and the need to think eternity and temporality together in their problematic, paradoxical relationship. See my paper "Heidegger's Encounter with Aristotle: A Theological Deconstruction of Metaphysics" presented at the 44th Annual Meeting of the Heidegger Circle, Stony Brook University, New York, May 2010. For an excellent overview of the Lutheran background to Heidegger's early thought, see the recent book by Dimitrios Yfantis: *Die Auseinandersetzung des frühen Heidegger mit Aristoteles* (Berlin: Duncker & Humblot, 2009).

32 And yet, this attitude differs from that which Heidegger refers to as "being-toward-death" (*Sein zum Tode*), for the latter merely serves a hermeneutic function, rather than characterizing the concrete existent. *Sein zum Tode* serves only to

bring Dasein's being as a whole into view, which is a precondition for carrying out the existential analytic of Dasein with a sufficient degree of originality. The existential analytic of Dasein itself is proposed as a propadeutic to the inquiry into being (*Seinsfrage*). The question of mortality is absent from Heidegger's thought, and when it does appear, as in the latter essays *The Origin of the Work of Art* and *Building, Dwelling, Thinking*, it is still bereft of all singularity. Heidegger, in pursuit of a philosophy as a "rigorous science," and seeking to avoid accusations of professing a *Lebensphilosophie*, would rather not talk about how one ought to live or die. He discounts philosophical *mūthos*, claiming: "The first philosophical step in understanding the problem of being consists in avoiding the *mython tina diēgeisthai*, in not 'telling a story,' that is, not determining beings as beings by tracing them back in their origins to another being—as if being had the character of a possible being." Martin Heidegger, *Being and Time*, trans. Joan Stambaugh (Albany, NY: SUNY Press, 1996), 5. However, in doing so, he loses sight of singularity altogether—as I will show later. In this, he could have learnt from Plato, who uses initiation in the sense of a near-death experience to mark the domain of singularity. See now Peter Kingsley, *The Dark Places of Wisdom* (Inverness, CA: Golden Sufi Center, 1999). Heidegger also conspicuously lacks a notion of natality, so that any putative singularity in Heidegger can, at best, be incomplete.

[33] Theodor Gomperz, *Greek Thinkers*, vol. 1, trans. Laurie Magnus (London: John Murray, 1901), 246–62.

[34] Ibid., 246–8.

[35] Ibid.

[36] Ibid.; emphasis added.

[37] Jan Bremmer, *Early Greek Concept of the Soul* (Princeton: Princeton University Press, 1987).

[38] C. P. Caswell, "Study of *Thumos* in Early Greek Epic," *Mnemosyne* Suppl. 144 (1990): 12.

[39] Ibid., 14.

[40] Ibid., 14. The passage is from *Iliad* ix.318–22 (trans. Caswell).

[41] Gomperz, *Greek Thinkers*, 249.

[42] I refer, of course, to the separation of emotion from purely cognitive functions in Descartes, arguably the first "modern" thinker in this respect. Contemporary scholars, however, such as Robert Solomon and Martha Nussbaum are more sensitive to the cognitive aspects of emotion.

[43] S. Darcus Sullivan, "How a Person Relates to θυμός in Homer," *Indogermanische Forschungen* 85 (1985): 142.

[44] Caswell, "Study of *Thumos* in Early Greek Epic," 22.

[45] Sullivan, "How a Person Relates to θυμός in Homer," 138.

[46] "All these things concern me, lady; but I should feel dreadfully ashamed before the Trojans and the Trojan women of the trailing robes if, like a coward, I should shrink from battle. Nor does my θυμός bid me, since I learned to be noble" (*Iliad* vi.441–5).

[47] See Sullivan, "How a Person Relates to θυμός in Homer."

[48] In the J & E documents of the early Hebrews, soul is likewise identified with the blood. The name of this "blood-soul" is Nephesh. Any shedding of blood including menstruation makes one unclean in as much as it is associated with death and its attendant pollution. In pre-seventh century BCE, this soul was

thought to leave the body upon death and was drained of its sanguinity in the Sheol. There was no individual existence in Sheol, which is called the realm of the shades. This ancient Hebraic thought was influenced later by Babylonian dualism and Alexandrian Greek influences. The consequent Hebraic eschatology differs from the earlier one in henceforth positing an afterlife where the individual soul in Sheol retains a discrete existence. The theological event of judgement after life with a possibility of resurrection has its roots in this later Pharasaic doctrine of the soul. See J. Pedersen, *Israel*, vol. 1 (London: Oxford University Press, 1929). For the purposes of my study here, "blood" is a metaphor for mortality, and I am not interested in the postmortem fate of Nephesh, *psukhē*, *ātman*, and other psychological entities that endure beyond the event of an individual's death.

49 Gomperz, *Greek Thinkers*, 249–50.

50 Erwin Rohde, *Psyche: The Cult of Souls and Belief in Immortality among the Greeks*, vol. 1, trans. W. B. Hillis (New York: Harper & Row, 1966), 50–1.

51 Sullivan, "How a Person Relates to θυμός in Homer," 142. The *thumos* was "an active agent in Homer . . . *thumos* actively performs a wide range of activities in a person. It engages in intellectual activity, feels emotion; it wills, hopes, desires, orders, and urges on. It can depart from a person causing his death. In all cases *thumos* is distinct from the person but by its activity can in large measure determine his behavior."

52 The proper explication of duplication as the necessary prerequisite for phenomenal appearing, perception, knowing, and thinking is beyond the scope of this study. It will be sufficient to note the "doubling" of the self in Parmenides' conversation with his *thumos*. Such a basic understanding of doubling persists in our vocabulary today in words like "reflection" in the sense of thinking. When I think I do not create another world in my head; I simply think the one world that exists phenomenally. Yet we use the term "reflection" as if there were a copy of the world in my head. The doubling of the self, implied in Parmenides' use of *thumos* in line 1 is universalized in the speech of the goddess when she says, the same are thinking and being (fr. 3). Thinking here is not a copy of being, or vice versa.

53 Caswell, "Study of *Thumos* in Early Greek Epic," 14.

54 Sullivan, "How a Person Relates to the θυμός in Homer," 138–50.

55 Sullivan, "How a Person Relates to the θυμός in Homer," 148. In Parmenides' poem, note that being, discussed in relation to *noos*, is "shackled" by *moira*. The discussion of being in relation to *thumos*, that is, in the proem, is capable of "reaching" the very limits of *dikē*, and transgressing these limits, albeit provisionally.

56 The blending of emotion and intellect, separated by Plato with long-lasting consequences, should not surprise us; notice, for example, in the *Old Testament*, the close relationship between shame and mortality, both of which arise from the same fruit.

57 S. Montiglio analyzes journey in this sense in early Greek thinkers in his "Wandering Philosophers in Classical Greece," *Journal of Hellenic Studies* 120 (2000): 86–105.

58 Aristotle wrestles with this. To explain motion, he posits a stable Prime Mover, itself unmoved. The love (*erōs*) of beings for the Prime Mover impels their motion. We might relate *erōs* and *thumos* here. Hegel, likewise, begins the dialectical-historical journey of the Spirit with Desire (B.iv.167). *Phenomenology of Spirit*, trans. A. V. Miller (Oxford: Oxford University Press, 1977), 105.

[59] To be sure, *methodos* had this meaning even in ancient Greek. Only in modern philosophy, however, does the method become the exclusive focus of the philosophical enterprise. The argument here is not etymological but descriptive in relation to the history of philosophy.

[60] The return is "tragic" because it embodies the tragic wisdom of Silenus which Nietzsche articulates in *The Birth of Tragedy*. But this tragic return is undertaken joyfully as a heroic act; the notion does not imply an attitude of *ressentiment* nor is it a return in an attitude of awaiting for some longed-after salvation. Thus my notion of return is ultimately closer to both Nietzsche's doctrine of "eternal recurrence" which stands at the end of metaphysics and the early Greek notion of transmigration of the soul which stands at its inception than to Heidegger's philosophy. Although I share Heidegger's concern with mortality, I reject his adoption of an eschatological notion of time ("ecstatic time" or "existential time" which is characterized by its relation to what remains "outstanding"). As I argue below (see the conclusion to this work), Heidegger's existential analytic ultimately draws heavily upon a Lutheran and Pauline interpretation of Christianity, whereas I would read Christ himself as articulating a tragic wisdom. The concept of singularity, as I understand it, is thus closer to the tragic aspects of Christ's passion than to the Pauline interpretation of salvation.

[61] I thus read Homer as a precursor of the Greek thinkers, in contrast to much of the subsequent tradition. I believe my reading to be supported by the fact that Plato clearly sees Homer as one of his great rivals: he repeatedly contrasts the Homeric philosophical and pedagogical approaches with his own program.

[62] Joydeep Bagchee's recent dissertation "Return to Transcendence: The Project of *Being and Time* and the Problem of Human Finitude" provides an original reading of Heidegger in that he uses the concept of authenticity in Heidegger to explore a breakdown in Heidegger's existential analyses. Bagchee uses this breakdown to break open the hermeneutic circle set up by Heidegger and interprets this move as a "return to transcendence." Bagchee thus implicitly opposes Heidegger's homecoming which is essentially political and bound up with *Volk* with a notion that has close resonances to Schürmann's notions of "dehiscence" and of singularity.

Chapter 2: Parmenides and His Importance as a Beginner

[1] The search for thematic consistency might itself be a typically modern obsession. For example, Pindar's *Odes* begin a certain theme, break off, and begin another. But in the case of Parmenides, consistency is demanded by the very content of the poem, which is brought out most clearly by the goddess' insistence on the principle of non-contradiction. Mortals, according to her, are led astray by their "two-headed" *logoi*.

[2] I explain this further in Chapter 6.

[3] The actual purpose may have been political, rather than a philosophical discussion. Peter Kingsley argues this in his *In the Dark Places of Wisdom*, but he has in mind the analogy of Gorgias' later visit to Athens.

⁴ Taran, *Parmenides: A Text with Translation*, 4; G. S. Kirk, J. E. Raven, and M. S. Schofield, eds., *The Presocratic Philosophers* (Cambridge: Cambridge University Press, 1983), 239–41; Patricia Curd, *The Legacy of Parmenides* (Princeton: Princeton University Press, 1998), 16.

⁵ Diogenes *Laertius* IX.23, relying on Apollodorus (cited in Taran, *Parmenides: A Text with Translation*, 3).

⁶ Diogenes *Laertius* states that Parmenides was taught by Ameinias the Pythagorean (D.L. IX.21). Kingsley develops this connection the most in his *In the Dark Places of Wisdom*.

⁷ Curd, *The Legacy of Parmenides*, 17, with reference to the work of D. Graham.

⁸ Friedrich Nietzsche, *Philosophy in the Tragic Age of the Greeks*, trans. M. Cowan (Washington, DC: Gateway Editions, 1962), 69.

⁹ David Gallop, *Parmenides of Elea: Fragments* (Toronto: University of Toronto Press, 1984), 3.

¹⁰ For the ordering and (to a large extent) the Greek text of the fragments, the edition of Diels-Kranz (known as DK: see Bibliography) has become canonical. Later scholars quibble about particular readings here and there, and sometimes the order of a few short fragments (for notable examples, see Taran and Coxon), or even attempt to identify new fragments (such as the so-called Cornford's fragment). This notwithstanding, almost all use the DK text as a starting-point. On Cornford's fragment, see Gallop, *Parmenides of Elea: Fragments*, 90–1.

¹¹ The dualism perhaps applies to the cosmology section. Some scholars believe that Aristotle interprets Parmenides as "an holistic monist, an advocate of the doctrine that 'all things are one'." Alexander P. D. Mourelatos, *The Route of Parmenides* (New Haven and London: Yale University Press, 1970), 130. For a full discussion, see Harold F. Cherniss, *Aristotle's Criticism of Presocratic Philosophy* (Baltimore: Johns Hopkins University Press, 1935). See also Guthrie, *A History of Greek Philosophy*, vol. 2, 55–7 and Taran, *Parmenides. A Text with Translation*, 269–91. Mourelatos, however, finds Taran's judgment ("Aristotle's testimony concerning Parmenides is of almost no value") "too harsh." I am more inclined to support Taran here.

¹² Alexander Nehamas, "On Parmenides' Three Ways of Inquiry," *Deukalion* (1981): 102.

¹³ Curd introduces the thesis on page 3 and argues it in detail throughout her book *The Legacy of Parmenides*.

¹⁴ Schürmann, "Tragic Differing," 5.

¹⁵ Ibid., 1.

¹⁶ Heidegger, "Moira," 100–1.

¹⁷ Heidegger, *Parmenides*, 1.

¹⁸ Schürmann, "Ultimate Double Binds," 213–36.

¹⁹ The tragic reading of Parmenides I have advanced here is not as far-fetched as may initially seem: Kouremenos has already noted that "The link between Parmenides and Aeschylus is the distinction between seeming and being, the cornerstone of Parmenidean metaphysics and theory of knowledge. This distinction appears prominently in Ag. 788–789." Theokritos Kouremenos, "Parmenidean Influences in the 'Agamemnon' of Aeschylus," *Hermes*, vol. 121, no. 3 (1993): 259. Kouremenos continues, "In Ag. 788–789 Aeschylus contrasts explicitly δοχεῖν

and εἶναι, a term introduced into philosophy by Parmenides and not attested in pre-Parmenidean thought." (ibid., 260). "The Aeschylean γλῶσσαν νέμων and Parmenidean γλῶσσαν νωμᾶν show the same degree of conceptual overlapping." (ibid., 264). "Parmenides chided mortals who confuse being and non-being thus bridging the two mutually exclusive notions of παλίντροπος . . . (6.9). Aeschylus used the non-epic, probably coined by Parmenides, adjective παλίντροπος (Ag. 777) in order to describe Dike's averting eyes as she shuns δοχεῖν in favor of εἶναι . . . Aeschylus' use of παλίντροπος seems to reflect the character of the relationship between Parmenides and Aeschylus: instead of banning out of existence the logically deplorable tension between being and non-being, δοχεῖν and εἶναι, Aeschylus conceived it in moral terms and emphasized the moral superiority of εἶναι following the logical and ontological principles of Parmenides" (ibid., 265). More recently, Reiner Schürmann also argued for an Aeschylean reading of Parmenides in his *magnum opus Broken Hegemonies*.

[20] "In essential history the beginning comes last." Heidegger, *Parmenides*, 1.

[21] Herrmann Diels, *Parmenides Lehrgedicht* (Berlin: Georg Reimer, 1897), 14–18.

[22] Walter Burkert, "Das Proömium des Parmenides und die Katabasis des Pythagoras," *Phronesis* 15 (1969): 1–30; translated by Joydeep Bagchee as "Parmenides' Proem and Pythagoras' Descent," in *Philosophy and Salvation in Greek Religion*, ed. Vishwa Adluri (Berlin: Walter de Gruyter, 2012).

[23] Kingsley, *In the Dark Places of Wisdom*.

[24] Kirk, Raven, and Schofield, *The Presocratic Philosophers*, 241.

[25] Heidegger, *Parmenides*, 70.

[26] Socrates also talks in the *Phaedrus* about the problem of how to read myths; see my discussion in Chapter 6.

[27] The first *muthos* is a narrative of journey, the second a narrative of unchanging being where no movement is possible. The poem joins together these two separate *muthoi* which would otherwise exclude each other on a common-sense or discursive level, introducing a new experience of journey—one specific to the poem.

[28] See, for example, Taran, *Parmenides: A Text with Translation*, 31: "As for the meaning of the proem, the wording of its text is sufficient to prove that Parmenides did not intend his journey to be taken as a reality in any sense . . . The proem is not a reference to a specific occasion . . . Neither is there symbolism in the proem . . . the goddess . . . only stands as a literary device implying that the 'revelation' is the truth discovered by Parmenides himself. Parmenides could not have attributed any reality to the goddess because for him there exists only one thing, the unique and homogenous Being . . . This definitely settles the question that the proem is only a literary device."

Chapter 3: The Mortal Journey:
Thumos (The Mortal Soul) and Its Limits

[1] In my work, I give a coherent account of all the fragments that are extant. There is a hermeneutic problem here: how can I give a complete account of an incom-

plete text? I am making the assumption that if the rest of the poem were available, it would not change the substance of my interpretation.

² As cited by W. K. C. Guthrie, *A History of Greek Philosophy*, 2 vols. (Cambridge: Cambridge University Press, 1962–65), 4.

³ Scholars have followed Diels in his division of the fragments into A: Testimonia (i.e., fragments about the author) and B: Fragmenta (i.e., what are thought to be genuine words of the author), although perhaps this division needs to be rethought. See J. Mansfeld, "Sources," in *The Cambridge Companion to Early Greek Philosophy*, ed. A. A. Long (Cambridge: Cambridge University Press, 1999), 22–44. In this study, I have attempted a coherent interpretation of the actual fragments, making little use of the testimonia.

⁴ This is O'Brien's translation; see now Denis O'Brien, *Études sur Parménide, Tome I* (Paris: Librairie Philosophique, 1987), 16. While it is true that *komizō* can mean "to attend, give heed to," which I think is appropriate (and safe) for this line, one cannot ignore its use as a verb of conveyance, especially as a verb of conveyance for the purpose of preservation. For full range of possible nuances, one should confer *LSJ*, s.v. *komizō*.

⁵ Mourelatos, *The Route of Parmenides*. Here is a good place to acknowledge the immense scholarship and wisdom of Prof. Mourelatos.

⁶ C. M. Bowra, "The Proem of Parmenides," *Classical Philology* 32 (1937): 97–112; Eric A. Havelock, "Parmenides and Odysseus," *Harvard Studies in Classical Philology* 63 (1958): 133–43; A. H. Coxon, *The Fragments of Parmenides* (Assen: Van Gorcum, 1986), 9–12.

⁷ Kingsley, *In the Dark Places of Wisdom*, 64.

⁸ Havelock, "Parmenides and Odysseus," 140.

⁹ When Odysseus arrives at his home on Ithaka, his old dog, Argus, first recognizes him. The dog wags his tail in faithful recognition and dies happily. This poignant image mirrors Odysseus' own faithfulness to his mortality. I thank John R. Lenz for this insight.

¹⁰ *Odyssey*, book xi. Here Odysseus' longing is precisely the opposite of the *kouros' thumos*: a return home rather than a journey into the unknown. Further, Odysseus is given a prophecy and the *kouros* a philosophical analysis, and the former is given a hint of death and the latter a hint of eternity. In fact Parmenides is turning Odysseus' underworld journey upside down. A reading placing the goddess high in the aether beyond the gates is more plausible as it is a suitable match for the goddess' message.

¹¹ Kingsley usefully points this out in his *In the Dark Places of Wisdom*. Havelock writes as if thought went straight from Homer to Parmenides in his "Parmenides and Odysseus," 133–43.

¹² Peter Kingsley, *Ancient Philosophy, Mystery, and Magic: Empedocles and Pythagorean Tradition* (Oxford: Clarendon Press, 1995).

¹³ Mourelatos, *The Route of Parmenides*, 41: "The myth and topography of the journey must have a certain impressionistic, sketchy, dreamy quality precisely to prevent identifications with persons and places familiar from the epic. Such identifications would have gotten in the way of using the traditional material to formulate new concepts. Parmenides can write clearly when he wants. The vagueness is intrinsic to the proem. The attempts of modern scholars to reconstruct itinerary and topography by inference could seem to go against the intent of the poet's

language." For attempts to chart the itinerary see, for example, J. Mansfeld, "Critical Note: Empedocles and His Interpreters," *Phronesis* 50 (1995): 109–15; Burkert, "Das Proömium des Parmenides und die Katabasis des Pythagoras," 1–30; Maja E. Pellikaan-Engel, *Hesiod and Parmenides. A New View on Their Cosmologies and on Parmenides' Proem* (Amsterdam: Adolf M. Hakkert, 1974); Kingsley, *In the Dark Places of Wisdom.*

[14] Mourelatos, *The Route of Parmenides*, 3.

[15] Heidegger, *Parmenides*, 2–3.

[16] Kingsley, *In the Dark Places of Wisdom*, 118.

[17] Charles Kahn, "The Thesis of Parmenides," *Review of Metaphysics* 22 (1969): 700–24.

[18] Ibid., 705.

[19] See Taran, *Parmenides: A Text with Translation*, 17–23, for criticisms of Sextus' interpretive methods.

[20] Ibid., 31.

[21] Ibid.

[22] Ibid., 9.

[23] Kingsley translates this "as far as longing can reach." *In the Dark Places of Wisdom*, 53. Gallop translates as "as far as impulse might reach." *Parmenides of Elea: Fragments*, 49. Both do not say that this emotion belongs to Parmenides in particular, but take it in general terms as a relative clause of characteristic, reading *thumos* generally as an attribute of humanity: as humanity's longing. Taran explains it in the same way, although he assumes the desire must be that of either Parmenides himself or of the mares, and argues for the former (9–10), correctly in my opinion, translating "as far as ever my heart may desire." *Parmenides: A Text and Translation*, 8. O'Brien, too, ascribes the longing to Parmenides, translating "aussi loin que puisse parvenir mon désir." *Études sur Parménide, Tome I*, 3.

[24] See, for example, Albin Lesky, *Greek Tragic Poetry*, trans. M. Dillon (New Haven: Yale University Press, 1983), 110–14. For an insightful analysis of the problem of double determination, see Arbogast Schmitt, "Self-Determination and Freedom: The Relationship of God and Man in Homer," in *Philosophy and Salvation in Greek Religion*, ed. Vishwa Adluri (Berlin: Walter de Gruyter, 2012). Schmitt argues against the modern prejudice that the Greek notion of double determination is the product of a deficiently self-conscious reflection on the nature of human autonomy.

[25] E. R. Dodds, *The Greeks and the Irrational* (Berkeley and Los Angeles: University of California Press, 1957).

[26] This view, famously associated with Bruno Snell has been challenged by Bernard Williams among others. See Bruno Snell, *The Discovery of the Mind*, trans. T. G. Rosenmeyer (Cambridge, MA: Harvard University Press, 1953). See also Bernard Williams, *Shame and Necessity* (Berkeley, CA: University of California Press, 1993).

[27] Snell's mistake, in my view, lies precisely herein. *The Discovery of the Mind*; see esp. chs. 1 and 3.

[28] Snell, *The Discovery of the Mind*; Williams, *Shame and Necessity*, 21–6.

[29] The journey "as far as *thumos* might reach" disproves Kingsely's argument that the journey is a *katabasis* to Hades. A journey to Hades is possible only for *psukhē*, as only the *psukhē* survives the terminal event of a mortal being: death. Unlike Odysseus, whose *katabasis* is undertaken to collect information, the Parmenidean

kouros desires to overcome his own mortality. Hence it is important to maintain the *psukhē* versus *thumos* distinction; Hades lies beyond the reach of the *thumos*. Kingsley is correct about the mortal connotations of this journey. However, the goddess does not "cure" mortality, especially through "magic." Conversely, by showing him that the desired immortality, as described by the goddess, is not available to him except in *logos*, the poem neutralizes the "magical," "pharmaka-logic" effects of metaphysical *logoi*.

30 On a textual problem in this line, see note to the translation. I take it that the *kouros* has become the "man who knows" before, and as a prerequisite to, the present journey.

31 Roberto Calasso, *The Marriage of Cadmus and Harmony* (New York: Vintage, 1993), 11–12.

32 Diels, *Parmenides Lehrgedicht*, 117–51. For Diels' interest in ancient technology, see the biographical essay in W. M. Calder III and W. Briggs, eds., *Classical Scholarship: A Biographical Encyclopedia* (New York: Garland, 1990). Interestingly, Diels' son received the Nobel Prize in Chemistry.

33 Kingsley, *In the Dark Places of Wisdom*, 127.

34 Ibid., 129–30.

35 In fact, a long metaphysical tradition of allegorizing *molu* as *logos*, a cure for the soul, or as *paideia*, grew up in antiquity, later Greek philosophy, and Christianity. See Hugo Rahner, *Greek Myths and Christian Mystery* (London: Burnes and Oates, 1963), 179–277; see esp. ch. 5, "Moly and Mandragora in Pagan and Christian Symbolism." See also Alfred Heubeck and Arie Hoekstra, eds., *A Commentary on Homer's Odyssey*, vol. II (Oxford: Oxford University Press, 1989), 61. However, this meaning of *molu* differs from mine. From the time of a poem in the Greek Anthology (cf. Rahner, *Greek Myths*, 182), *molu* was allegorized as a charm for mortal men to reach immortality. I stress the delimiting boundary between mortals and immortals. Odysseus here protects himself against immortal powers (Circe's), just as he rejects the immortality of Kalypso. *Molu* is apotropaic. The word may be cognate with Sanskrit *mulam*, "root" (cf. Heubeck and Hoekstra, *A Commentary on Homer's Odyssey*, 60).

36 See Chapter 7. All *logoi* are potentially *pharmaka*, not merely writing. Their pharmaka-logic properties are related to the temporal *aporia*, where mortality and immortality intersect.

37 I have modified the usual classicist's view of *phusis* and *tekhnē* as exclusive opposites. For the generally accepted views on nature/culture, *phusis/nomos* distinctions, see Guthrie, *A History of Greek Philosophy*, vol. 1. See also Bruce S. Thornton, *Erōs: The Myth of Ancient Greek Sexuality* (Boulder, CO: Westview Press, 1998).

38 Of course technical objects also change, decay. But as with the gods, all we can perceive is that their *aiōn* exceeds ours. In the case of technical objects, strictly speaking, we cannot speak about an *aiōn*. For mortals, technical objects seem to endure. The relevant point here is the relationship between human mortality and technical objects, which seem to mortals to be immune to mortality.

39 Kingsley, *In the Dark Places of Wisdom*.

40 A slightly different account of ritual as technology is presented by Bruce Thornton. He writes "Hence ancient ritual and worship are important 'technologies,' for they attempt to control for the practitioner's benefit the numinous power embodied in the god or goddess." *Erōs: The Myth of Ancient Greek Sexuality*, 7.

41 This differs from the dominant view of Greek sacrifice which, following Durkheim, sees it as purely social. See, for example, Walter Burkert, *Homo Necans*, trans. Peter Bing (Berkeley: University of California Press, 1983) and Marcel Détienne and Jean-Pierre Vernant, *The Cuisine of Sacrifice among the Greeks*, trans. Paula Wissing (Chicago: University of Chicago Press, 1989).

42 Plato accuses the Sophists of making *logos* into a pure *tekhnē* (cf. the criticism of Lysias' speech in the *Phaedrus*), whereas he grounds *logos* in *phusis*.

43 I believe Plato immortalizes the domination of *thumos* by *psukhē*.

44 It is thus misguided to downgrade Heidegger's longing for a community and for a *Heimat* as being a purely idiosyncratic longing, whether for a Nazi state or for a rustic hut in the Black Forest. To preserve a *nostos* and to escape being constituted by technology, we need only identify ourselves with what technology excludes: our radical individuality, *thumos*, and mortality. To succumb to those definitions that exceed mortal *aiōn*, and to define the other as German, Muslim, Woman or Homosexual is dangerous. Heidegger's entanglement with National Socialism teaches us that large and profound philosophies do not insulate us from the ethics of mortality, where individuals encounter each other as *singulars*. My relating the Heideggerian *Heimat* to *nostos* is textually based on Heidegger's definition of philosophy. Following Novalis' insight, "Philosophy is really home-sickness, an urge to be at home everywhere," Heidegger defines homesickness as the "fundamental attunement of philosophizing." *The Fundamental Concepts of Metaphysics*, trans. W. McNeill and N. Walker (Bloomington, IN: Indiana University Press, 1995), 5. Two parallels between my thesis and Heidegger's are: "Urge" translates the German *Trieb*. Heidegger makes much use of this word and its cognates in analyzing "pre-philosophical" states, such as boredom and animal life (ibid., part 2). I prefer the Greek idiom, and my analysis of *thumos* translates it as "urge" to be sure, but without regarding this urge as something purely 'pre' philosophical: it is the agent that has at its disposal the technology—*poiēsis* and *logos*—by which it seeks to metaphysically overcome its mortality.

Philosophy, in the sense that I champion, is closer to *thumos* than *nous* or critical thinking. Obviously, the latter faculties are in the service of *thumos*. In "mortal rectitude," these sophisticated faculties critique themselves and expose the *thumos* to itself as fleeing mortality—first in grief and then in anxiety. Mortal rectitude as destruction of metaphysics allows the philosopher to transcend metaphysical immortality.

A second parallel is the notion of individuation. Heidegger writes, "If we wish to truly become what we are, we cannot abandon this finitude or abandon it, we must safeguard it. In becoming finite, however, there ultimately occurs an individuation of man with respect to his Dasein. Individuation—this does not mean that man clings to his frail little ego that puffs itself up against something or another which it takes to be the world. This individuation is rather the solitariness in which each human being first of all enters into a nearness to what is essential in all things, a nearness to the world . . . solitude where each human being will be as though unique . . ." (ibid., 6). Individuation begins for me biologically, with birth, and here I am closer to Hannah Arendt. Singularity, as I have defined it here in terms of life-span, as disclosed by and to *thumos*, is not the alienation one feels in the process of philosophy, rather it is the reason for philosophy, it is the positive given-ness of an *aiōn* which is unsubsumable by metaphysical *logoi*.

45 An oft-quoted line in twentieth-century German philosophy, "Where there is danger, grows the saving power also . . ." (*Nah ist / und schwer zu fassen der Gott / Wo aber Gefahr ist, wächst das Rettende auch*; Hölderlin "Patmos" (1802, variants in 1803)).

46 Kalypso "charms" (*thelgei*) Odysseus with *malakoisi logoisi*, that is, she attempts to persuade him to remain with her and forget his homecoming to Ithaka (*nostos*; *Odyssey* i.56). As we learn in the work, this includes her offer to make him immortal, which he refuses. Here too, it is a matter of bridging the divide between mortals and immortals through words (*logos*).

Chapter 4: In the Realm of the Goddess: *Logos* and Its Limits

1 In tragedy as well, the dialogue form was exploited for philosophical reasons, when the protagonists made contrasting arguments. The Sophists were known for developing paired antithetical speeches or *dissoi logoi*.

2 See, for example, Guthrie, *A History of Greek Philosophy*, vol. 1 and G. E. L. Owen, *Logic, Science and Dialectic* (Ithaca: Cornell University Press, 1986), 3–44. See also, Jonathan Barnes, *The Presocratic Philosophers* (London: Routledge, 1979), esp. 155–230 and Curd, *The Legacy of Parmenides*.

3 Kingsley, *In the Dark Places of Wisdom*.

4 G. Santillana, "Prologue to Parmenides," in *Lectures in Memory of Louise Taft Semple* (Princeton: Princeton University Press, 1967), 50.

5 Karl Reinhardt quoted in Santillana "Prologue to Parmenides," 50. To be sure, the "Sphinx of Metaphysics" is a characterization of the entire poem, but I find that it describes the goddess herself aptly.

6 Ibid.

7 Ibid., 51. See also Giovanni Cerri, *Parmenide di Elea, Poema sulla natura, Introduzione, testo, traduzione e note* (Milano: Biblioteca Universale Rizzoli, 1999)—a work I have unfortunately been unable to consult. I, however, thank the author for making his unpublished paper "Parmenides' Physical Theory," which summarizes the main argument of the book, available to me.

8 Heidegger, *Parmenides*, 12–14.

9 Schürmann, *Heidegger on Being and Acting*, 170.

10 Here, "accused" is used to evoke the accusation of *katagorein*. For a discussion of Heidegger's etymology of this word, see Schürmann, *Heidegger on Being and Acting*, 161.

11 Empedocles, fr. 17.

12 G. E. L. Owen, "Eleatic Questions," in *Logic, Science and Dialectic* (Ithaca, NY: Cornell University Press, 1986), 23.

13 It is not surprising that Owen has Descartes fully in view: "The comparison with Descartes' *cogito* is inescapable . . .". Owen, "Eleatic Questions," 16.

14 Curd, *The Legacy of Parmenides*, 26.

15 Charles Kahn as quoted in Curd, *The Legacy of Parmenides*, 27.

16 Ibid.

17 I follow Curd (*The Legacy of Parmenides*, 53). There is a substantial controversy about the number and description of the three routes. Curd provides a concise summary and a good bibliography on this issue.

[18] For example, we search helplessly for a noun in this passage and try to supply a subject for *estin*.

[19] Charles H. Kahn, *Essays on Being* (New York: Oxford University Press, 2009), 28–9.

[20] Charles H. Kahn, "Greek Verb 'To Be' and the Concept of Being," *Foundations of Language*, vol. 2, no. 3 (August 1966): 245–65.

[21] Ibid.

[22] Curd, *The Legacy of Parmenides*, 28.

Chapter 5: At Home in the *Kosmos*: The Return

[1] For further commentary on these passages, see the Appendix to this work.

[2] This method of preserving the self through dialogue clearly had an enormous impact on Plato, in whose writings the contribution of the interlocutor, however unscientific, and the human dimension of Socrates, no matter how philosophic, are preserved in the phenomenal priority of an existential encounter.

[3] Taran is a classic example; see his *Parmenides: A Text with Translation*.

[4] I thank J. R. Lenz for this point.

[5] Conventionally, Parmenides' poem is read as an allegory of enlightenment similar to Plato's Allegory of the Cave, light representing metaphysical truth, I read this as a passage from phenomena into their obscurity.

[6] Curd, *The Legacy of Parmenides*, 123.

[7] Curd speaks of "a system of enantiomorphic opposites." *The Legacy of Parmenides*, 123.

[8] Cf. Jean Beaufret, *Le poème de Parménide* (Paris: Presses universitaires de France, 1955), 8: "un des plus beaux de la langue grecque," cited in Mourelatos, *The Route of Parmenides*, 224.

[9] O' Brien's translation (*Études sur Parménide*, Tome I, 69). My translation (in the Appendix) reads: "Night-lighting, astray around earth, a borrowed light."

[10] *Iliad* xiv.258–61, as translated in Kirk, Raven, and Schofield, *The Presocratic Philosophers*, 17.

[11] W. K. C. Guthrie, *Orpheus and Greek Religion* (Princeton: Princeton University Press, 1993), 258–60.

[12] We have two different and perhaps contradictory testimonia concerning what Parmenides thought about the composition of the moon, both from Aëtius. The moon is "fiery" (Testimonium A42); it is also "denser or colder" than the sun (A43). For the texts, see Gallop, *Parmenides of Elea: Fragments*, 118.

[13] Sedley, for instance, writes, "for example, that the sky *is* blue and *is not* grey." "Parmenides and Melissus" in *Cambridge Companion to Early Greek Philosophy*, ed. A. A. Long (Cambridge: Cambridge University Press, 1999), 115.

[14] Taran, *Parmenides*, 225.

[15] In the *Iliad* the word *mēnis* is only used of gods and Akhilleus. See my comments on Akhilleus' transcendence toward divinity.

[16] Although this may seem to be reading a lot into one word, the first word of a work was deeply significant for the Greeks; for example, the first word of Plato's *Republic* (*kateben*) is a motif that structures the whole text. For a more extensive discussion, see my "Initiation into the Mysteries: Experience of the Irrational in Plato," *Mouseion*, series III, vol. 6 (2006): 407–23.

17 Not of course in the trivial sense of anarchy. For a full philosophical definition of this term, see Schürmann, *Heidegger on Being and Acting*, 253, 280.

18 The seat of emotions such as anger.

19 Akhilleus only apparently desire the immortality of fame, as becomes clear from his lament to Odysseus: "About death, do not try to comfort me, bright Odysseus! I would rather be the living slave of a peasant, than the king of all the dead" (*Odyssey* xi.489–91). It would seem, rather, that he too desires true immortality, that is, immortality that transcends fame and glory.

20 M. P. Nilsson, *The Mycenaean Origin of Greek Mythology* (Berkeley, CA: University of California Press, 1972), 203.

21 Unique exceptions are: Menelaus is prophesied to live on in the Elysian Fields, rather than dying (in *Odyssey* iv), and, in the Nekuia (*Odyssey* xi), some individuals retain their bodies in Hades; this is the case with Minos and Rhadamanthys (the two, formerly mortal, rulers of the dead) and Sisyphus and the few individuals punished with eternal torments, although this last is rarely adequately recognized by scholarship.

22 A similar formula is found in Sanskrit as well.

23 The goddess' entire argument is agonistic. She herself refers to her demonstration in 7.5 as *poludeiron elengkhon*.

24 See, for example, Euripides' *Hippolytus* and *Bacchae*.

25 Kingsley stresses Parmenides' descent (*katabasis*) to her realm in his *In the Dark Places of Wisdom*.

Chapter 6: Reading Plato's *Phaedrus*: Socrates the Mortal

1 Martin Heidegger, *Nietzsche*, 2 vols., trans. David Farrell Krell (New York: Harper, 1981), 191.

2 John Palmer, *Plato's Reception of Parmenides* (Oxford: Oxford University Press, 1999).

3 Gallop, *Parmenides of Elea: Fragments*, 3.

4 See, for example, Palmer, *Plato's Reception of Parmenides*.

5 Cf. Cornford, *Plato's Theory of Knowledge*.

6 See, for example, Stanley Rosen, *Sophist: The Drama of Original and Image* (South Bend, IN: St. Augustine's Press, 1999).

7 Taran, *Parmenides: A Text with Translation*; Owen, *Logic, Science and Dialectic*; Barnes, *The Presocratic Philosophers*.

8 Curd, *The Legacy of Parmenides*.

9 Jacques Derrida, "Plato's Pharmacy," in *Dissemination*, trans. Barbara Johnson (Chicago: University of Chicago Press, 1981).

10 Kingsley, *In the Dark Places of Wisdom*.

11 Taran, *Parmenides: A Text with Translation*, 18.

12 Paul Natorp, *Platons Ideenlehre. Eine Einführung in den Idealismus* (Leipzig: Verlag der Dürr'schen Buchhandlung, 1903).

13 Perceval Frutiger, *Les Mythes de Platon. étude philosophique et littéraire* (Paris: F. Alcan, 1930).

14 Léon Robin, *Platon: Œuvres complètes*, vol. 2 (Paris: Gallimard, 1943).

[15] For a recent overview of scholarship on this issue and an analysis from an inter-textual perspective, see Svetla Slaveva-Griffin, "Of Gods, Philosophers, and Charioteers: Content and Form in Parmenides' Proem and Plato's Phaedrus," *Transactions of the American Philological Association (1974–)* 133.2 (Autumn, 2003): 227–53.

[16] R. Hackforth, *Plato's Phaedrus. Translated with an Introduction and Commentary* (Cambridge: Cambridge University Press, 1993), 76–7.

[17] Taran, *Parmenides: A Text with Translation*, 18–19.

[18] Santillana, "Prologue to Parmenides," 2.

[19] Palmer, *Plato's Reception of Parmenides*.

[20] Taran, *Parmenides: A Text with Translation*.

[21] However, the term *pharmakon* does not occur in the extant text anywhere.

[22] For a good description of the dramatic setting and its meanings, see Rosen, *Sophist: The Drama of Original and Image*. Debra Nails provides a useful analysis of Plato's use of distinct "voices"; see Debra Nails, *The People of Plato* (Indianapolis/Cambridge: Hackett, 2003); also see the same author's "Mouthpiece, Shmouth-piece," in *Who Speaks for Plato: Studies in Platonic Anonymity*, ed. Gerald A. Press (Oxford: Rowman & Littlefield Publishers, 2000).

[23] Stanley Rosen, *Plato's Sophist* (New Haven: Yale University Press, 1983). See also Stanley Rosen, *The Quarrel between Philosophy and Poetry* (London: Routledge, 1988), where he summarizes his method for reading a Platonic Dialogue. "The method is simplicity itself; it amounts to the careful and reflective consideration of every aspect of the dialogue under study. As is especially appropriate in the study of a dialogue devoted to the perfect writing [*Phaedrus*], I assume nothing more than that Plato knew what he was doing, and that all portions of the written text are meant to convey their meaning to the careful reader. In this way, Plato, rather than the interpreter or contemporary academic fashion, becomes the standard for what is important in a Platonic dialogue; namely everything" (78).

[24] Seth Benardete, *The Being of the Beautiful: Plato's Theaetetus, Sophist, and Statesman* (Chicago: University of Chicago Press, 1984), xvi.

[25] Note that necessity is experienced as a temptation in Parmenides.

[26] Nails, "Mouthpiece, Shmouthpiece," *passim.*

[27] Contrast, however, Lysias' writings, which are clearly orphaned as Socrates argues (275e). See also Derrida, "Plato's Pharmacy."

[28] All translations, unless otherwise specified, are from William S. Cobb, *Plato's Erotic Dialogues* (Albany, NY: SUNY Press, 1993).

[29] Phaedrus' "conversion" to philosophy at the conclusion of the dialogue is open to interpretation. Hackforth, for example, takes an optimistic view. "And Phaedrus' last words, in their moving simplicity, show us once more that the devotee of clever but hollow oratory has become one in heart and mind with the lover of truth, the genuine ψυχαγωγός." *Plato's Phaedrus. Translated with an Introduction and Commentary*, 169.

[30] For a recent and influential example, see Hannah Arendt who makes this distinction in *Responsibility and Judgment* (New York: Schocken Books, 2003), 83–7. See also *The Human Condition*.

[31] The concept of personal autopsy is especially relevant in historical writing, as intro-duced by Herodotus. I thank John Lenz for relating this point to the Platonic dialogue. "So far the Egyptians themselves have been my authority; but in what follows I shall relate what other people, too, are willing to accept in the history of

this country, with a few points added from my own observation" (*Histories* II.147; Sélincourt trans.).

³² For example, he is explicitly not present in the *Phaedo*, the dialogue that recounts the death of Socrates.

³³ See Jean-Pierre Vernant, *Myth and Society in Ancient Greece*, trans. Janet Lloyd (New York: Zone Books, 1990), 205. Recent scholarship has questioned the degree to which Classical Athens (i.e., fifth and fourth centuries BCE) was a literate culture. However, these limitations need not apply to Plato, since his own accomplishment go beyond simply following popular standards. Since Plato has chosen to adopt writing, especially in contrast to his teacher, he uses writing to analyze the implications of writing for philosophy and pedagogy.

³⁴ Ibid.

³⁵ Cf. Jack Goody, *The Interface between the Written and the Oral* (Cambridge: Cambridge University Press, 1987); Walter J. Ong, *Orality and Literacy: The Technologizing of the Word* (London: Routledge, 1988); Eric Alfred Havelock, *The Literate Revolution in Greece and Its Cultural Consequences* (Princeton: Princeton University Press, 1982).

³⁶ Rowe commenting on 227a5, is cynical about Acumenus and his advice. Christopher Rowe, *Plato: Phaedrus* (London: Penguin Classics, 2005), 136, see also 137 on 227d4. I have chosen to read Plato without assuming irony.

³⁷ See, for instance, William S. Cobb, who writes: "Phaedrus was actually in exile from Athens between 415 and 409, as a result of his alleged involvement in the infamous destruction of the Herms. Lysias left Athens as a child and did not return until after 411, and Lysias' brother Polemarchus was murdered in 404." Hence, this dialogue could not depict an actual historical conversation, since in the dialogue Lysias is in Athens (227b), Polemarchus is alive (257b), and Phaedrus is not in exile." *Plato's Erotic Dialogues*, 193.

³⁸ Cf. Jean-Pierre Vernant, *Myth and Thought among the Greeks* (London: Routledge & Kegan Paul, 1983), 37.

³⁹ G. R. F. Ferrari calls Phaedrus a "ubiquitous salon presence." *Listening to the Cicadas* (Cambridge: Cambridge University Press, 1987), 5. R. Burger draws parallels between Morychus' gluttony and Phaedrus' passion for speeches in *Plato's Phaedrus* (Tuscaloosa, AL: University of Alabama Press, 1980).

⁴⁰ Herodicus' advice to walk to Megara and back (227d) applies equally to Phaedrus and Socrates.

⁴¹ Although the *Republic* is set in the wealthy citizen Cephalus' house, the setting is nevertheless not private for it is colored by Cephalus' comments on being a good citizen, and discharging his civic duties appropriately. Further, the dialogue unfolds following Cephalus' explicit request that Socrates instruct his son. The pedagogical setting, and the fact that the discussion is initiated at the behest of a good citizen, makes Socrates' task a civic one. The dialogue's theme is, appropriately, explicitly political.

⁴² Stanley Rosen, "Erotic Ascent," *Graduate Faculty Philosophy Journal* 17 (1994): 37–57.

⁴³ Rosen, *The Quarrel between Philosophy and Poetry*, 102: "Plato seems to think of philosophy as composed of two [apparently] incompatible aspects . . . If we are aware that the terms are tentative and metaphorical, I believe we shall not be wrong in calling these aspects the poetic and the mathematical."

⁴⁴ Theaetetus, like Phaedrus, is introduced as resembling Socrates (143e). Whereas the resemblance between Socrates and Phaedrus is "psychological," the

resemblance is physical in the case of Theaetetus. Moreover, the latter, like Socrates, cares very little about material possessions (144d).

[45] Thus, whereas the *Theaetetus* approaches the question of *epistēmē* using mathematical axioms, the *Phaedrus* expresses the theory of Forms mytho-poetically.

[46] Vernant writes: "In Plato, the myths about memory are integrated into a general theory of Knowledge." Vernant, *Myth and Thought among the Greeks*, 84. "Both these features of mythical memory: escape from time and union with gods, are to be found in the Platonic theory of anamnesis. In Plato, recollections no longer focus upon the primeval past nor upon previous lives. It has as its object those truths which together constitute reality" (ibid., 92). "Memory in Plato . . . retains a function similar to that which is exalted in myth . . . What he asks of memory is not knowledge of his own past but the means of escape from time and to be reunited with the divine" (ibid., 93).

[47] Stanley Rosen, "The Non-Lover in Plato's Phaedrus," *Man and His World 2* (1969): 423–37, and *Phaedrus* 279b–c.

[48] See Snell, *The Discovery of the Mind*, especially chapter 9: "Myth to Logic, The Role of Comparison." However, I do not agree with Snell entirely on this point.

[49] The Silenius image, according to Alkibiades, applies equally to Socrates' speeches. The comparison of Socrates' speech and Lysias' speech would lead to other areas, which exceed my present concerns.

[50] In the analogy, the place of divine *erōs*.

[51] For further reading in the relationship between *paideiea* and *paiderasteia*, see H. I. Marrou, *A History of Education in Antiquity*, trans. George Lamb (Madison, WI: University of Wisconsin Press, 1982). He says "For the Greeks, education—παιδεία—meant, essentially, a profound and intimate relationship, a personal union between a young man and an elder who was at once his model, his guide and his initiator—a relationship on which the fire of passion threw warm and turbid reflections" (31). Also see John Boswell, *Same Sex Unions in Premodern Europe* (New York: Vintage, 1995) for a learned account of Greek homosexuality. This account supersedes Dover's (Kenneth James Dover, *Greek Homosexuality* [Cambridge, MA: Harvard University Press, 1978]).

[52] Derrida suggests the ambivalent nature of writing by comparing it to a *pharmakon*, arguing that writing both vivifies and kills. I see no reason why such an analysis should apply only to writing and not to philosophy in general. In fact, Socratic philosophy is more effective in leading Socrates to death than in averting his mortal fate.

[53] The *Symposium* is a homosexual banquet, where previously even the flute girls have been dismissed. The topic of this conversation is homosexual erotic love, and in some sense, praising the god of love. Diotima is a poor guest for disrespecting the rules of the house.

[54] *Phaedrus*, 230d, 274e, 275a.

[55] Derrida, "Plato's Pharmacy," 61–171.

[56] Ibid., 117.

[57] Ibid., 70.

[58] Jane Ellen Harrison, *Prolegomena to the Study of Greek Religion* (Princeton: Princeton University Press), 95–6.

[59] Schürmann, "Ultimate Double Binds," 216–18.

[60] Harrison, *Prolegomena to the Study of Greek Religion*, 104.

61 As quoted in Harrison, *Prolegomena to the Study of Greek Religion*, 105.

62 Harrison, *Prolegomena to the Study of Greek Religion*, 97; my italics.

63 Theocritus, quoted in Harrison, *Prolegomena to the Study of Greek Religion*, 101.

64 Ibid.

65 See Harrison's discussion of the practice of the city maintaining at its expense, certain very ugly individuals, who were to be sacrificed as part of purifications to rid the city of its ailments (ibid., 95–6).

66 This is, on my view, a Platonist conceit.

67 For an interpretation of the erotic journey as an ascent, see Rosen, "Erotic Ascent," 37–57.

68 Charles L. Griswold, Jr., *Self-Knowledge in Plato's Phaedrus* (University Park, PA: Pennsylvania University Press, 1996), 75.

69 Graeme Nicholson, *Plato's Phaedrus: The Philosophy of Love* (West Lafayette, IN: Purdue University Press, 1999), 156. Nicholson reads this phrase as "every soul" rather than "all souls" collectively. Thus he makes a distinction between a collective or distributive meaning of the word *panta*. In my interpretation, it does not make a difference, because in either event, what is crucial is the introduction of plurality and motion into being.

70 T. M. Robinson, *Plato's Psychology*, 2nd ed. (Toronto: University of Toronto Press, 1995), 111.

71 A. F. Festugière, "Platon et l'Orient," *Revue de Philologie* 3 (1947): 5–45.

72 D. D. McGibbon, "The Fall of the Soul in Plato's Phaedrus," *Classical Quarterly* 14 (1964): 56–63.

73 Gregory Vlastos, "The Individual as Object of Love in Plato," in *Platonic Studies* (Princeton: Princeton University Press, 1981), 3–42.

74 Robinson, *Plato's Psychology*, 111.

75 Derrida, "Plato's Pharmacy," 67.

76 Ibid.

77 Ibid., 71.

78 Cf. Diogenes Laertius, III.52: "Now where he has a firm grasp Plato expounds his own view and refutes the false one, but, if the subject is obscure, he suspends judgement. His own views are expounded by four persons, Socrates, Timaeus, the Athenian Stranger, the Eleatic Stranger. These strangers are not, as some hold, Plato and Parmenides, but imaginary characters without names, for, even when Socrates and Timaeus are the speakers, it is Plato's doctrines that are laid down." *The Lives of Eminent Philosophers*, vol. 1, trans. R. D. Hicks (Cambridge, MA: Harvard University Press, 1950), 323.

79 Glenn R. Morrow and John M. Dillon, trans., *Proclus' Commentary on Plato's Parmenides* (Princeton: Princeton University Press, 1987), 83.

Conclusion: Returning to Parmenides

1 See Heidegger's lecture *Parmenides*, especially the section titled "Outset and Beginning."

2 For a discussion of these three rough stages in Heidegger's thought, see Reiner Schürmann, "How to Read Heidegger," *Graduate Faculty Philosophy Journal* 19.1 (1997).

³ Martin Heidegger, *The End of Philosophy*, trans. Joan Stambaugh (Chicago: University of Chicago Press, 1973), x.

⁴ See Heidegger's *Nietzsche* lectures, esp. the chapter "Nietzsche's Overturning of Platonism" in *Nietzsche*.

⁵ On Heidegger's relation to the pre-Socratics, see Joseph Seidel, *Martin Heidegger and the Pre-Socratics: An Introduction to His Thought* (Lincoln, NE: University of Nebraska Press, 1964) and David C. Jacobs, ed., *The Presocratics after Heidegger* (Albany, NY: SUNY Press, 1999); see esp. Jacob's contribution "The Ontological Education of Parmenides" where he argues that Parmenides' poem presents the *kouros* undergoing an ontological education.

⁶ Heidegger, *Being and Time*, 22–3; my emphasis. In this quote, Heidegger goes on to assert that "time itself is taken to be one being among others." As my interpretation of mortality shows, this characterization of Parmenides' understanding of time by Heidegger is manifestly incorrect. The claim is repeated throughout Heidegger's early writings in various forms, most dramatically in his essay "Phenomenological Interpretations of Aristotle: An Indication of the Hermeneutic Situation." Heidegger writes: "Parmenides was the first to have brought the being of being into view, though in ontological terms things remained at this first 'impression of being.' With this first, though decisive view, ontological seeing was already at its end." "Phenomenological Interpretations of Aristotle: An Indication of the Hermeneutic Situation," in *Supplements: From the Earliest Essays to* Being and Time *and Beyond*, ed. John van Buren (Albany, NY: SUNY Press, 2002), 141.

⁷ Heidegger explains the "fourfold" (*das Gevierte*), namely, earth, sky, mortals, and divinities in the essay "Bauen, Denken, Wohnen" (1951; English title: "Building, Dwelling, Thinking").

⁸ From the point of view of the *thumos*, history is the hall of the dead populated by the concerns of the living.

⁹ Adluri, "Heidegger's Encounter with Aristotle."

¹⁰ For an excellent overview of Heidegger's interest in Luther see John van Buren, "Martin Heidegger, Martin Luther," in *Reading Heidegger from the Start*, ed. T. Kisiel and J. van Buren (Albany, NY: SUNY Press, 1994), 159–74. Yfantis' recent book, *Die Auseinandersetzung des frühen Heidegger mit Aristoteles*, provides a provocative and insightful analysis of Heidegger's Lutheran background—see esp. sections 1.1.5.1 and 1.1.5.2. Yfantis notes, "The turn to liberal Protestantism is of decisive significance for the direction and basic tendency of Heidegger's thought during his early lectureship in Freiburg (1919–23) since the lectures of Schleiermacher and Dilthey have undoubtedly contributed essentially to the hermeneutic-historical turn in his thought. However, above all one must point to the intensive study of Luther's writings, which diverse biographic sources document and which several passages in the early Freiburg lectures let us intuit. How powerful the influence in particular of the young Luther and his understanding of early Christianity was on the thought of the young Heidegger lets itself, however, only be assessed through a direct comparison of the central termini, concepts, and intellectual motivations of both thinkers that provides detailed testimony that the conceptuality and use of language in the early Freiburg lectures . . . arose, to a great extent, out of translations and reinterpretations of concepts and termini

that Heidegger already found in Luther's writings." *Die Auseinandersetzung des frühen Heidegger mit Aristoteles,* 72; all translations mine.

11 See Heidegger's *The Basic Problems of Phenomenology,* trans. Albert Hofstadter (Bloomington, IN: Indiana University Press, 1982), 232–56 for his explication of the Aristotelian doctrine of time and pages 256–74 for the "derivation" of "vulgar time" out of "original time."

12 Romolo Perrotta, *Heideggers Jeweiligkeit: Versuch einer Analyse der Seinsfrage anhand der veröffentlichen Texte* (Würzburg: Königshausen und Neumann, 1999); see also Kisiel's note on his translation of *Prolegomena zur Geschichte des Zeitbegriffs.* Kisiel calls *Jeweiligkeit,* which he translates with either "the particular while" or "temporal particularity," the "most central of the characters of Dasein." Martin Heidegger, *Prolegomena to the History of the Concept of Time,* trans. Theodor Kisiel (Bloomington, IN: Indiana University Press, 1985), 153.

13 Heidegger, *Being and Time,* 23.

14 Since the soul is not an entity separate from the body in Aristotle's thought, there could be no transmigration for him (cf. especially *De anima* 2.1 412b5, where Aristotle defines the soul as "the first actuality of a natural body that is possessed of organs").

15 Especially illuminating here is Heidegger's engagement with Nietzsche, since Nietzsche precedes Heidegger with his critique of Christianity. But whereas Nietzsche's critique of Christianity defuses the need for personal salvation (since everything repeats eternally, there is no individual being here in need of personal salvation), Heidegger's critique of Christianity fundamentally aims at a retrieval of a more original, that is, non-Hellenized, experience of Christianity. Nietzsche's critique could thus more properly be called an attack on Christianity, while Heidegger's critique represents a retrieval or even a revitalization of faith.

16 Heidegger critiques the Aristotelian conception of time as infinite in two places. In *Being and Time,* he claims that "Only because primordial time is *finite* can the 'derived' time temporalize itself as *infinite*" (331; emphasis in original). Although he does not specifically refer to Aristotle here, it is clear that his target is the Aristotelian thesis, as is confirmed by an almost identical claim made in *The Basic Problems of Phenomenology.* In section 19, following a historical orientation and an overview of the Aristotelian treatise on time, identified here with the "vulgar understanding of time," Heidegger again repeats the thesis that "Only because temporality in the authentic sense is finite is inauthentic time in the sense of common time infinite." Heidegger, *The Basic Problems of Phenomenology,* 273.

17 In my view, Thanassas' reading of Parmenides succumbs to the same error of dismissing the *aporia* for a happy resolution; see my recent review of *Parmenides, Cosmos, and Being: A Philosophical Interpretation,* by Panagiotis Thanassas, *Bryn Mawr Classical Review* March 18, 2010; http://bmcr.brynmawr.edu/2010/2010–03-18.html.

18 Although I cannot enter into a longer discussion here, it seems to me that Heidegger misunderstands Greek thought when he claims it covers over *Jeweiligkeit.* There are three ways to thematize *Jeweiligkeit*: (1) as *erōs,* where I understand and value the other *qua* singular, (2) in myth where the unique life of an individual acquires paradigmatic status (e.g., Akhilleus in Homer or

Socrates in the Platonic dialogues), and (3) as a soteriological moment, where this individual being bound for death is concerned with its salvation. Since Heidegger does not have *erōs* and rejects myth, he can only thematize *Jeweiligkeit* as a soteriological moment.

[19] The Kierkegaardian resonances in *Being and Time* have been frequently noted, but here I specifically mean Heidegger's dedication of the text *Phenomenological Interpretations of Aristotle* to Kierkegaard with the words: "Motto, along with a grateful indication of the source." Martin Heidegger, *Phenomenological Interpretations of Aristotle: Initiation into Phenomenological Research*, trans. Richard Rojcewicz (Bloomington, IN: Indiana University Press, 2001), 137. The motto, taken from Kierkegaard's *Exercises in Christianity* reads: "All of modern philosophy is based on something which both ethics and Christianity would consider a frivolity. Instead of deterring people and calling them to order by speaking of despair and exasperation, it has winked at people and invited them to pride themselves on doubting and having doubted. For the rest, philosophy, as abstract, floats in the indeterminateness of the metaphysical. Instead of admitting this to itself and then pointing people (individuals) to the ethical, the religious, and the existential, philosophy has given rise to the pretence that humans could, as is said prosaically, speculate themselves out of their own skin and into pure appearance" (ibid.).

[20] The emphasis on salvation becomes increasingly explicit in the later writings, including references to the "saving power" in his essay "The Question Concerning Technology" and the famous claim made in the *Der Spiegel* interview (also in the context of a rejection of technicity): "Only a god can save us."

[21] The emphasis on facticity and its temporality are clearly underscored by theologians deeply influenced by Heidegger. For example, Bultmann writes: "Thus, theological thinking—the theology of the New Testament—begins with the *kerygma* of the earliest Church and not before. But the fact that Jesus had appeared and the message which had proclaimed were, of course, among its historical presuppositions; and for this reason Jesus' message cannot be omitted from the delineation of New Testament theology." Bultmann Rudolf, *Theology of the New Testament*, trans. Kendrick Grobel (New York: Scribner, 1951), 3. Thus, Bultmann stresses the *kerygma* even in relation to the appearance of Jesus. What is this *kerygma*? "*That the earliest Church regarded itself as the Congregation of the end of days.*" (ibid., 37). The Heideggerian analysis of *Jeweiligkeit* is transparent in Bultmann's statements about Jesus: "Basically, therefore, *he in his own person is the 'sign of the time' . . . He in his own person signifies the demand for decision*" (ibid., 9; emphasis in original).

[22] Nietzsche is an important exception here, since I see him as holding on to the thought of *Jeweiligkeit* in the doctrine of the "eternal recurrence of the same." Thus contrary to Heidegger's characterization of Nietzsche as "the last metaphysician," Nietzsche criticizes Christianity precisely for devaluing existence here and now in favor of an afterlife. Interestingly, when Heidegger turns to Nietzsche in the 1930s, he insists upon the "will to power" as Nietzsche's central thought, downplaying the doctrine of the eternal recurrence of the same.

[23] On the concept of *persona*, see Hannah Arendt, *Revolution* (New York: Penguin Books, 1986), 107. Arendt develops a concept of *persona* drawn from the ancient

theatrical practice of wearing masks that covered the actors' faces but let their voice through to clarify the private individual from the public identity.

[24] Thus, Burkert notes, "To summarize: Parmenides' journey is neither a transition from night to light nor an ascent; it is also not a collection of heterogenous symbols, which would only be comprehensible in relation to the theoretical content [of the text], and still less a purely literary device without deeper meaning. Parmenides travels on the path of the daimon to the edge of the world, where, at the boundary between heaven and earth, a towering gateway divides this world from the hereafter. The Heliades approach him from the house of night, they accompany him through the gate into the great 'open', where the goddess receives him. Everything falls of necessity into place, as soon as one resolutely lays the path upward and the path to the light, these Platonic-Christian symbols, to the side. The journey should rather—with Morrison—be called a katabasis." Walter Burkert, "Parmenides' Proem and Pythagoras' Katabasis," trans. Joydeep Bagchee, in *Philosophy and Salvation in Greek Religion*, ed. Vishwa Adluri (Berlin: Walter de Gruyter, 2012).

[25] See, for example, the conclusion to Burkert's article "Das Proömium des Parmenides und die Katabasis des Pythagoras," 29, where he argues that Parmenides combines Pythagorean elements and elements from mystery religions with "logically consistent thinking." The contribution of this new mode of thought notwithstanding, the real experience of thought is motivated by a desire to transform the content or insight of the religious experience into a new form.

[26] The "tragic" reading of the Greeks first advanced in Schürmann and further articulated here by me thus becomes an important corrective to this one-sided and dogmatically motivated interpretation of ancient ontology. As I have shown in this work, the pre-Socratics and Plato do not permit us to easily reduce them to either thinkers of static being (either as "monists," or "metaphysical thinkers," or "logicians") without any intuition of the complex interplay of change, temporality, pluri-vocity, dialogue, and, above all, of *mortal* knowledge in every endeavor to say something philosophical about being. But nor are Parmenides and Plato easily reducible to a stage of prescientific thinking predating Aristotle and contemporary phenomenology.

[27] As Yfantis notes, "Primordial Christian religiosity—according to Heidegger—*lives temporality* [*Zeitlichkeit*] (the verb understood in an intransitive sense), which is fundamentally different from the fallen objective concept of time insofar as it does not signify a definite schematism, but is rooted in the context of unfolding [*Vollzugszusammenhang*] itself and constitutes the meaning of its facticity. This unfolding itself is carried by the awaiting of the second coming of Christ, so that every moment of such original experience of life attains its signification through the reference to the event of the end of days. The original meaning of the primordial Christian temporality [*Zeitlichkeit*], however, has been falsified through the covering over of the eschatological problem and the penetration of Greek philosophy into Christianity, and this has led to specific theological problems, e.g., that of the eternity of god, which were no longer appropriately understood in the Middle Ages." Yfantis, *Die Auseinandersetzung des frühen Heidegger mit Aristoteles*, 89–90.

Yfantis continues, "Heidegger sees the specific character of primordial Christian temporality [*Zeitlichkeit*] unmistakeably expressed in the passage where Paul expresses himself concerning the question of the time of the second coming of Christ (παρουσία). In his interpretation, he emphasizes that the Apostle not only does not make any statements as to the time and keeps the Thessalonians from indulging themselves in brooding and speculating about it, but rather, he sharply contrasts two fundamental attitudes to the event of the end of days: on the one hand, the fallen flight of the damned in the face of the constant insecurity of facticity into calculation and expectation according to one's feelings and, on the other, the sober awaiting of the saved in the unfolding of Christian life. The day of the lord will not surprise them; in contrast, it will suddenly befall the others. Heidegger concludes from this that the question of the time of the παρουσία for Paul neither points to an objective time nor to objective outcomes, but rather, points to the individual unfolding of the life of the Christian and to the way he relates to the παρουσία. Therein lies the fundamental character of Christian temporality [*Zeitlichkeit*]" (ibid., 90).

28 Of Scotus, Heidegger writes, "He discovered a greater and finer proximity (*haecceitas*) to real life in its multiplicity and potential for tension as the scholastics before him. He simultaneously knows how to turn his attention to abstract mathematics with the same lightness drawn from the fullness of life. The 'forms of life' are just as familiar (to the extent this was at all the case in the Middle Ages) to him as the 'grey on grey' of philosophy." Martin Heidegger, *Frühe Schriften* (Frankfurt a.M.: Vittorio Klostermann, 1972), 145; I thank Joydeep Bagchee for this passage from his forthcoming translation, *The Doctrine of Categories and Meaning of Duns Scotus* (Bloomington, IN: Indiana University Press, forthcoming).

29 Throughout this work, I have been critical of *logos* understood as textuality that does not refer to a mortal singular. The valorization of *logos* as evidenced in literal and fundamentalist interpretations of scripture implies a loss of tragic wisdom as can be seen from dogmatic and historical interpretations of texts in the history of philosophy—but there is a price to be paid for this fetishization of the text. Although emancipatory in many ways, Luther's turn to the text has unanticipated consequences; as William L. Shirer notes, "It is difficult to understand the behavior of most German Protestants in the first Nazi years unless one is aware of two things: their history and the influence of Martin Luther. The great founder of Protestantism was both a passionate anti-Semite and a ferocious believer in absolute obedience to political authority." *The Rise and Fall of the Third Reich* (New York: Simon & Schuster, 1990), 236.

Appendix: Translation and Textual Notes
of Parmenides' *Peri Phuseōs*

* I thank J. R. Lenz for his generous help with this translation. Without his philological expertise, my philosophical comments would have gone astray. I am, however solely responsible for any errors.

1 O'Brien's translation of lines 6–10 must be rendered here for its exceptional clarity, let alone poignancy: "The axle a-blaze in the axle-boxes *was sending out* a cry from the hollow hub of the wheel as from a shepherd's pipe, for it was being hurtled forward by the two wheels spinning on either side of it, as the young girls, daughters of the Sun, were hastening to bring me on my way, once they had left

behind the realms of night to pass into the light and had flung back with their hands the coverings from their heads." *Études sur Parménide, Tome I*, 4.

[2] Gallop, *Parmenides of Elea: Fragments*. All references hereafter to this edition.

[3] Coxon, *The Fragments of Parmenides*. All references hereafter to this edition.

[4] Taran, *Parmenides: A Text with Translation*. All references hereafter to this edition.

[5] Kingsley, *In the Dark Places of Wisdom*. All references hereafter to this edition.

[6] Burkert, "Das Proömium des Parmenides und die Katabasis des Pythagoras," 1–30. All references hereafter to this edition.

[7] Curd, *The Legacy of Parmenides*. All references hereafter to this edition.

[8] For O'Brien's thorough justification for his translation of this line see *Études sur Parménide, Tome I*, 12–15.

[9] Kurt von Fritz, "Nous, Noein, and Their Derivatives in Pre-Socratic Philosophy (Excluding Anaxagoras): Part I. From the Beginnings to Parmenides," *Classical Philology*, vol. 40, no. 4 (October 1945): 223–42.

[10] David Sider and Henry W. Johnstone, *The Fragments of Parmenides* (Bryn Mawr, PA: Bryn Mawr Greek Commentaries, 1986). All references hereafter to this edition.

[11] Personal communication.

[12] Schürmann, *Being and Acting*, 170; see also 355, n. 9.

[13] Barnes, *The Presocratic Philosophers*, 178; cf. Gallop, 65, note *ad loc.*

[14] Mourelatos, *The Route of Parmenides*. All references hereafter to this edition.

[15] Kingsley, *Ancient Philosophy, Mystery, and Magic*, 16–18.

[16] For this and other Orphic references in the poem, see Kingsley, *The Dark Places of Wisdom*.

[17] Guthrie, *A History of Greek Philosophy*, vol. 2.

[18] I thank J. R. Lenz for this reference.

[19] Matt Newman, "Remembering Tradition, Transforming Remembrance" (unpublished, 2008).

Bibliography

I have included a more extensive bibliography of more traditional interpretations of Parmenides to balance my own reading.

Abraham, W. E. "The Nature of Zeno's Argument against Plurality in DK 29 B 1." *Phronesis* 17 (1972): 40–52.

Adam, J. *The Republic of Plato: Edited with Critical Notes, Commentary and Appendices.* 2nd ed. 2 vols. Cambridge: Cambridge University Press, 1965.

Adluri, V. "Derrida, Textuality, and Sacrifice." *Southwest Philosophical Studies* 29 (Spring 2007): 9–19.

—. ed. *Philosophy and Salvation in Greek Religion.* Berlin: Walter de Gruyter, 2012.

—. "Heidegger's Encounter with Aristotle: A Theological Deconstruction of Metaphysics." Proceedings of the 44th Annual Meeting of the Heidegger Circle, Stony Brook University, New York, May 2010.

—. "Heraclitus on *Thanatos.*" *Abstracts of the 136th Annual Meeting of the American Philological Association*, Philadelphia 2005.

—. "Initiation into the Mysteries: Experience of the Irrational in Plato." *Mouseion*, Series III, vol. 6 (2006): 407–23.

—. "The Perils of Textual Transmission: Decapitation and Recapitulation." *Seminar*, no. 608, special issue titled *The Enduring Epic: A Symposium on Some Concerns Raised in the Mahābhārata* (April 2010): 48–54.

—. "Review of *Parmenides, Cosmos, and Being: A Philosophical Interpretation,* by Panagiotis Thanassas." *Bryn Mawr Classical Review* March 18, 2010. http://bmcr.brynmawr.edu/2010/2010–03-18.html.

Algra, K. *Concepts of Space in Greek Thought.* Leiden: E. J. Brill, 1995.

Allen, R. E. "Participation and Predication in Plato's Middle Dialogues." *Studies in Plato's Metaphysics.* Ed. R. E. Allen. London: Routledge & Kegan Paul, 1965. 43–60.

—. *Plato's "Parmenides": Translation and Analysis.* Minneapolis: University of Minnesota Press, 1983.

Ambrose, Z. P. "The Homeric *Telos.*" *Glotta* 43 (1965): 38–62.

Arendt, H. *The Human Condition.* Chicago: University of Chicago Press, 1958.

—. *Responsibility and Judgment.* New York: Schocken Books, 2003.

—. *Revolution.* New York: Penguin Books, 1986.

Aristotle. *The Physics.* Trans. F. M. Cornford and P. H. Wicksteed. London: Heinemann. New York: Putnam, 1929.

Ast, F. *Lexicon Platonicum.* 2 vols. Lipsiae: in libraria Weidmanniana, 1835–38.

Aubenque, P., ed. *Études sur Parménide.* 2 vols. Paris: J. Vrin, 1987.

Augustine. *The Confessions of St. Augustine.* Trans. J. K. Ryan. New York: Image Books, 1960.

Austin, J. L. *How to Do Things with Words.* Oxford: Clarendon Press, 1962.

—. *Philosophical Papers.* Oxford: Clarendon Press, 1961.

—. *Sense and Sensibilia.* Oxford: Clarendon Press, 1962.

Austin, S. "Genesis and Motion in Parmenides: B8.12–13." *Harvard Studies in Classical Philology* 87 (1983): 151–68.

—. *Parmenides: Being, Bounds, and Logic.* New Haven: Yale University Press, 1986.

Bagchee, J., trans. *The Doctrine of Categories and Meaning of Duns Scotus.* Bloomington, IN: Indiana University Press, forthcoming.

—. "Return to Transcendence: The Project of *Being and Time* and the Problem of Human Finitude." Ph.D. diss., New School for Social Research, 2009.

Baldes, R. W. "'Divisibility' and 'Division' in Democritus." *Apeiron* 12 (1978): 1–12.

Ballew, L. "Straight and Circular in Parmenides and the 'Timaeus.'" *Phronesis* 19 (1974): 189–209.

Barnes, J. *Early Greek Philosophy.* Harmondsworth: Penguin Books, 1987.

—. "Parmenides and the Eleatic One." *Archiv für Geschichte der Philosophie* 61 (1979): 1–21.

—. *The Presocratic Philosphers.* 2 vols. London: Routledge & Kegan Paul, 1979.

Barrett, W. S. *Euripides: Hippolytos. Edited with Introduction and Commentary.* Oxford: Clarendon Press, 1964.

Beaufret, J. *Le poème de Parménide.* Paris: Presses universitaires de France, 1955.

Becker, O. "Das Bild des Weges und verwandte Vorstellungen im frühgriechischen Denken." *Hermes* Einzelschriften 4. Berlin, 1937.

Benardete, S. *The Being of the Beautiful: Plato's Theaetetus, Sophist, and Statesman.* Chicago: University of Chicago Press, 1984.

—. "*Khrē* and *dei* in Plato and Others." *Glotta* 43 (1965): 285–98.

—. *Plato's Theaetetus.* Chicago: University of Chicago Press, 1968.

Bergk, T. *Kleine philologische Schriften.* Ed. R. Peppmüller. 2 vols. Halle: Buchhandlung des Waisenhauses, 1884–86.

Bicknell, J. "A New Arrangement of Some Parmenidean Verses." *Symbolae Osloenses* 42 (1968): 44–50.

—. "Parmenides, DK 28 B4." *Apeiron* 13 (1979): 115.

—. "Parmenides, DK 28 B5." *Apeiron* 13 (1979): 9–11.

—. "Parmenides, Fragment 10." *Hermes* 98 (1968): 629–31.

—. "Parmenides's Refutation of Motion and an Implication." *Phronesis* 12 (1967): 1–5.

—. "Zeno's Arguments on Motion." *Acta Classica* 6 (1963): 81–105.

Blank, D. L. "Faith and Persuasion in Parmenides." *Classical Antiquity* 1 (1982): 167–79.

Blümner, H. *Technologie und Terminologie der Gewerbe und Künste bei Griechen und Römern.* 4 vols. Leipzig: B.G. Teubner, 1875.

Bodnar, I. *Being Bound: A Parmenidian Journey.* Budapest, 1990.

Boeder, H. "Der frühgriechische Wortgebrauch von *Logos* und *Aletheia*." *Archiv für Begriffsgeschichte* 4 (1959): 82–112.

—. *Grund und Gegenwart als Frageziel der frühgriechischen Philosophie.* The Hague: Martinus Nijhoff, 1962.

Bollack, J. "La Cosmologie parménidéenne de Parménide." *Herméneutique et Ontologie: Mélanges en homage à Pierre Aubenque.* Ed. R. Brague. Paris: Presses Universitaires de France, 1990. 17–53.

—. *Empédocle.* 3 vols. Paris: Les Editions de Minuit, 1965–69.

Bormann, K. *Parmenides: Untersuchungen zu den Fragmenten.* Hamburg: Felix Meiner Verlag, 1971.

—. "Perpetual Duration and Atemporal Eternity in Parmenides and Plato." *Monist* 62 (1979): 43–53.

Boswell, J. *Same Sex Unions in Premodern Europe.* New York: Vintage, 1995.

Boudouris, K., ed. *Ionian Philosophy.* Athens: International Association for Greek Philosophy, 1989.

Bowra, C. M. "The Proem of Parmenides." *Classical Philology* 32 (1937): 97–112.

Bremmer, J. *Early Greek Concept of the Soul.* Princeton: Princeton University Press, 1987.

Brentlinger, J. "Incomplete Predicates and the Two-World Theory of the Phaedo." *Phronesis* 17 (1972): 61–79.

Bultmann, R. and A. Weiser. *Faith, Bible Key Words from Gerhard Kittel's Theologisches Wörterbuch zum Neuen Testament.* Trans. D. M. Barton. Ed. P. R. Ackroyd. London: A. & C. Black, 1961.

—. *Theology of the New Testament.* Trans. Kendrick Grobel. New York: Scribner, 1951.

Burger, R. *Plato's Phaedrus.* Tuscaloosa, AL: University of Alabama Press, 1980.

Burkert, W. *Homo Necans.* Trans. Peter Bing. Berkeley: University of California Press, 1983.

—. *Lore and Science in Ancient Pythagoreanism.* Trans. E. L. Minar, Jr. Cambridge: Harvard University Press, 1972.

—. "Das Proömium des Parmenides und die Katabasis des Pythagoras." *Phronesis* 15 (1969): 1–30. Trans. Joydeep Bagchee as "Parmenides' Proem and Pythagoras' Descent." *Philosophy and Salvation in Greek Religion.* Ed. Vishwa Adluri. Berlin: Walter de Gruyter, 2012.

Burnet, J. *Early Greek Philosophy.* 4th ed. London: Adam and Charles Black, 1930.

Burnyeat, M. F. "Idealism and Greek Philosophy. What Descartes Saw and Berkeley Missed." *Philosophical Review* 91 (1982): 3–40.

Calasso, R. *The Marriage of Cadmus and Harmony.* New York: Vintage, 1993.

Calogero, G. "Parmenide di Elea." *Enciclopedia italiana.* Rome: Istuto Giovanni Treccani, 1929–36.

—. "La regola di Socrate." *La cultura* I (1963): 182–96.

—. *Storia della Logica Antica,* vol. I. *L'Età arcaica.* Bari: Laterza, 1967.

—. *Studi sull'eleatismo.* 2nd ed. Firenze: La Nuova Italia, 1977.

Calvert, B. "Meno's Paradox Reconsidered." *Journal of the History of Philosophy* 12 (1974): 143–52.

Calvo, T. "Truth and *Doxa* in Parmenides." *Archiv für Geschichte der Philosophie* 59 (1977): 245–60.

Caswell, C. P. *Study of* Thumos *in Early Greek Epic* (*Mnemosyne* Suppl. 144). Leiden: Brill, 1990.

Cerri, G. *Parmenide di Elea, Poema sulla natura, Introduzione, testo, traduzione e note.* Milano: Biblioteca Universale Rizzoli, 1999.

—. "Parmenides' Physical Theory." Unpublished paper.

Chalmers, W. R. "Parmenides and the Beliefs in Morals." *Phronesis* 5 (1960): 5–22.

Chantraine, P. *Dictionnaire étymologique de la langue grec.* 4 vols. Paris: Editions Klincksieck, 1968.

Cherniss, H. *Aristotle's Criticism of Presocratic Philosophy.* Baltimore: Johns Hopkins Press, 1935.

—. "The Characteristics and Effects of Presocratic Philosophy." *Journal of the History of Ideas* 12 (1951): 319–45.

—. ed. and trans. "Concerning the Face Which Appears in the Orb of the Moon." *Plutarch's Moralia 920A–945D*. Loeb Classical Library. Cambridge, MA: Harvard University Press, 1957.

—. "Parmenides and the *Parmenides* of Plato." *The American Journal of Philology* 53 (1932): 122–38.

—. "Timaeus 38a8–b5." *Journal of Hellenic Studies* 77, Part 1 (1957): 18–23.

Clark, R. J. "Parmenides and Sense-Perception." *Revue des études grècques* 82 (1969): 14–32.

Clarke, M. *Flesh and Spirit in the Songs of Homer.* Oxford: Oxford University Press, 1999.

Classen, C. J. "Licht und Dunkel in der frühgriechischen Philosophie." *Studium generale* 18 (1965): 97–116.

Cobb, W. S. *Plato's Erotic Dialogues.* Albany, NY: SUNY Press, 1993.

Collobert, C. *L'être de Parménide ou le refus de temps.* Paris: Edition Kimé, 1993.

Cordero, N.-L. "Les Deux Chemins de Parménide dans les fragments 6 et 7." *Phronesis* 24 (1979): 1–32.

—. "L'histoire du Texte de Parménide." *Études sur Parménide*, vol. 1. Ed. Pierre Aubenque. Paris: J. Vrin, 1987. 3–24.

—. "Zénon d'Elée, Moniste ou Nihiliste?" *La Parola del Passato* 43 (1983): 100–26.

—. *By Being, It is: The Thesis of Parmenides.* Las Vegas: Parmenides Publishing, 2004.

Cornford, F. M. "Anaxagoras' Theory of Matter." *Studies in Presocratic Philosophy*, vol. 2. Ed. D. J. Furley and R. E. Allen. London: Routledge & Kegan Paul, 1975. 275–322.

—. *From Religion to Philosophy.* London: Edward Arnold, 1912.

—. "A New Fragment of Parmenides." *Classical Review* 49 (1935): 122–3.

—. "Parmenides' Two Ways." *Classical Quarterly* 27 (1933): 97–111.

—. *Plato and Parmenides.* London: Routledge & Kegan Paul, 1939.

—. *Plato's Cosmology.* London: Routledge & Kegan Paul, 1937.

—. *Plato's Theory of Knowledge.* London: Routledge & Kegan Paul, 1935.

Cosgrove, M. R. "The *Kouros* Motif in Parmenides: B 1.24." *Phronesis* 19 (1974): 81–94.

Couloubaritsis, L. "Considération sur la notion de 'Noûs' chez Démocrite." *Archiv für Geschichte der Philosophie* 62 (1980): 129–45.

Coxon, A. H. *The Fragments of Parmenides.* Assen: Van Gorcum, 1986.

—. "The Manuscript Tradition of Simplicius' Commentary on Aristotle's *Physics* i–iv." *Classical Quarterly*, n.s., 18 (1968): 70–5.

—. "Parmenides on Thinking and Being." *Mnemosyne* 4th series, 56, fasc. 2 (2003): 210–12.

—. "The Philosophy of Parmenides." *Classical Quarterly* 28 (1934): 134–44.

—. "The Text of Parmenides: Fr. 1.3." *Classical Quarterly*, n.s., 18 (1968): 69.

Croissant, J. "Le Début de la doxa de Parménide." *Mélanges offerts a A. -M. Desrousseaux par ses amis et ses élèves.* Paris: Librarie Hachett, 1937. 99–104.

Crystal, I. "Parmenidean Allusions in *Republic V*." *Ancient Philosophy* 16 (1996): 351–63.

—. "The Scope of Thought in Parmenides." *Classical Quarterly*, n.s., 52.1 (2002): 207–19.

Cunliffe, R. J. *A Lexicon of the Homeric Dialect.* Norman, OK: University of Oklahoma Press, 1963.

Curd, M. V. "Showing and Telling: Can the Difference between Right and Left Be Explained in Words?" *The Philosophy of Right and Left: Incongruent Counterparts and the Nature of Space.* Ed. J. Van Cleve and R. E. Frederick. Dordrecht: Kluwer Academic Publishers, 1991. 195–201.

Curd, P. K. "Deception and Belief in Parmenides' *Doxa.*" *Apeiron* 25 (1992): 109–33.

—. "Eleatic Arguments." *Method in Ancient Philosophy.* Ed. J. Gentzler. Oxford: Oxford University Press, 1997. 1–28.

—. "Eleatic Monism in Zeno and Melissus." *Ancient Philosophy* 13 (1993): 1–22.

—. "Knowledge and Unity in Heraclitus." *The Monist* 74 (1991): 531–49.

—. *The Legacy of Parmenides.* Princeton: Princeton University Press, 1999.

—. "Parmenidean Monism." *Phronesis* 36 (1991): 241–64.

—. "Socratic Empiricism." *The Philosophy of Socrates,* vol. 1. Ed. K. Boudouris. Athens: International Association for Greek Philosophy, 1991. 208–16.

—. "Some Problems of Unity in the First Hypothesis of the *Parmenides.*" *Southern Journal of Philosophy* 27 (1989): 347–59.

Denniston, J. D. *The Greek Particles.* 2nd ed. Oxford: Clarendon Press, 1954.

Derrida, J. "Plato's Pharmacy." *Dissemination.* Trans. Barbara Johnson. Chicago: University of Chicago Press, 1981.

Descartes, R. *The Philosophical Works of Descartes.* Trans. E. S. Haldane and G. R. T. Ross. Cambridge: Cambridge University Press, 1911.

—. *The Philosophical Writings of Descartes,* vol. 2. Trans. J. Cottingham et al. Cambridge: Cambridge University Press, 1984.

Détienne, M. *The Daily Life of the Greek Gods.* Stanford: Stanford University Press, 2000.

Détienne, M. and Jean-Pierre Vernant. *The Cuisine of Sacrifice among the Greeks.* Trans. Paula Wissing. Chicago: University of Chicago Press, 1989.

—. *Ruses de l'intelligence: La Métis des grecs.* Paris: Flammarian, 1974. Trans. J. Lloyd as *Cunning Intelligence in Greek Culture.* Atlantic Highlands, NJ: Humanities Press, 1978.

Diels, H. *Doxographi Graeci.* 4th ed. 1879. Berlin: Walter de Gruyter, 1965.

—. *Parmenides: Lehrgedicht.* Berlin: Georg Reimer, 1897.

Diels, H. and W. Kranz, eds. *Die Fragmente der Vorsokratiker.* 3 vols. 1951–52, reprint of 6th ed. Berlin: Weidnamm, 1974.

Diller, H. "Die dichterische Form von Hesiods Erga." *Akademie der Wissenschaften und der Literatur in Mains: Abhandlungen der Geistes- und Sozialwissenschaftlichen Klasse.* No. 2. Jahrgang: 1962. 41–69.

—. "Der vorphilosophische Gebrauch von *kosmos* und *kosmein.*" *Festschrift Bruno Snell.* Munchen: C. H. Beck, 1956. 47–60.

Dillon, J. "Proclus and the Forty *Logoi* of Zeno." *Illinois Classical Studies* 11 (1986): 35–41.

Diogenes Laertius. *The Lives of Eminent Philosophers,* vol. 1. Trans. R. D. Hicks. Cambridge: Harvard University Press, 1950.

Dodds, E. R. *The Greeks and the Irrational.* Berkley and Los Angeles: University of California Press, 1951.

Dolin, E. F., Jr. "Parmenides and Hesiod." *Harvard Studies in Classical Philology* 66 (1962): 93–8.

Dover, K. J. *Greek Homosexuality.* Cambridge: Harvard University Press, 1978.

Dumont, J.-P. "Les Abdéritains et le non être." *Bulletin de la Société française de Philosophie* 77 (1983): 39–58, discussion reported on 58–76.

Dunbar, H. *A Complete Concordance to the Odyssey of Homer.* Ed. B. Marzullo. Hildesheim: G. Olms, 1962.

Eagleton, T. *Sweet Violence: The Idea of the Tragic.* Malden, MA: Blackwell, 2003.

Eaton, R. M. *Symbolism and Truth.* Cambridge, MA: Harvard University Press, 1925.

Eliade, M. *Shamanism: Archaic Technique of Ecstasy.* Trans. W. R. Trask. New York: Bollingen Foundation, 1964.

English, R. B. "Parmenides' Indebtedness to the Pythagoreans." *Transactions and Proceedings of the American Philological Association* 42 (1912): 81–94.

Ferrari, G. R. F. *Listening to the Cicadas.* Cambridge: Cambridge University Press, 1987.

Ferwerda, R. *La Signifation des images et des métaphors dans la pensée de Plotin.* Groningen: J. B. Wolters, 1965.

Festugière, A. F. "Platon et l'Orient." *Revue de Philologie* 3 (1947): 5–45.

Finkelberg, A. "The Cosmology of Parmenides." *American Journal of Philology* 107 (1986): 303–17.

—. "Like by Like' and Two Reflections of Reality in Parmenides." *Hermes* 114 (1986): 405–12.

—. "Parmenides: Between Material and Logical Monism." *Archiv für Geschichte der Philosophie* 70 (1988): 1–14.

—. "Parmenides' Foundation of the Way of Truth." *Oxford Studies in Ancient Philosophy* 6 (1988): 39–67.

Floyd, E. D. "Why Parmenides Wrote in Verse." *Ancient Philosophy* 12 (1992): 251–65.

Forrester, J. W. "The Argument of the 'Porphyry Text.'" *Journal of the History of Philosophy* 11 (1973): 537–39.

Fournier, H. *Les Verbes "dire" en grec ancien.* Paris: C. Klincksieck, 1946.

Fowler, H. W. *A Dictionary of Modern English Usage.* 2nd ed. New York: Oxford University Press, 1965.

Francotte, A. "Les disertes Juments de Parménide." *Phronesis* 3 (1958): 83–94.

Fränkel, E. *Aeschylus: Agamemnon. Edited with a Commentary.* 3 vols. Oxford: Clarendon Press, 1950.

Fränkel, H. *Early Greek Philosophy and Poetry.* Trans. M. Hadas and J. Willis. Oxford: Basil Blackwell, 1975.

—. "Studies in Parmenides." *Studies in Presocratic Philosophy,* vol. 2 Ed. D. J. Furley and R. E. Allen. London: Routledge & Kegan Paul, 1975. 1–47.

—. "Zeno of Elea's Attacks on Plurality." *Studies in Presocratic Philosophy,* vol. 2. Ed. D. J. Furley and R. E. Allen. London: Routledge & Kegan Paul, 1975. 102–42.

Frede, M. "Prädikation und Existenzaussage." *Hypomnemata* 18, Gottingen: Vandenhoeck und Ruprecht, 1967.

Freudenthal, G. "The Theory of Opposites and an Ordered Universe: Physics and Metaphysics in Anaximander." *Phronesis* 31 (1986): 197–228.

Friedländer, P. *Plato: An Introduction.* Trans. H. Meyerhoff. New York: Harper & Row, 1958.

—. *Platon.* 3rd ed. 2 vols. Berlin: W. de Gruyter, 1964.

Frutiger, P. *Les Mythes de Platon: étude philosophique et littéraire.* Paris: F. Alcan, 1930.

Fujisawa, N. "*'Ekhein, metekhein* and Idioms of 'Paradigmatism' in Plato's Theory of Forms." *Phronesis* 20 (1975): 30–49.

Furley, D. J. "Anaxagoras and the Naming of Parts." Unpublished manuscript.

—. "Anaxagoras in Response to Parmenides." *Cosmic Problems: Essays on Greek and Roman Philosophy of Nature.* Ed. D. J. Furley. Cambridge: Cambridge University Press, 1989. 47–65.

—. *Cosmic Problems: Essays on Greek and Roman Philosophy of Nature.* Cambridge: Cambridge University Press, 1989.

—. "From Anaxagoras to Socrates." *The Philosophy of Socrates*, vol. II. *Elenchus, Ethics, and Truth.* Athens: International Center for Greek Philosophy and Culture, 1992. 74–80.

—. *The Greek Cosmologists*, vol. I. *The Formation of the Atomic Theory and Its Earliest Critics.* Cambridge: Cambridge University Press, 1987.

—. "Melissus of Samos." *Ionian Philosophy.* Ed. K. Boudouris. Athens: International Association for Greek Philosophy, 1989. 114–22.

—. "Notes on Parmenides." *Cosmic Problems: Essays on Greek and Roman Philosophy of Nature.* Ed. D. J. Furley. Cambridge: Cambridge University Press, 1989. 27–37.

—. "Parmenides of Elea." *Encyclopedia of Philosophy*, vol. 5. Ed. P. Edwards. New York: Macmillan Co. and the Free Press, 1967. 47–51.

—. "Truth as What Survives the *Elengkhos.*" *Cosmic Problems: Essays on Greek and Roman Philosophy of Nature.* Ed. D. J. Furley. Cambridge: Cambridge University Press, 1989. 38–46.

Furley, D. J. and R. E. Allen. *Studies in Presocratic Philosophy.* 2 vols. London: Routledge & Kegan Paul, 1970–75.

Furth, M. a. "Elements of Eleatic Ontology." *Journal of the History of Philosophy* 7 (1968): 111–32.

—. "Elements of Eleatic Ontology." *The Pre-Socratics.* Ed. A. P. D. Mourelatos. Garden City, NY: Doubleday, 1974; reprint, Princeton: Princeton University Press, 1993. 241–70.

—. "A 'Philosophical Hero?' Anaxagoras and the Eleatics." *Oxford Studies in Ancient Philosophy* 9 (1991): 95–129.

Gadamer, H-G. "Um die Begriffswelt der Vorsokratiker." *Wege der Forschung* 9. Darmstadt: Wissenschaftliche Buchgesellschaft, 1968.

—. "Plato und die Vorsokratiker." *Epimelia: Die Sorge der Philosophie um den Menschen (Festschrift Helmut Kuhn).* Ed. F. Weidmann. Munchen: Pustet, 1964. 127–42.

—. "Zur Vorgeschichte der Metaphysik." *Anteile: Festschrift Martin Heidegger.* Frankfurt a.M.: Vittorio Klostermann, 1950. 51–79.

—. "Retraktationen zum Lehrgedicht des Parmenides." *Varia Variorum: Festschrift Karl Reinhardt.* Munster/Koln: Bohlau, 1952. 58–68.

Gallop, D. " 'Is or Is Not'?" *The Monist* 62 (1979): 61–80.

—. *Parmenides of Elea: Fragments.* Toronto: University of Toronto Press, 1984.

Gigon, O. *Der Ursprung der griechischen Philosophie von Hesiod bis Parmenides.* Basel: B. Schwabe & Co., 1945.

Gill, M. L. and P. Ryan. *Plato: Parmenides.* Indianapolis: Hackett, 1996.

Goldin, O. "Parmenides on Possibility and Thought." *Apeiron* 26 (1993): 19–35.

Gomperz, T. *Greek Thinkers*, vol. 1. Trans. Laurie Magnus. London: John Murray, 1901. 246–62.

Goody, J. *The Interface between the Written and the Oral.* Cambridge: Cambridge University Press, 1987.

Graham, D. A. "Heraclitus and Parmenides." Unpublished manuscript.

—. "The Postulates of Anaxagoras." *Apeiron* 27 (1994): 77–121.

—. "Symmetry in the Empedoclean Cycle." *Classical Quarterly* 38 (1988): 297–312.

Graz, L. "Le Feu dans l'Illiade et l'Odyssée: *pyr:* Champ d'emploi et signification." *Études et commentaries* 60. Paris: C. Kincksieck, 1965.

Griswold, C. L., Jr. *Self-Knowledge in Plato's Phaedrus.* University Park: Pennsylvania State University Press, 1996.

Groarke, L. "Parmenides' Timeless Universe." *Dialogue* 24 (1985): 535–41.

—. "Parmenides' Timeless Universe, Again." *Dialogue* 26 (1987): 549–52.

Guazzoni Foà, V. "Per l'interpretazione di aidelos nel fr. 10 di Parmenide." *Giornale di metafisica* 19 (1964): 558–62.

Guthrie, W. K. C. *A History of Greek Philosophy.* 2 vols. Cambridge, Cambridge University Press, 1962–65.

Hackforth, R. *Plato's Phaedrus. Translated with an introduction and commentary.* Cambridge: Cambridge University Press, 1993.

Harrison, J. E. *Prolegomena to the Study of Greek Religion.* Princeton: Princeton University Press, 1991.

Havelock, E. A. *The Literate Revolution in Greece and Its Cultural Consequences.* Princeton: Princeton University Press, 1982.

—. "Parmenides and Odysseus." *Harvard Studies in Classical Philology* 63 (1958): 133–43.

—. *Preface to Plato.* Cambridge: Harvard University Press, 1963.

—. "Pre-Literacy and the Pre-Socratics." *Institute of Classical Studies, University of London* Bulletin No. 13 (1966): 44–67.

—. "Thoughtful Hesiod." *Yale Classical Studies* 20 (1966): 44–67.

Heath, P. L. "Nothing." *The Encyclopedia of Philosophy,* vol. 5. Ed. P. Edwards. New York: Macmillan Co. and the Free Press, 1967.

—. *The Philosopher's Alice.* New York: St. Martin's Press, 1974.

Heidegger, M. *The Basic Problems of Phenomenology.* Trans. Albert Hofstadter. Bloomington, IN: Indiana University Press, 1982.

—. *Being and Time.* Trans. Joan Stambaugh. Albany, NY: SUNY Press, 1996.

—. "Das Ding." *Vorträge und Aufsätze.* Pfullingen: Neske, 1954.

—. *Early Greek Thinking.* Trans. David Farrell Krell and Frank A Capuzzi. San Francisco: Harper, 1984.

—. *The End of Philosophy.* Trans. Joan Stambaugh. Chicago: University of Chicago Press, 1973.

—. *Frühe Schriften.* Frankfurt a.M.: Vittorio Klostermann, 1972.

—. *The Fundamental Concepts of Metaphysics.* Trans. W. McNeill and N. Walker. Bloomington, IN: Indiana University Press, 1995.

—. *An Introduction to Metaphysics.* Trans. R. Manheim. New Haven: Yale University Press, 1959.

—. *Nietzsche.* 2 vols. Trans. David Farrell Krell. New York: Harper, 1981.

—. *On Time and Being.* Trans. J. Stambaugh. New York: Harper & Row, 1972.

—. *Parmenides.* Trans. A. Schuwer and R. Rojcewicz. Bloomington, IN: Indiana University Press, 1992.

—. *Pathmarks.* Ed. William McNeill. Cambridge: Cambridge University Press, 1999.

—. "Phenomenological Interpretations of Aristotle: An Indication of the Hermeneutic Situation." *Supplements: From the Earliest Essays to* Being and Time *and Beyond.* Ed. John van Buren. Albany, NY: SUNY Press, 2002.

—. *Phenomenological Interpretations of Aristotle: Initiation into Phenomenological Research.* Trans. Richard Rojcewicz. Bloomington, IN: Indiana University Press, 2001.

—. *Prolegomena to the History of the Concept of Time.* Trans. Theodor Kisiel. Bloomington, IN: Indiana University Press, 1985.

—. "The Question Concerning Technology." *Basic Writings.* Ed. David Farrell Krell. San Francisco: Harper, 1993. 307–41.

Hegel, G. W. F. *Phenomenology of Spirit.* Trans. A. V. Miller. Oxford: Oxford University Press, 1977.

Heidel, W. "On Certain Fragments of the Pre-Socratics: Critical Notes and Elucidations." *Proceedings of the American Academy of Arts and Sciences* 48 (1913): 681–734.

—. "*Peri phuseōs*: A Study of the Conception of Nature among the Pre-Socratics." *Proceedings of the American Academy of Arts and Sciences* 45 (1910): 79–133.

—. "Qualitative Change in Pre-Socratic Philosophy." *Archiv für Geschichte der Philosophie* 19, n.s., 12 (1906): 333–79.

Heinimann, F. *Nomos und Physis: Herkunft und Bedeutung einer Antithese im griechischen Denken des 5. Jahrhunderts.* Basel: F. Reinhardt, 1945.

Heitsch, E. "Die nicht-philosophische *aletheia.*" *Hermes* 90 (1962): 24–33.

—. "Das Wissen des Xenophanes." *Rheinisches Museum fur Philologie* 109 (1966): 193–235.

Hermann, A. *To Think Like God: Pythagoras and Parmenides. The Origins of Philosophy.* Las Vegas, NV: Parmenides Publishing, 2004.

Hershbell, J. P. "Parmenides and *Outis* in *Odyssey* 9." *Classical Journal* 68 (1972–73): 178–80.

—. "Parmenides' Way of Truth and B16." *Apeiron* 4 (1970): 1–23.

Heubeck, A. and A. Hoekstra, eds. *A Commentary on Homer's Odyssey,* vol. 2. Oxford: Oxford University Press, 1989.

Hintikka, J. "*Cogito, Ergo Sum*: Inference or Performance?" *Philosophical Review* 71 (1962): 3–32.

Hölscher, U. "Anaximander and the Beginnings of Greek Philosophy." *Studies in Presocratic Philosophy,* vol. 1. Ed. D. J. Furley and R. E. Allen. London: Routledge & Kegan Paul, 1975. 281–322.

—. *Anfängliches Fragen: Studien zur frühen griechischen Philosophie.* Göttingen: Vandenhoeck u. Ruprecht, 1968.

—. "Grammatisches zu Parmenides." *Hermes* 84 (1956): 385–97.

—. "Weltzeiten und Lebensyklus: Eine Nachprüfung der Empedokles-Doxographie." *Hermes* 93 (1965): 7–33.

Hussey, E. *The Pre-Socratics.* New York: Charles Scribner's Sons, 1972.

Inwood, B. "Anaxagoras and Infinite Divisibility." *Illinois Classical Studies* 11 (1986): 17–33.

—. "The Origins of Epicurus' Concept of Void." *Classical Philology* 76 (1981): 273–85.

—. *The Poem of Empedocles: A Text and Translation with an Introduction.* Toronto: University of Toronto Press, 1992.

Jacobs, D. C., ed. *The Presocratics after Heidegger.* Albany, NY: SUNY Press, 1999.

Jaeger, W. *The Theology of the Early Greek Philosophers.* Oxford: Clarendon Press, 1947.

Jameson, G. "Well-Rounded Truth and Circular Thought in Parmenides." *Phronesis* (1958): 15–30.

Johnson, M. R. "Review of *The Legacy of Parmenides*, by Patricia Curd." *Bryn Mawr Classical Review* June 21, 1999.

Jöhrens, O. *Die Fragmente des Anaxagoras.* Bochum-Langendreer: Druck, Heinrich Pöppinghaus o. H. G., 1939.

Jones, B. "Parmenides' "Way of Truth.' " *Journal of the History of Philosophy* 11 (1973): 287–98.

Kahn, C. H. *Anaximander and the Origins of Greek Cosmology.* Philadelphia: Centrum Philadelphia, 1985.

—. *The Art and Thought of Heraclitus.* Cambridge: Cambridge University Press, 1979.

—. "The Beautiful and the Genuine." *Oxford Studies in Ancient Philosophy* 3 (1985): 261–87.

—. "Being in Parmenides and Plato." *La Parola del Passato* 43 (1988): 237–61.

—. "Democritus and the Origins of Moral Psychology." *American Journal of Philology* 106 (1985): 1–31.

—. "The Greek Verb 'To Be' and the Concept of Being." *Foundations of Language* 2 (1966): 245–65.

—. "The Historical Position of Anaxagoras." *Ionian Philosophy.* Ed. K. Boudouris. Athens: International Association for Greek Philosophy, 1989. 203–10.

—. "More on Parmenides." *Review of Metaphysics* 22 (1968/69): 333–40.

—. "Pythagoras and Pythagoreanism before Plato." *The Pre-Socratics.* Ed. A. P. D. Mourelatos. Garden City, NY: Doubleday, 1974; reprinted Princeton: Princeton University Press, 1993. 161–85.

—. "Retrospect on the Verb 'To Be' and the Concept of Being." *The Logic of Being.* Ed. S. Knuuttila and J. Hintikka. Dordrecht: D. Reidel, 1986. 1–28.

—. "Review of *Parmenides: A Text with Translation, Commentary and Critical Essays*, by L. Taran." *Gnōmon* 40 (1968): 123–33.

—. "The Thesis of Parmenides." *Review of Metaphysics* 23 (1969/70): 700–24.

—. *The Verb "Be" in Ancient Greek; Foundations of Language*, Supplementary Series, vol. 16. Dordrecht: Reidel, 1973.

—. "Why Existence Does Not Emerge as a Distinct Concept in Greek Philosophy." *Archiv für Geschichte der Philosophie* 58 (1978): 323–34.

Kember, O. "Right and Left in the Sexual Theories of Parmenides." *Journal of Hellenic Studies* 91 (1971): 70–9.

Kerferd, G. B. "Anaxagoras and the Concept of Matter before Aristotle." *The Pre-Socratics.* Ed. A. P. D. Mourelatos. Garden City, NY: Doubleday, 1974; reprinted Princeton: Princeton University Press, 1993. 489–503.

Kerschensteiner, J. *Kosmos: Quellenkritische Untersuchungen zu den Vorsokratikern.* München: C. H. Beck, 1962.

Ketchum, R. J. "Parmenides on What There Is." *Canadian Journal of Philosophy* 20 (1990): 167–90.

Kingsley, P. *Ancient Philosophy, Mystery, and Magic: Empedocles and Pythagorean Tradition.* Oxford: Clarendon Press, 1995.

—. *In the Dark Places of Wisdom.* Inverness, CA: Golden Sufi Center, 1999.

Kirk, G. S. *Heraclitus: The Cosmic Fragments.* Cambridge: Cambridge University Press, 1954.

—. "Men and Opposites in Heraclitus." *Museum Helveticum* 14 (1957): 155–63.

Kirk, G. S. and M. C. Stokes. "Parmenides' Refutation of Motion." *Phronesis* 5 (1960): 1–22.

Kirk, G. S., J. E. Raven, and M. S. Schofield, eds. *The Presocratic Philosophers.* 2nd ed. Cambridge: Cambridge University Press, 1983.

Kirwan, C. "Review of *Parmenides: A Text with Translation, Commentary and Critical Essays,* by L. Taran." *Mind* 79 (1970): 308–10.

Kittel, G., ed. *Theologisches Wörterbuch zum Neuen Testament,* 7 vols. Stuttgart: W. Kohlhammer, 1949.

Kleingünther, A. *Protos Euretes: Untersuchungen zur Geschichte einer Fragestellung. Philologus.* Supplementary Vol. 26, No. 1. Leipzig, 1933.

Kneale, W. "Time and Eternity in Theology." *Proceedings of the Aristotelian Society,* n.s., 61 (1960–61): 87–108.

Knight, T. S. "Parmenides and the Void." *Philosophy and Phenomenological Research* 19 (1958–59): 524–31.

Knox, B. *The Heroic Temper.* Sather Classical Lectures 35. Berkeley: University of California Press, 1964.

Kouremenos, T. "Parmenidean Influences in the 'Agamemnon' of Aeschylus." *Hermes* 121.3 (1993): 259–65.

Kripke, S. "Identity and Necessity." *Naming, Necessity, and Natural Kinds.* Ed. S. P. Schwartz. Ithaca: Cornell University Press, 1977. 66–101.

Krischer, T. "*Etumos* und *alēthēs.*" *Philologus* 109 (1965): 161–74.

Kühner, R. and B. Gerth. *Ausführliche Grammatik der griechischen Sprache.* 4 vols. 3rd ed. 1890–1904. Hannover: Hahnsche Buchhandlung, 1976.

Lacey, A. R. "The Eleatics and the Aristotle on Some Problems of Change." *Journal of the History of Ideas* 26 (1965): 451–68.

Laks, A. *Diogéne d'Apollonie: La Dernière Cosmologie présocratique.* Lille: Presses Universitaires de Lille, 1983.

Latona, M. J. "Reining in the Passions: The Allegorical Interpretation of Parmenides B Fragment 1." *The American Journal of Philology* 129.2 (Summer, 2008): 199–230.

Lattimore, R., trans. *The Odyssey of Homer.* New York: Harper & Row, 1965.

Lee, E. N. "On the Metaphysics of the Image in Plato's *Timaeus.*" *The Monist* 50 (1966): 341–68.

Lesher, J. H. "The Emergence of Philosophical Interest in Cognition." *Oxford Studies in Ancient Philosophy* 12 (1994): 1–34.

Lesky, A. *Greek Tragic Poetry.* Trans. M. Dillon. New Haven: Yale University Press, 1983.

Lloyd, G. E. R. *Methods and Problems in Greek Science.* Cambridge, Cambridge University Press, 1991.

Loenen, J. H. M. M. *Parmenides, Melissus, Gorgias.* Assen: Van Gorcum, 1959.

Long, A. A. "Empedocles' Cosmic Cycle in the 'Sixties'." *The Pre-Socratics.* Ed. A. P. D. Mourelatos. Garden City, NY: Doubleday, 1974; reprinted Princeton: Princeton University Press, 1993. 397–425.

—. "The Principles of Parmenides' Cosmogony." *Studies in Presocratic Philosophy,* vol. 2. New Jersey: N. J. Humanities Press, 1975.

Longrigg, J. "Elements and After: A Study in Presocratic Physics of the Second Half of the Fifth Century." *Apeiron* 19 (1985): 93–115.

Lovejoy, A. O. "The Meaning of *phusis* in the Greek Physiologers." *The Philosophical Review* 18 (1909): 369–83.

Lukacher, N. *Time-Fetishes: The Secret History of Eternal Recurrence.* Durham, NC: Duke University Press, 1998.

Luther, W. *Weltansicht und Geistesleben.* Göttingen: Vandenhoeck und Ruprecht, 1954.

Mackenzie, M. M. "Heraclitus and the Art of Paradox." *Oxford Studies in Ancient Philosophy* 6 (1988): 1–37.

—. "Parmenides' Dilemma." *Phronesis* 27–8 (1982–83): 1–12.

Malcolm, J. "Plato's Analysis of *to on* and *to me on* in the *Sophist.*" *Phronesis* 12 (1967): 130–46.

Manchester, P. B. "Parmenides and the Need for Eternity." *The Monist* 62 (1979): 81–106.

Mannsperger, D. *Physis bei Platon.* Berlin: de Gruyter, 1969.

Mansfeld, J. "Critical Note: Empedocles and His Interpreters." *Phronesis* 50 (1995): 109–15.

—. "Sources." *The Cambridge Companion to Early Greek Philosophy.* Ed. A. A. Long. Cambridge: Cambridge University Press, 1999. 22–44.

Marcovich, M. *Heraclitus: Greek Text with a Short Commentary (Editio Maior).* Merida, Venezuela: Los Andes University Press, 1967.

Marrou, H. I. *A History of Education in Antiquity.* Trans. George Lamb. Madison: University of Wisconsin Press, 1982.

Mason, R. "Parmenides and Language." *Ancient Philosophy* 8 (1988): 149–66.

Matthen, M. "A Note on Parmenides' Denial of Past and Future." *Dialogue* 25 (1986): 553–7.

McKirahan, R. *Philosophy before Socrates.* Indianapolis: Hackett, 1994.

Meinwald, C. C. *Plato's Parmenides.* New York, Oxford University Press, 1991.

Merleau-Ponty, M. *Phenomenology of Perception.* Trans. Colin Smith. London: Routledge & Kegan Paul, 1962.

Meuli, K. "Scythica." *Hermes* 70 (1935): 121–76.

Miller, F. D., Jr. "Parmenides on Mortal Belief." *Journal of the History of Philosophy* 15 (1977): 253–65.

Millerd, C. E. *On the Interpretation of Empedocles.* 1908. New York: Garland, 1980.

Minar, E. L., Jr. "Parmenides' and the World of Seeming." *American Journal of Philology* 70 (1949): 41–55.

Monteil, P. *La Phrase relative en grec ancien. Études et commentaries* 47. Paris: C. Klincksieck, 1963.

Montiglio, S. "Wandering Philosophers in Classical Greece." *Journal of Hellenic Studies* 120 (2000): 86–105.

Moorhouse, A. C. "*Den* in Classical Greece." *Classical Quarterly* 12.2 (1962): 235–38.

Morrison, J. S. "Parmenides and Er." *Journal of Hellenic Studies* 75 (1955): 59–68.

Morrow, G. R. and J. M. Dillon, trans. *Proclus' Commentary on Plato's Parmenides.* Princeton: Princeton University Press, 1987.

Mouliner, L. *Le Pur et l'impur dans la pensée des Grecs. Études et commentaries* 11. Paris: C. Klincksieck, 1952.

Mourelatos, A. P. D. "*Demokritos: philosophos tēs morphēs.*" *Proceedings of the First International Congress on Democritus,* vol. 1. Xanthi: International Democritean Foundation, 1984. 109–19. English abstract, "Democritus, Philosopher of Form," 118–19.

—. *The People of Plato*. Cambridge: Hackett Press, 2003.

—. ed. *The Pre-Socratics*, Garden City, NY: Doubleday, 1974; reprinted Princeton: Princeton University Press, 1993.

—. *The Route of Parmenides*. New Haven and London: Yale University Press, 1970.

Nails, D. "Mouthpiece, Shmouthpiece." *Who Speaks for Plato: Studies in Platonic Anonymity*. Ed. Gerald A. Press. Oxford: Rowan and Littlefield Publishers, 2000. 15–26.

Natorp, P. *Platons Ideenlehre: Eine Einführung in den Idealismus*. Leipzig: Verlag der Dürr'schen Buchhandlung, 1903.

Nehamas, A. "Meno's Paradox and Socrates as a Teacher." *Oxford Studies in Ancient Philosophy* 3 (1985): 1–30.

Newman, M. "Remembering Tradition, Transforming Remembrance." Unpublished paper, written at Yale University, New Haven, 2008.

Newton, I. *Philosophiae Naturalis Principia Mathematica* Third edition (1726) with variant readings (in two volumes). Ed. Alexandre Koyré et al. Cambridge, MA: Harvard University Press, 1972.

Nicholson, G. "On Parmenides' Three Ways of Inquiry." *Deukalion* (1981): 102.

—. *Plato's Phaedrus: The Philosophy of Love*. West Lafayette: Purdue University Press, 1999.

Nietzche, F. *Philosophy in the Tragic Age of the Greeks*. Trans. M. Cowan. Washington, DC: Gateway Editions, 1962.

—. *The Twilight of the Idols*. Cambridge: Cambridge University Press, 2005.

Nilsson, M. P. *The Mycenaean Origin of Greek Mythology*. Berkeley: University of California Press, 1972.

Notopoulos, J. A. "Parataxis in Homer: A New Approach to Homeric Literary Criticism." *Transactions of the American Philological Society* 80 (1949): 1–23.

Nussbaum, M. C. "Eleatic Conventionalism and Philolaus on the Conditions of Thought." *Harvard Studies in Classical Philology* 83 (1979): 63–108.

O'Brien, D. *Empedocles' Cosmic Cycle: A Reconstruction from the Fragments and Secondary Sources*. Cambridge: Cambridge University Press, 1969.

—. *Études sur Parménide, Tome I*. Paris: Librairie Philosophique, 1987.

Oguse, A. "A propos de la Syntaxe de *peithō* et de *pisteuo*." *Revue des études grecques* 78 (1965): 513–41.

Oliver, J. H. *Demokratia, the Gods, and the Free World*. Baltimore: Johns Hopkins Press, 1960.

Ong, W. J. *Orality and Literacy: The Technologizing of the Word*. London: Routledge, 1988.

Onians, R. B. *The Origins of European Thought*. Cambridge: Cambridge University Press, 1951.

Osborne, C. "Empedocles Recycled." *Classical Quarterly* 37 (1987): 24–50.

Owen, G. E. L. "Eleatic Questions." *Logic, Science, and Dialectic*. Ed. G. E. L. Owen and M. Nussbaum. Ithaca: Cornell University Press, 1986. 3–26.

Owens, J. *A History of Ancient Western Philosophy*. New York: Appleton-Century-Crofts, 1959.

Page, D. L. *The Homeric Odyssey*. Oxford: Clarendon Press, 1955.

Palmer, J. A. *Plato's Reception of Parmenides*. Oxford: Oxford University Press, 1999.

Panofsky, E. "Iconography and Iconology: An Introduction to the Study of Renaissance Art." *Meaning in the Visual Arts*. Ed. E. Panofsky. Garden City, NY: Doubleday, 1955. 26–54.

Pater, W. *Plato and Platonism.* Whitefish, MT: Kessinger Publishing, 2004.

Patin, A. *Parmenides im Kampfe gegen Heraklit. Jahrbücher für klassische Philologie.* Suppl. vol. 25 (1899): 489–660.

Paulson, J. *Index Hesiodus.* 1890. Hildesheim: G. Olms, 1962.

Pedersen, J. *Israel,* vol. 1. London: Oxford University Press, 1929.

Pellikaan-Engel, M. E. *Hesiod and Parmenides: A New View on Their Cosmologies and on Parmenides' Proem.* Amsterdam: Adolf M. Hakkert, 1974.

Pepe, G. M. "Studies in *Peitho.*" PhD diss., Princeton University, 1966.

Perrotta, R. *Heideggers Jeweiligkeit: Versuch einer Analyse der Seinsfrage anhand der veröffentlichen Texte.* Würzburg: Königshausen und Neumann, 1999.

Perry, B. M. "On the Cornford-Fragment (28B8.38*)." *Archiv für Geschichte der Philosophie* 71 (1989): 1–9.

Peterson, S. "Zeno's Second Argument against Plurality." *Journal of the History of Philosophy* 16 (1978): 261–70.

Pfeiffer, H. *Die Stellung des Parmenideischen Lehrgedichtes in der epischen Tradition.* Bonn: Habelt, 1975.

Philip, J. A. "Parmenides' Theory of Knowledge." *The Phoenix* 12.2 (1958): 63–6.

Phillips, E. D. "Parmenides on Thought and Being." *Philosophical Review* 64 (1955): 546–60.

Picht, G. "Die Epiphanie der ewigen Gegenwart." *Festschrift Wilhelm Szilasi.* München: Francke, 1960. 201–44.

Plato. *Theaetetus.* Trans. J. McDowell. Oxford: Oxford University Press, 1973.

Podlecki, A. J. "Guest-Gifts and Nobodies in *Odyssey* 9." *Phoenix* 15 (1961): 125–33.

Popper, K. R. "Back to the Pre-Socratics" *Proceedings of the Aristotelian Society,* n.s., 59 (1958–59): 1–24. *Studies in Presocratic Philosophy,* vol. 1. Ed. D. J. Furley and R. E. Allen. London: Routledge & Kegan Paul, 1975. 130–53.

Porter, H. N. "The Early Greek Hexameter." *Yale Classical Studies* 12 (1951): 3–63.

Powell, J. E. *A Lexicon to Herodotus.* Cambridge: Cambridge University Press, 1938.

Prendergast, G. L. *A Complete Concordance to the Iliad of Homer.* Ed. and rev. B. Marzullo. Hildesheim: G. Olms, 1962.

Prior, W. J. "Zeno's First Argument Concerning Plurality." *Archiv für Geschichte der Philosophie* 60 (1978): 247–56.

Rahner, H. *Greek Myths and Christian Mystery.* London: Burnes and Oates, 1963.

Ramnoux, C. *La Nuit et les enfants de la Nuit dans la tradition grecque.* Paris: Flammarion, 1959.

Redard, G. "Du grec *dekomai* 'je reçois' au Sanskrit *atka-* 'manteau': Sens de la racine **dek-.*" *Sprachgeschichte und Wortbedeutung: Festschrift Albert Debrunner.* Berne: A. Francke, 1954. 351–62.

Reilly, T. J. "Parmenides Fragment 8.4: A Correction." *Archiv für Geschichte der Philosophie* 58 (1976): 57.

Reinhardt, K. "The Relation between the Two Parts of Parmenides' Poem." *The Pre-Socratics.* Ed. A. P. D. Mourelatos. Garden City, NY: Doubleday, 1974; reprinted Princeton: Princeton University Press, 1993. 293–311.

Renehan, R. "Review of *The Fragments of Parmenides,* by A. H. Coxon." *Ancient Philosophy* 12 (1992): 395–409.

Robbiano, C. *Becoming Being: On Parmenides' Transformative Philosophy.* International Pre-Platonic Studies, vol. 5. Sankt Augustin: Academia Verlag, 2006.

Robin, L. *Platon: Œuvres complètes,* vol. 2. Paris: Gallimard, 1943.

Robinson, J. M. *Contrasting Arguments: An Edition of the Dissoi Logoi.* New York: Arno, 1979.

Robinson, T. M. " 'Is' or 'Is not?' " *Monist* 62 (1979): 61–80.

—. *Plato's Psychology.* 2nd ed. Toronto: University of Toronto Press, 1995.

Rohde, E. *Psyche: The Cult of Souls and Belief in Immortality among the Greeks.* Trans. W. B. Hillis. London: K. Paul, Trench, and Trubner, 1925.

Rosen, S. "Erotic Ascent." *Graduate Faculty Philosophy Journal* 17 (1994): 37–57.

—. "The Non-Lover in Plato's *Phaedrus.*" *Man and His World* 2 (1969): 423–37.

—. *Plato's Sophist.* New Haven: Yale University Press, 1983.

—. *The Quarrel between Philosophy and Poetry.* London: Routledge, 1988.

—. *Sophist: The Drama of Original and Image.* South Bend, IN: St. Augustine's Press, 1999.

Ross, W. D. *Aristotle's Metaphysics.* Oxford: Clarendon Press, 1924.

Rowe, C. *Plato: Phaedrus.* London: Penguin Classics, 2005.

Rumpel, J. *Lexicon Pindaricum.* Leipzig: n.p., 1883.

Russel, B. *Logic and Knowledge: Essays 1901–1950.* Ed. Robert C. Marsh. London: George Allen, 1956.

Ryle, G. *The Concept of Mind.* London: Hutchinson's University Library, 1949.

Sanders, K. R. "Much Ado about 'Nothing': *meden* and *me eon* in Parmenides." Unpublished manuscript.

Santillana, G. "Prologue to Parmenides." *Lectures in Memory of Louise Taft Semple,* 50. Princeton: Princeton University Press, 1967.

Sayre, K. *Plato's Late Ontology: A Riddle Resolved.* Princeton: Princeton University Press, 1983; second edition with a new introduction and the essay, "Excess and deficiency at Statesman 283C–285C." Las Vegas: Parmenides Publishing, 2005.

Schmidt, C. E. *Parallel-Homer oder Index aller Iterati in lexikalischer Anordnung.* Göttingen: 1885.

Schmitt, A. "Self-Determination and Freedom: The Relationship of God and Man in Homer." *Philosophy and Salvation in Greek Religion.* Ed. Vishwa Adluri. Berlin: Walter de Gruyter, 2012.

Schofield, M. "The Antinomies of Plato's *Parmenides.*" *Classical Quarterly,* n.s., 27 (1977): 139–58.

Schofield, M. C. "Did Parmenides Discover Eternity," *Archiv für Geschichte der Philosophie* 52 (1970): 113–35.

Schreckenberg, H. *Ananke: Untersuchungen zur Geschichte des Wortgebrauchs.* Zetemata 36. München: C. H. Beck, 1964.

Schürmann, R. *Broken Hegemonies.* Trans. Reginald Lilly. Bloomington, IN: Indiana University Press, 2003.

—. *Des Hégémonies Brisées.* Mauvezin: Trans-Europ-Repress, 1996.

—. *Heidegger on Being and Acting: From Principles to Anarchy.* Trans. Christine-Marie Gros. Bloomington, IN: Indiana University Press, 1990.

—. "How to Read Heidegger." *Graduate Faculty Philosophy Journal* 19.1 (1997).

—. "Symbolic Difference," *Graduate Faculty Philosophy Journal* 19.2–20.1 (1997).

—. "Tragic Differing: The Law of One and the Law of Contraries in Parmenides." *Graduate Faculty Philosophy Journal* 13.1 (1988).

—. "Ultimate Double Binds." *Graduate Faculty Philosophy Journal* 14.2–15.1 (1991).

Schwabl, H. "Hesiod und Parmenides: zur Formung des parmenideischen Prooimions." *Rheinisches Museum für Philologie,* n.s., 106 (1963): 134–42.

Schwartz, E. *Die Odyssee.* München: Hueber, 1924.

Seidel, G. J. *Martin Heidegger and the Pre-Socratics: An Introduction to His Thought.* Lincoln, NE: University of Nebraska Press, 1964.

Sherover, C. M. *The Human Experiences of Time.* New York: New York University Press, 1975.

Shirer, W. L. *The Rise and Fall of the Third Reich.* New York: Simon & Schuster, 1990.

Sider, D. "Confirmation of Two 'Conjectures' in the Pre-Socratics: Parmenides B12 and Anaxagoras B15." *Phoenix* 33 (1979): 67–69.

Sider, D. and H. W. Johnstone, Jr. *The Fragments of Parmenides.* Bryn Mawr, PA: Bryn Mawr Greek Commentaries, 1986.

Siegel, R. "Parmenides and the Void: Some Comments on the Paper of Thomas S. Knight." *Philosophy and Phenomenological Research* 22 (1961–62): 264–66.

Sinnige, T. *Matter and Infinity in the Presocratic Schools and Plato.* Assen: Van Gorcum, 1971.

Slaveva-Griffin, S. "Of Gods, Philosophers, and Charioteers: Content and Form in Parmenides' Proem and Plato's *Phaedrus.*" *Transactions of the American Philological Association (1974–)* 133.2 (Autumn, 2003): 227–53.

Smyth, H. W. *Greek Grammar.* 1920. Ed. G. M. Messing. Cambridge: Harvard University Press, 1956.

Snell, B. *Die Ausdrücke für den Begriff des Wissens in der vorplatonischen Philosophie.* Berlin: Weidmann, 1924.

—. *The Discovery of the Mind.* Trans. T. G. Rosenmeyer. Cambridge: Cambridge University Press, 1993.

Sorabji, R. *Time, Creation, and the Continuum.* Ithaca: Cornell University Press, 1983.

Sprague, R. K. *Plato's Use of Fallacy: A Study of the Euthydemus and Some Other Dialogues.* London: Routledge, 1962.

Sprute, J. *Der Begriff der doxa in der platonischen Philosophie.* Göttingen: Vandenhoeck und Ruprecht, 1962.

Stanford, W. B. *Ambiguity in Greek Literature: Studies in Theory and Practice.* Oxford: Blackwell, 1939.

Stannard, J. "Parmenidean Logic." *Philosophical Review* 69 (1960): 526–33.

Steele, L. D. "Mesopotamian Elements in the Proem of Parmenides? Correspondences between the Sun-Gods Helios and Shamash." *Classical Quarterly*, n.s., 52.2 (2002): 583–8.

Stein, H. "Die Fragmente des Parmenides *Peri phuseōs.*" *Festschrift Friedrich Ritschl.* Part II. Leipzig, 1867.

Stein, H. "Newtonian Space-Time." *The* Annus Mirabilis *of Sir Isaac Newton 1666–1966.* Ed. Robert Palter. Cambridge, MA: MIT Press, 1967.

Stough, C. "Parmenides' Way of Truth, B8.12–13." *Phronesis* 13 (1968): 91–107.

Strang, C. "The Physical Theory of Anaxagoras." *Studies in Presocratic Philosophy*, vol. 2. Ed. D. J. Furley and R. E. Allen. London: Routledge & Kegan Paul, 1975. 361–80.

Sullivan, S. D. "How a Person Relates to θυμός in Homer." *Indogermanische Forschungen* 85 (1985): 138–42.

Tannery, P. *Pour l'histoire de la science hellène.* 2nd ed. Paris: Gauthier-Villars, 1930.

Taran, L. *Parmenides: A Text with Translation, Commentary and Critical Essays.* Princeton: Princeton University Press, 1965.

Tarrant, H. A. S. "The Conclusion of Parmenides' Poem." *Apeiron* 17 (1983): 73–84.

Teodorsson, S.-T. *Anaxagoras' Theory of Matter.* Göteborg: Acta Universitatis Gothoburgensis, 1982.

Thanassas, P. *Parmenides, Cosmos, and Being: A Philosophical Interpretation.* Milwaukee, WI: Marquette University Press, 2007.

Thornton, B. S. *Erōs: The Myth of Ancient Greek Sexuality.* Boulder: Westview Press, 1998.

Tilghman, B. R. "Parmenides, Plato and Logical Atomism." *Southern Journal of Philosophy* 7 (1969): 151–60.

Tolstoy, L. *The Death of Ivan Ilych and Master and Man.* Trans. Ann Pasternak Slater. New York: Modern Library, 2003.

Tugwell, S. "The Way of Truth." *Classical Quarterly,* n.s., 14 (1964): 36–41.

Ustinova, Y. *Caves and the Ancient Greek Mind: Descending Underground in the Search for Ultimate Truth.* Oxford/New York: Oxford University Press, 2009.

van Buren, J. "Martin Heidegger, Martin Luther." *Reading Heidegger from the Start.* Ed. T. Kisiel and J. van Buren. Albany, NY: SUNY Press, 1994.

van Cleve, J. and R. E. Frederick, eds. *The Philosophy of Right and Left: Incongruent Counterparts and the Nature of Space.* Dordrecht: Kluwer Academic Publishers, 1991.

van Groningen, B. A. *La composition littéraire archaique grecque.* Amsterdam: Noord-Hollandsche Uitg. Mij., 1958.

Verdenius, W. J. "Der *Logos*begriff bei Heraklit und Parmenides, II." *Phronesis* 12 (1967): 99–117.

—. *Parmenides, Some Comments on his Poem.* Groningen: Bij J. B. Wolters' Uitgevers Maatschappij, 1942.

Vernant, J.-P. *Myth and Society in Ancient Greece.* Trans. Janet Lloyd. New York: Zone Books, 1990.

Versényi, L. *Heidegger, Being, and Truth.* New Haven: Yale University Press, 1965.

Vlastos, G. "Degrees of Reality in Plato." *Platonic Studies.* Ed. G. Vlastos. Princeton: Princeton University Press, 1973. 58–75.

Voigt, C. "*Peitho.*" *Realencyclopädie der classischen Altertumswissenschaft.* Ed. Pauly-Wissowa. Half Vol. 37. Stuttgart: J. B. Metzler, 1937. 194–217.

von Fritz, K. "Nous, Noein, and Their Derivatives in Pre-Socratic Philosophy (Excluding Anaxagoras): Part I. From the Beginnings to Parmenides." *Classical Philology* 40.4 (October 1945): 223–42.

—. "Review of *Studi sull' eleatismo,* by G. Calogero." *Gnōmon* 14 (1938): 91–109.

Vos, H. "Die Bahnen von Nacht und Tag." *Mnemosyne* 16 (1963): 18–34.

Wardy, R. B. B. "Eleatic Pluralism." *Archiv für Geschichte der Philosophie* 70 (1988): 125–46.

Warren, J. *Presocratics: Ancient Philosophies.* Stocksfield: Acumen, 2007.

Weiss, H. "Democritus' Theory of Cognition." *Classical Quarterly* 32 (1938): 47–56.

West, M. L. *Early Greek Philosophy and the Orient.* Oxford: Clarendon Press, 1971.

Wheeler, S. C. III. "Megarian Paradoxes as Eleatic Arguments." *American Philosophical Quarterly* 20 (1983): 287–95.

Whittaker, J. *God, Time and Being: Two Studies in the Transcendental Tradition in Greek Philosophy. Symbolae Osloenses* Supplementary vol. XXIII. Oslo, 1971.

Wilamowitz-Moellendorff, U. v. *Die griechische Literatur des Altertums. Die griechische und lateinische Literatur und Sprache.* Ed. U. v. Wilamowitz-Moellendorff. Berlin: B. G. Teubner, 1905.

Williams, B. A. O. "The Legacy of Greece: Philosophy." *The Legacy of Greece: A New Appraisal.* Ed. M. I. Finley. Oxford: Clarendon Press, 1981. 219–25.

—. *Shame and Necessity.* Berkeley: University of California Press, 1993.

Wilson, J. R. "Parmenides, B 8.4." *Classical Quarterly* 20 (1970): 32–4.

Wittgenstein, L. *Tractatus Logico-Philosophicus.* Trans. D. F. Pears and B. F. McGuinness. London: Routledge, 1961.

Woodbury, L. "Anaxagoras and Athens." *Phoenix* 35 (1981): 295–315.

—. "Parmenides on Names." *Essays in Ancient Greek Philosophy.* Ed. J. P. Anton and G. L. Kustas. Albany, NY: SUNY Press, 1972.

Wright, M. R. *Empedocles: The Extant Fragments.* New Haven: Yale University Press, 1981.

Yfantis, D. *Die Auseinandersetzung des frühen Heidegger mit Aristoteles.* Berlin: Duncker & Humblot, 2009.

Zhmud', L. J.-A. " 'All is Number'?" *Phronesis* 34 (1989): 270–92.

Index